Lauren Hough

Leaving Isn't the Hardest Thing

Lauren Hough was born in Germany and raised in seven countries and West Texas. She's been an airman in the U.S. Air Force, a green-aproned barista, a bartender, a livery driver, and, for a time, a cable guy. Her work has appeared in *Granta*, *The Wrath-Bearing Tree*, *The Guardian*, and *HuffPost*. She lives in Austin.

Leaving Isn't
the Hardest Thing

Leaving Isn't the Hardest Thing

ESSAYS

Lauren Hough

VINTAGE BOOKS
A DIVISION OF PENGUIN RANDOM HOUSE LLC
NEW YORK

A VINTAGE BOOKS ORIGINAL, APRIL 2021

Copyright © 2021 by Good Dog Harper LLC

All rights reserved. Published in the United States
by Vintage Books, a division of Penguin Random House LLC,
New York, and distributed in Canada by Penguin Random
House Canada Limited, Toronto.

Vintage and colophon are registered
trademarks of Penguin Random House LLC.

Some stories originally appeared, in slightly different
form, in the following publications: "Cable Guy" as "I Was
a Cable Guy. I Saw the Worst of America." in *HuffPost* (December 30, 2018); "Pet Snakes" as "My Drug Dealer's Snake" in *Gay
Magazine* (May 16, 2019); and "Solitaire" in *The Wrath-Bearing
Tree* (December 4, 2017 and January 1, 2018).

The Cataloging-in-Publication Data is on file
at the Library of Congress.

**Vintage Books Trade Paperback ISBN: 978-0-593-08076-4
eBook ISBN: 978-0-593-08077-1**

Book design by Nicholas Alguire

www.vintagebooks.com

Printed in the United States of America
10 9 8 7 6 5 4 3 2 1

For my grandmothers, Nell and Barbara

Contents

Author's Note

We used to carry a book of Bible verses to memorize, a new verse every day. Then there were entire prayers and psalms and chapters any good Family kid should know. For a time, when I'd get in trouble, I'd be assigned something like Hebrews 11 to memorize. I got in trouble a lot. I am really good at memorizing. Yet I know, in the jumble of words and lines I've gone over again and again to commit them to memory, quoted to myself as a test, and sometimes a prayer, I've added, changed, and deleted words. If I were to look up a verse now, a verse I know, it'll be different from the one in my head. The meaning will be the same. But I'll have swapped a "thee" and a "thou," a "shall" and a "will." I'll be sure this is a revision, the New International Version maybe, the words on the page can't be right.

My memories aren't much different. They're stories I've told myself so many times that I've added lines and deleted people. Added weather and deleted a smell. Added a taste and deleted the walls. The meaning hasn't changed for me. But my memories aren't a collection of verses. They aren't even memories of events. They're memories of memories.

I have tried to be as accurate and truthful as possible. But the truth I know is the memory of a memory and a story I told myself to make sense of it all.

I've changed the names of the guilty and the innocent, and one too many Kyles. I've changed small details to provide my loved ones a bit of camouflage. But as anyone with siblings knows, you can experience the same event, and none of you will agree on what happened. Unfortunately for them, I'm the one telling the stories. The best I can tell you is, if your kid ever tells you she wants to be a writer, send her to live with the cousins.

Leaving Isn't
the Hardest Thing

Solitaire

If you ask me where I'm from, I'll lie to you. I'll tell you my parents were missionaries. I'll tell you I'm from Boston. I'll tell you I'm from Texas. Those lies, people believe. I'm better at lying than I am at telling the truth because the lies don't make me nervous. It's the truth, the thought of telling it, that triggers my awkward laugh and my sweaty palms, makes me not want to look you in the eye. I know I won't like what I'll see.

When Sheriff Horton moseyed up to the front porch, past my car smoldering in the driveway, I figured I should stick as close to the truth as possible. I'd been watching him talk to the firemen out on the lawn, but with the rain coming down in sheets, I couldn't make out but a few words.

I was sitting on the steps drying my hair with a towel. Didn't take much to dry it. I'd chopped off most of my hair that summer when the South Carolina air hit 100 degrees with 100 percent humidity and walking outside was like opening a dishwasher mid-cycle and climbing in.

Horton took his hat off, beat it against his thigh to shake off the water. I stood and realized he was shorter than me. I stepped back. I'm six feet tall, and guys don't like feeling short. I offered him my hand, which he crushed in his own meaty grip.

"Looks like arson," he said and stared at me like I was supposed to respond with something more than "No shit."

So I said, "Yeah, I can smell the gas." I mimicked his accent.

Sometimes the mimicry's unintentional. The way someone talks is the fastest way to tell someone isn't like you. Come back from years overseas to a place like Amarillo, Texas, for example, and you'll learn that accent *real* fast. South Carolina isn't much different. If you don't sound like them, people start asking you questions, like "Where are you from?" After a while, you mimic without even thinking about it. It's safer when people don't think you're different.

I lit a Marlboro, something to do with my hands because I knew better than to put them in my pockets. Southern rules follow military rules. You don't talk to an authority figure with your hands in your pockets.

I offered him a cigarette. He asked if I thought that was a good idea, nodded over to where my car sat, still steaming. The firemen were packing up their hoses, shouting and joking on the lawn. I said I doubted there was much risk of combusting. He asked if maybe we should go inside. I raised the cigarette like that was the reason we would not be going inside. He raised his eyebrows like that wasn't a good reason. I told him it wasn't my house, I couldn't give permission, because I thought that seemed reasonable. I don't know what he expected to find.

He asked me if I knew who'd done it. I said it was probably the same person who'd been leaving me death threats. He pulled out his notepad and asked for names. I told him I didn't have any. He asked with a smirk on his face why someone would threaten me, but he already knew.

I should've been more concerned when only a month before this night, someone fingered the words "Die Dike" into the dust on my rental car. I should've told someone.

I was a twenty-three-year-old senior airman, a combat rescue controller. Sounds like a cool job. Makes you picture me jumping out of a helicopter, returning enemy fire, and saving a pilot. What I really did was read, play a lot of solitaire, and, once a week, sit in the corner of the briefing room, clicking next on PowerPoint slides.

When I found that first threatening message, my unit was on an exercise in Egypt, a welcome trip away from my duty station, Shaw Air Force Base, in South Carolina. An exercise is when you go somewhere else to play solitaire on your computer because you're not allowed to read at your desk—that would look unprofessional. You spend your off-hours pranking each other—gluing sleeping bags shut, dropping raw eggs into someone's boots, duct-taping people to cots with cardboard "Free Blow Job" signs.

That first note, I wanted to believe someone just had a bad sense of humor. I rubbed the dust off the car, hoping no one had seen it. And I forgot about it because something else happened while I was in Egypt: I got orders to Araxos Air Base in Greece.

I'd been at Shaw two years, I was due for new orders, but considering the Air Force had already stuck me in South Carolina, I'd been half expecting to be sent to another shitty stateside base, South Dakota maybe.

All I had to do was go back to Shaw for a bit, keep my mouth shut about the stupid prank that read like a threat, and in two months, I'd move to Greece. I'd swim in the sea. I'd drink ouzo. I'd play more solitaire. I'd be more careful about who I told I was gay. I'd become someone else—something I'd been doing as long as I can remember. New country. New town. New story.

I returned to Shaw and hoped, nearly believed, I'd left that problem in Egypt. Maybe it wasn't even someone from Shaw. Could've just as easily been a marine from Camp Lejeune or a soldier from Fort Bragg who'd come to the exercise. Then I woke up one morning to four flat tires. Flat tires aren't a fucking prank. I should've called the cops then. Should've saved the next note, the one on paper, stuck under my windshield wiper, the one that said I'd burn, or the one after that said they were going to kill me.

The night my car burst into flames, I'd agreed to babysit for my supervisor, Sergeant Peters, because it meant spending a couple nights with HBO and without roommates arguing about who emptied the dishwasher last or what movie to watch. I liked Sergeant Peters. He was a big corn-fed-looking guy who had only hit on me once and only sulked about my rejection when he was drinking. I'd been in the Air Force long enough to know that's about as much as you can hope for in a military guy. They took rejection easier if I told them I was gay. That's likely why most of my small unit knew about me, or at least thought they did. I didn't exactly make an announcement. But telling one person, if only to convince him he didn't have a chance, was as good as telling twenty others. But other than some unfunny jokes, the rumors hadn't been a problem. Anyway, I liked Peters well enough, his kid wasn't too much of a pain, but mostly I liked his two German shepherds.

That night, I'd sent his kid to bed, popped *EDtv* into the VCR—because I was lesbian and required to watch every Ellen movie—and I settled in on the couch in the family room at the back of the house. Then I heard the windows rattle in their frames. The dogs went nuts. I ran to the front window and saw my new, shiny black Acura Integra engulfed in flames.

The kid wandered into the hallway, half asleep in her pajamas. I think she was twelve at the time. I told her to go out back. I didn't know if the house was on fire, but if it wasn't, it would be soon—I hadn't parked but two feet from the garage. I was trying to get ahold of the dogs when I saw her open the *front* door.

I got her turned around. I ushered the dogs and her out back and ran inside for the phone, and a blanket so she wouldn't freeze. I called 9-1-1 and watched a fireball shoot into the air high enough I could see it over the roof.

The firemen came, doused the flames, and called the sheriff. They told me the house was safe. I sent the kid to bed. I called Sergeant Peters, and he said not to let anyone inside. Peters liked his guns and maybe they weren't all legal.

So there I was talking to a redneck sheriff in backwoods South Carolina, in 1999, where the Rebel flags outnumbered American flags, and I knew his smirk when he asked who would do this was an insinuation.

I took a drag off my cigarette to buy enough time to decide on an answer. I said someone thought I was gay. I didn't say I was gay.

He asked me if I was gay.

I said, "Hey, don't ask, don't tell, right?" The punch line of the '90s.

I'm not always this cool and collected, not even usually. This is what happens when I'm facing an authority figure. I can't meet their eyes. But I wouldn't show fear. I know better. I'd been through this before. Not with the cops, but I when I was growing up, interrogation was something I was used to. I knew the drill: Stay calm. See the question behind the question. Stick as close to the truth as possible. Don't give too much away or they'll think you're hiding something—liars always explain too much.

Sheriff Horton didn't laugh. He said he didn't have a problem with gay people. He liked Ellen.

I told him, "I can't answer that. You know I can't answer that."

He asked me if anything was wrong with the car.

"Other than it's smoldering in the driveway? No." And I remembered what my brother, Mikey, said when I last saw him at our grandfather's funeral that August. I hadn't owned the Acura a month. I'd been circling the restaurant parking lot where my mom and the aunts said to meet for dinner, searching for a spot my doors might be safe from other car doors. "Seriously," Mikey said, "I'm gonna get out and kick one of your doors in and you'll thank me 'cause you won't have to worry about it anymore." I said, "The fuck you will."

I think the sheriff caught me smiling at the memory.

He took down some information on his notepad with a pen he held with four fingers: name, insurance company, number, address. There wasn't much more to tell him. He tried to be my buddy then, like we'd go out for beers after. Asked me where I was from. That question. I never know how to answer. I'd been telling people I was from Boston. I said Texas because guys like Sheriff Horton aren't too fond of Yankees.

I asked Sheriff Horton if I could get my things out of the trunk, see if anything survived—the chem-warfare suit I'd been issued for Egypt that I still hadn't returned; souvenirs I'd bought in Giza: a chess set for my dad, a painting on papyrus for my mom, a hookah for Mikey, little trinkets for my sister's kids. He said I'd have to wait until they were done processing the car. Everything was evidence now.

He asked how I liked South Carolina, the Air Force. I said it was all right. But I was going to Greece in a month.

He said, "We'll see about that." And he snapped his notebook shut.

———

It's hard to think of even now. I was so close to leaving that damn base. I never could figure out why I'd been sent to Shaw in the first place. I was the only one in my graduating class to volunteer for an overseas assignment and the only one assigned stateside. I'd hoped for Germany, would've settled for England. I got fucking South Carolina.

Shaw was a fighter base, but I worked at CENTAF, the Air Force part of CENTCOM. It doesn't matter. What matters is I worked in a tiny office in one of those tiny units with a separate mission from the main base, a unit where everyone knew everyone else. The officers worked on their promotions. The NCOs worked on networking with contractors. The airmen drank and counted days to their next assignment.

I'd hated Shaw upon my arrival two years before. I'd only been there a few weeks when I heard this guy who worked in my building complaining at the smoke pit that he'd been handed orders for a three-month stint in Saudi Arabia. His wife was pregnant. They didn't have a car. I told him I'd go for him if he could get permission to switch.

He tried to convince me otherwise. I didn't blame him. I can relate to a suspicion of altruism. But I wasn't motivated by altruism. No one joins the Air Force because they're dying to see more of South Carolina. I wanted to travel, even if that meant Saudi. But more than that, I needed somewhere to keep me out of trouble.

I was gay and didn't know what to do about it. I needed time. It's not that I'd put much thought into going to

Saudi. But, determined to avoid the problem I couldn't solve, I saw three months in Saudi as the perfect way to buy that time.

We shook on it. And I went to Saudi. I left him my car keys while I was gone. I preferred Saudi Arabia to Shaw. I preferred being locked on a base that we only got to leave twice, and only in full-body abayas with the hijab. And because we were all locked on base, I'd had something of a social life. I'd go to the base bar where they served near beer and play cards with all the others who had nothing better to do.

When I returned to Shaw, nothing had changed. But slowly, I did. I turned twenty-one and could escape to gay bars in Columbia and Florence, larger cities where, for a few hours, I didn't have to hide who I was. I bought a Gateway computer and spent hours each night in my room, chatting on AIM and Gay.com, where a world outside South Carolina seemed to be racing forward, quickly becoming less dangerous for someone like me. People in New York, D.C., and Boston told me they could walk down the street holding hands without catching a beating.

The Air Force was a job, not an adventure, not my life. Just a job. And when I took off my uniform, I was almost myself. I occasionally tried to make friends, and when I did, I occasionally told them I was gay. It seemed like an interesting thing about me. No one cared, or it didn't feel like they did. Sure, I'd have to answer the standard 101 questions you've always wanted to ask a lesbian—is scissoring real? But this was the late '90s—*Friends* aired a lesbian wedding, Ellen came out on national television, and sure, they canceled her, but then *Will & Grace* aired and Will was okay because he was handsome and celibate, Tammy Baldwin was elected to Congress, and okay, Clinton signed DOMA, but he didn't mean it. Don't Ask, Don't Tell was still the law, but my early paranoia seemed unfounded. I thought, *As long as I'm careful, don't date other military, don't give anyone details, don't trust the wrong person, as long as I'm careful, it'll be okay.*

The part of my life spent in uniform, in an office playing solitaire, seemed less important, almost temporary, like the world outside the gates was changing so fast, it was only a matter of time before the Air Force changed too, and either way, I wouldn't be at Shaw forever.

A couple years passed without major incident. Then the threats started on that trip to Egypt. But like I said, I had orders to Greece. I couldn't even tell you which came first. But I returned to Shaw and tried to keep my head down. Some asshole sending me threats wouldn't matter once I left.

A few days after the fire, my new buddy Sheriff Horton called my office. He said someone had seen a white car speeding away from the house. Asked if I knew who drove a white car. I couldn't think of anyone. Then he asked me take a polygraph.

I'd watched plenty of television and read enough legal thrillers to know I was a suspect. I called the base legal office. The base lawyer told me I shouldn't be too worried, but I should stop talking to the cops. Tell them to talk to her. Call her back if anything changed.

That's when the Air Force took over the investigation. I waited as the investigators asked every airman on base if they knew Senior Airman Hough was being harassed, if they knew Senior Airman Hough was gay. She's gay. I waited while investigators showed up at my grandma's door in Texas. But they didn't know she'd been an Air Force wife. She'd had about enough of the Air Force somewhere between the Korean and Vietnam Wars. They didn't even finish introducing themselves before she slammed the door in their faces and called me.

"Lauren, the OSI just knocked on my door. And I knew it was them before they showed their stupid badges. They have a smell." My grandma never had much patience for small talk.

I said I was sorry they bothered her. And I was.

"Never mind that. What do they want?" she asked.

"They didn't say?"

She laughed. "I never gave them the chance."

So I explained about the car, about the death threats. And I shit you not, she said, "Oh. Good. I was worried you'd done something stupid like have an affair with an officer's wife."

Here's the thing you need to know about my grandma: when I lived with her in Amarillo, she was the only Democrat I'd ever met. I was half convinced she was Amarillo's sole liberal, who practiced all manner of lunatic beliefs like recycling and yoga and feminism and gay rights. She caught hell for it—from the neighbors; from the old biddies at the First Presbyterian; from her own family, who regularly referred to her as "that crazy old bitch"—but she never gave a shit. In fairness, she wasn't what anyone would describe as "nice," or even "nurturing." Oh, she'd give you the shirt off her back if you needed it. Then swear at you for your pathetic posture. When we were little and Mom was working late at the restaurant, she'd let us stay up to all hours watching *Dallas* and *Miami Vice*. She'd answer any question we had, with no regard for what might be age appropriate. I knew more about hookers and blow than any kid in second grade. She'd take us on archaeological digs and show us how to dig up fossils. Then drop all four of us at the dollar theater with three wet dollar bills she'd pulled from her bra because she had a bridge game. She could play Chopin without looking at the music. She held several degrees. She'd read everything. She forgot nothing. And she was one of the first people I'd come out to, before my own parents even, because I knew she would never judge me.

So while I was pissed that they'd worried her, I was a lot more pissed they'd knocked on her door for no other reason I could imagine than to humiliate me by outing me to my grandma.

The investigation took another bad turn when they talked to my roommate. He said I was a liar. Sometimes when we watched a movie set in a place I'd lived, I'd say, "Hey, I've been there." I grew up all over the place—Japan, Switzerland, Argentina, Chile. Sometimes I forget that some people never stray too far from home. Most people know where home is. But I didn't understand why he thought I was a liar just because I said "I've been there" unless I'd slipped.

It could be hard sometimes to keep my lies straight, hazard of the trade. The trade—that is, being a fucking liar, whatever the reason—keeps you apart. Even the

most basic of initial friendship-interview questions like
"Where are you from?" required a lie, or at least omis-
sion. But I wanted to tell. I wanted to have a story like
everyone else. And sometimes, just sometimes, I'd let a
little thing slip. "I was born in Berlin" or "I used to live
in Osaka." "My parents were missionaries." *Here's a thing
about me. I'm someone too. Please like me.* But maybe I'd
switched stories.

With all the chaos, I moved back into the dorms on
base that I'd been so eager to leave. Senior airmen were
allowed to move off base, and I had taken advantage of
that. Off base, there were no dorm inspections, no first
sergeants trolling the common areas for underage drinkers or dayroom blow jobs. I liked thinking that gave me
some privacy, but I'd been wrong. I'd let my guard down,
trusted the wrong people with little bits of information.
Nothing that would out me as having grown up in a cult.
But enough maybe to join a conversation.

It hadn't been a year since Barry Winchell, an Army private, had been beaten to death with a baseball bat in a
barracks hallway at an Army post in Kentucky because
he was gay. I was scared before. But the worst I feared
was getting kicked out of the Air Force. Even the act of
torching my car seemed like a far leap from murder; a
beatdown seemed more likely. That is, until June, six
months after my car was torched, when I got the next
note: "Gun knife or bat I can't decide which one."

In the months since the car fire, it had seemed whoever torched my car was finished with me. I thought

they'd leave me alone now that I was being investigated, keep their ass clean and get away with it. Maybe they'd transferred to another base.

The Air Force's investigation had stalled. My car insurance company, frustrated with the lack of an outcome, sent their own investigator. He looked at the evidence the cops had, interviewed me and a few people on base, called Sheriff Horton some names, which I appreciated, and cleared me of wrongdoing in two days.

My insurance paid off the car, a massive relief. I figured the Air Force investigators had given up trying to pin the arson on me. I'd missed my deployment date in January and had assumed someone else took my slot in Greece. But when I talked to the staff sergeant who was to be my new supervisor at Araxos, he said they'd never filled the slot. He said he'd try to push for new orders. And just before I got that new threat, true to his word, I received new orders to Greece. I thought the Air Force would let me go, if only to wash their hands of the problem.

But with this most recent note, being stuck at Shaw or getting kicked out of the Air Force was no longer my biggest fear, or the most likely outcome. The note clarified my priorities. I thought of Winchell. And I was terrified.

I called the Air Force investigators. They asked me if I'd touched the note. They took me over to their office, then led me down a hallway, into a room, told me to sit there in an office chair.

The room wasn't very intimidating. No mirror on the wall. No metal chairs. Just a government-issue gray desk and three blue office chairs. Investigator Campbell was built like a linebacker, all shoulders and forehead. He was wearing a navy suit in mid-June. I wondered how many times the FBI had turned down his application before he took this job, Air Force Office of Special Investigations. He'd be playing bad cop. To his side was Investigator Maldonado. She was pregnant and getting into the role of good cop. Campbell waited while Maldonado tried to adjust her chair—the paddle that lowered the seat wasn't working, so her legs didn't reach the floor.

They switched places.

I stared at the gold cross that had slipped out of Maldonado's blouse during the chair ordeal. She played nice, but I knew she'd push for execution if she could. She tucked the necklace back in, cleared her throat, opened a folder. I half expected her first words to be, "Should we pray?" But they just sat there looking at me like it was a game to see who'd speak first. I looked at my hands. I asked for a lawyer from base legal. Even airmen have a right to a lawyer. I said I'd already spoken to one. Maldonado said I wasn't a suspect. I shouldn't need a lawyer. Not a very convincing good cop.

"When did you find the note? Who left the note? Is this the first time this has happened?"

"I want a lawyer. The base lawyer told me not to answer questions."

"You're not a suspect. This isn't about your car. This is about the threats. We're trying to help you."

And the tears filled my eyes and I wiped them with the back of my hand. I wasn't crying. My eyes were leaking. There is, in fact, a difference. The leaking happens when I'm frustrated.

Maldonado asked me, "Why are you so upset if you didn't do anything?"

I told them I wanted a lawyer.

They gave up after a while. Wrote some notes down in the folder. Maldonado said she had to eat something. Campbell took me to another room where another agent, a lab rat with dandruff and a yellow collar, spread ink on my hands and arms and took impressions. He pulled hair from random spots on my head for a DNA test.

I knew then they weren't looking for who sent me death threats. They didn't believe me. Though their initial investigation had stalled, they were still convinced I'd torched my own car.

They wanted my DNA because a rag had been stuffed in the gas tank. The rag never ignited. Whoever did torch my car filled it with gas and lit it that way after trying to light a rag in the pouring rain. The cops had found a hair on the rag. Campbell had mentioned it earlier, hoping for a reaction.

They let me go then. But I was pretty sure I was fucked. And I was really damn sure I wasn't ever going to Greece.

One thing I learned late in life is there are people who are shocked when bad things happen to them. More than that. They expect good things to happen. There are others who tell you to think positive thoughts and focus on something pretty and the universe will hand it to you, like you have any significance, like the universe is a benevolent soul who cares about sweet little you with your pretty thoughts. Those are the same people who after something bad happens will tell you they totally had a dream about that. But no one ever calls to tell you not to go to work today because Steve from IT can't get laid so he's bringing a shotgun to work. No one tells you not to get on that plane. Only after your dog runs in front of a car will that friend, the friend who talks a lot about her journey, tell you she had a really bad feeling. She wishes she'd said something.

I'm not one of those people. Sometimes I think I'd like to be. I'd like to have lived a life that allows me to believe if I want something bad enough, if I visualize positivity or whatever it is these people tell you, I'll be rewarded with an easy life. Sometimes. Most of the time, I figure it's better to know the universe doesn't pay out favors for magical thinking. I've learned, if not to expect the worst, to not be surprised by the worst. I'll cry in frustration when my Internet's out, but when my car bursts into flames, well, that seems about right. When I'm blamed for it, yeah, that tracks. You can call it cynicism. I call it growing up in cult.

The Children of God was one of the many cults that sprang up in the late '60s and early '70s. This one was founded by David Berg, a failed Pentecostal preacher and wildly successful alcoholic. In some other timeline they might've locked him up in a place he'd have to wear a bathrobe. In mine, he was free to try a number of career paths—soldier, legal secretary, taxi driver, preacher—until he found his calling. Referred to as Dad, Grandpa, or Moses David, he finally landed on a lifestyle that let him wear bathrobes all day.

If I wanted to play armchair psychologist, I'd slap a label of malignant narcissist on him. Maybe he truly saw visions and heard voices. Maybe he truly believed he could talk to God. Doesn't really matter. What matters is, in 1968, in Huntington Beach, California, while the war was raging in Vietnam and the country seemed ready to tear itself apart, David Berg started preaching to the hippies at the Teens for Christ coffee shop on the strip.

Berg's kids were in their late teens, and he used them as bait. They'd sing a few songs, offer coffee, stale donuts, and shelter. Berg tested his new brand of Gospel: Jesus was a long-haired hippie like them. Jesus was a social-ist. Jesus was the biggest radical ever. The mainstream churches hadn't caught the youth-ministry fever yet. Those who heard him back then will tell you they'd never heard anything like him before. He was offering more than an answer to the materialism they already loathed. He gave them what they'd never known: unconditional love and purpose. Around fifty of them followed him around the country, half starved and living in buses and rotting canvas tents. They protested the war. They preached the Gospel he'd taught them: follow Jesus, forsake all. "All" meant everything and everyone from your past life.

In '71, about 150 members moved onto a ranch in Texas, about an hour east of Dallas, called the Texas Soul Clinic. The members lived communally in absolute poverty. There was no sex, no drugs. They were high on Jesus and freezing in shacks. Berg, however, relocated himself to a sweet pad in Dallas, where he replaced his wife with his secretary (because everything's a cliché) and took on a few concubines.

The Children of God sent out teams to colleges and universities across the country, to bus stations, anywhere they could find converts. They donned sackcloth and smeared ashes on their foreheads and lined up in front of the UN, the White House, the middle of Times Square.

Time magazine called them Jesus Freaks. And kids kept joining up. By the time they left the ranch, Berg had amassed over 1,400 followers. My parents were among them.

By 1972, Berg communicated only by edicts called Mo Letters. Imagine the crazy guy who comments on your local news Facebook page, ranting about spaceships, vaccines, George Soros, and Hollywood pedophiles. Now imagine (and this was likely more difficult prior to 2016) someone following him around with a little tape recorder, transcribing all his alcohol-infused nuggets of wisdom, printing them, and sending them out to his disciples. Essentially, some drunk asshole's completely fucking insane diatribes on every subject from car engines to shitting habits to biblical theory to dream interpretation. That's a Mo Letter. And every word he said was law. There's a paragraph in one—and there are entire volumes of these, enough to fill a pickup bed—where the old bastard says he only eats with spoons. Forks aren't really necessary. Matter of fact, forks can be dangerous. At that moment, every fucking Children of God home around the world threw away their forks. Another Mo Letter declared America as Babylon, the Whore of Satan. God was going to destroy the continent, he said. So naturally everyone went to Europe—England first, then Scandinavia, Germany, France, and the rest—spreading farther as they gained followers.

Anytime the authorities or press got a little too close for Berg's comfort, he'd get a prophecy. The first prophecy sent him into hiding, and from then on, only a few senior members would know his location. Later on, his prophecies would disband the group, change the name, move countries, continents, regroup, whatever Berg needed.

By the time I was born in '77, there were over 130 communes around the world and they'd changed their name to the Family of Love. That's right about the time Berg instituted his Law of Love.

Which brings us to the main reason—aside from its more famous alumni: Jeremy Spencer from Fleetwood Mac, who vanished the night before what was supposed to be the band's big break, a show at the Whiskey A Go Go, to join up; Rose McGowan; River and Joaquin Phoenix—the main reason anyone's heard of this cult, by any name. Berg waited until he had his followers completely dependent. He had them sever all ties. Most everyone had kids, no jobs, and now lived in foreign countries. His crowning message was simple: Anything done in love was good. Which sounds like an Instagram caption. But it had a dark twist. Go out to nightclubs and lure rich men into bed. It's not prostitution if you tell them about Jesus. Someone wants to fuck you or your husband, we're all one family now. Incest, that's just the devil making you feel ashamed. God's only law is love, man.

A cult is your textbook abusive relationship—love-bomb, isolate, create dependence, and your victim won't have the power to leave, even if staying in the relationship means buying into the new Gospel of David Berg. In short, in the eyes of the world, the Children of God, now the Family of Love, became a sex cult.

Enough people had a problem with his message that the press got wind of his new ministry. Mo Letters with titles like "God's Whores" and "The Devil Hates Sex" made their way into the wrong hands. And Berg did what he did best. He got another prophecy. Fired his leadership team, anyone who spoke against him. Told everyone the cult was disbanded. No more massive communes. Europe was a lost cause. Go to the third world, what we now call developing countries. What was the Children of God, then the Family of Love, became simply, the Family.

This is probably why the memories I have of my early years in a cult look a little more idyllic than you'd imagine. We lived in campgrounds in Chile, in Argentina. A bus in Buenos Aires my dad built into an RV. A farm in Mendoza with goats. A house in Santiago with hay on the roof.

Our little family—my parents, my two older sisters, and our little brother—teamed up with another small family. Other members would pass through occasionally. But for the most part, it was just us. And we were often desperately poor.

Sometimes, when we were strapped for cash, my mom and dad would head out to a local pool hall or pub. My dad's as affable as a golden retriever, tall and handsome in that inoffensive way that makes you trust him. And he can talk to anyone. Which helped temper my mom's presence. Her coal-black hair offsets those pale blue eyes she'll lock on you, making your bones shiver. There's an intensity to her beauty, like a coiled snake. But they'd order a drink and rack a game. And my mom would biff the break. My dad would patiently remind her to watch the cue ball. And he'd strike up a conversation with the guys waiting on the table. "How about a friendly game? Sure, we can put a little money on it. Make it interesting." No one minds taking money from a couple of dumb American tourists. That's when my mom, with skills earned from a misspent youth in NCO clubs and Berlin dives, would attack. My dad's not bad at pool either. But he rarely got a chance to shoot before she'd cleared the table. Beginner's luck.

They were a perfect team, or so I thought. But they fought, had affairs, split up, got back together, and had more affairs. Yet I remember being happy.

I remember busking on street corners, and strangers would give us money and food. I remember playing in the campgrounds, one infested with tarantulas, and one down by a beach where we played in the ocean, and one near an outdoor movie theater where we'd pile our blankets on the roof of our bus and watch movies we couldn't hear. My dad got me a dog. We went to school where I got to wear a tie, even though it was just a clip-on. But I was younger than my sisters. If you ask them, Ann, my other middle, with whom, as is the law of middles, I fought with constantly, or Valerie, the oldest, who at seven cooked our meals and washed our clothes and nursed our wounds, they have different memories of that time. Mikey, who was doted on like all boys smart enough to be born last—maybe it's better he doesn't remember at all.

Then, right before I turned seven, we left.

My parents thought if they left the cult, they could salvage their marriage. But moving to Texas doesn't save marriages, not theirs certainly. My dad once told me they'd married without ever having a conversation. They were traveling around England, living in a double-decker bus with "Children of God" painted on the side in that groovy, flower-power lettering, when someone said they should have a mass wedding. It would be revolutionary, man. My dad asked my mom because she was pretty and seemed nice. Their marriage only makes sense knowing they'd put exactly as much thought into it as choosing a movie to watch.

Soon after we arrived in Texas, right after my seventh birthday, my dad left, went back to the cult in Germany, where my sisters soon joined him. I was fucking devastated. They shouldn't have split us up. When you're raised with siblings, you're not so much an individual as part of a whole. And they fucking cut us in half. Might also have helped if they'd explained. I don't think they ever told us. Valerie did, in the back of our grandma's closet, where we'd hide behind a stack of *National Geographic*s. Valerie didn't know why, though. She just said the word "divorce," and this being the '80s, we knew that meant the end of us. All I knew was my dad left me, and then half of me, my sisters, were gone too.

For a few years there, Mikey and I had a pretty typical American childhood circa 1984–1987, complete with an asshole stepdad, Gabe. Gabe was younger, only twenty-three when Mom met him at the chain steakhouse where they both worked. He was cool at first, like a big brother. He rode dirt bikes and always had change for the *Pac-Man* machine when we had to wait for Mom to get off work. We moved out of Grandma's house in Amarillo, to an apartment in Oklahoma City.

We rejoined the cult when I was nine. By the way, if your kid hasn't seen her real dad in three years and you tell her you're all going to Dallas to meet someone, but it's a surprise, that surprise better fucking be her dad. That surprise was not my dad.

The Family I knew no longer existed. They'd grown to ten thousand members and lived in houses now where they'd cram in as many people as possible—closets and hallways were used as bedrooms. In Dallas we shared a room with maybe fifteen kids, and I shared a bed with a nose-picker named Melody.

There were rules for everything, from how many sheets of toilet paper you used to what to say when someone gave you a compliment (not "thank you" but "praise the Lord," because you didn't do anything good, God did, although God wasn't responsible if you did something wrong). The home was run by elders called shepherds who controlled everything we did and how we did it. My parents were replaced by a shepherd named Mercy, or that was her Family name. Family names were usually something biblical, or a cure for physical or spiritual sickness. I once knew a Victory, named so medicinally to treat her asthma. As a cure, the name was as effective as "Mercy."

There was no television and few games. The cult had its own music, its own books, its own language of code words and acronyms to keep us apart from the System, the outside world, and the Systemites—that's you. There wasn't any school since we already knew how to read and write, all you need to fulfill your godly roles. Kids had a purpose—cleaning the homes, taking care of the other kids, memorizing Bible verses, and studying Family doctrine to prepare for the End Time. We had to leave America.

In 1987, we flew to Osaka, where they changed my name again, and again. Another country, another name. It didn't matter anymore. One day blurred into another. Changing diapers. Begging. Going door-to-door selling posters and videotapes, Family music, and low-budget music videos meant to spread their message—Jesus loves you, the Antichrist is coming, don't kill your baby. We memorized the Bible. We memorized the zodiac. (Berg—Grandpa, the old pervert, whatever you want to call him—thought the whole zodiac thing was witch-craft. But he should've thought of that before he started a hippie cult.)

They'd sworn off some of the sex shit by then—fear of AIDS, problems with local authorities.

The Family was focused on the End Time, Revela-tion, the coming Apocalypse. They were training us, the second generation, to fight the Antichrist. Could've been worse. We could've ended up like Waco. But our luna-tic cult leader chose to tell us we'd use our superpowers instead of actual weapons. Maybe Berg *was* a vision-ary. Maybe we were just lucky he'd hated his time in the Army. Anyway, who needs assault rifles when you can shoot laser beams from your fingers. (The Family comic books could be entertaining, but we were sup-posed to take them as gospel, training manuals for the End Time. And they were not kidding about the lasers, or the flying.)

Since we didn't have our superpowers yet, they con-centrated on training us for the very real possibility that we'd be questioned by the police and the media about our beliefs and practices. The training stuck. When homes were eventually raided and the kids questioned, the authorities never found evidence of abuse. That fear of police they drilled into us stuck too. So did the other interrogations, the times we weren't practicing, the times they were trying to get me to confess to breaking the rules, the countless times I was accused of being too loud, too quiet, too stubborn, too masculine. If it wasn't one thing, it was another.

Long story, right? And you still have questions. Maybe it's easier to see why I might just tell you I'm from Texas and leave it at that. Considering my history, maybe it's not hard to imagine why I might be reticent to discuss my past, might even reflexively lie to hide it, and why being questioned by the OSI felt a little too fucking familiar.

When the OSI let me go, I walked across the street to the base legal office and sat down to wait for a lawyer. A lawyer could make them stop asking me questions I couldn't answer.

The lawyer said to stop talking to the investigators, but that he couldn't represent me. He'd just transferred from the prosecuting side, where he'd been involved in my investigation. If there was to be a court-martial, they'd have to send a defense attorney from another base. I hadn't considered there would be a court-martial, at least not with me as the defendant. Up until that conversation, I assumed they'd either figure out who did it or drop the investigation, because I hadn't done anything.

I had always slept with a knife by my bed—too many

nights when some drunk airman tried my doorknob. But given the recent developments, I replaced the knife with a little snub-nosed .38 I bought at one of the ten pawn-shops between the base and Sumter, the nearest town.

When I bought it, I drove into the country and prac-ticed a few shots on a row of beer bottles. The bottles remained intact. I'd barely qualified with a rifle back in basic training. I wouldn't have qualified with a 9 mm, if the good ol' boy major beside me at the range hadn't pitied my piss-poor shooting, said, "Aw shit," and blown a few more holes in my target. His grouping was so tight, his shots had made a single hole dead center of his own target. He could spare the rounds to help me out. I hoped I wouldn't need the gun. I'd end up killing my television or someone across the hall.

The next week, they told me I couldn't work in my office anymore. My security clearance was suspended because of the investigation. They moved me to the gym, where I traded IDs for towels, where no one looked me in the eye.

One morning in August, I was told to report to the com-mander's office. I called base legal. They said they'd assign me a lawyer now that I was going to be court-martialed. Don't say a word. You'll have to sign the charge sheet. Call us back.

Even in a small unit like mine, a command unit where officers outnumbered airmen, I'd only met my com-manding officer once—one of those walk-throughs, like when you get a new regional manager and he comes by your office to shake everyone's hand. His secretary gave me a sympathetic look and told me, "He'll want you to do your reporting statement, hon."

I hadn't done that sort of thing in years. But it's not something you forget after the way they drill it into you in basic training and tech school. It's not meant as a kindness. But it is easier, when your face feels hot and your hands are shaking, to revert to the stone-faced airman they trained you to be—march in, square off, stand at attention, salute, "Sir, Airman Hough reports as ordered."

One of the strange things about the military justice system is that a commanding officer is the final authority on whether or not someone is charged with a crime. They'll usually go along with the recommendation from the judge advocate. But as a lot of men accused of rape or spousal abuse can tell you, a commanding officer makes the final decision. Colonel Young either hadn't yet come to terms with the idea he'd never get his general's star and was being careful, or he didn't want to save me.

He read the charges: Arson with intent to defraud. And something about conduct unbecoming, but I hear they always add that. If there's a crime becoming of a U.S. airman, I'm guessing they wouldn't charge anyone for it. My eyes were stuck on the first line: "United States Air Force vs. Senior Airman Lauren Hough." There it was, completely absurd and fucking terrifying.

I signed the charge sheet, the colonel dismissed me, and I marched out. Kept right on walking across the street to base legal, where I locked myself in the bathroom and cried. I was going to have to call my parents.

The legal office let me use a desk and a phone. I called

my mom first because I didn't know how to reach my dad. When I'd told her about the car back when it happened, she said, "Oh, Jesus, Lauren. This lesbian thing. I don't know about it."

I was worried she'd tell me more about how this lesbian thing wasn't a good idea—"You can't have kids, it's just hedonism, Lauren." Hedonism would require some degree of happiness. Mom hadn't had much time to get used to what she called "this lesbian thing." When I'd told her a couple years before this, she said she hoped I'd change my mind. Since those first arguments, when it seemed like all she did was cry on the phone, and I'd cry after we hung up, we'd agreed to a sort of Don't Ask, Don't Tell policy of our own.

But she didn't say any of that. She said she'd pray for me. She said she'd come to the trial. She asked me if I needed money for a lawyer. I told her the Air Force was providing one.

"I'll be okay. I need a number for Dad." She said to ask Valerie. She might know.

Valerie was still at work when I called. I left a message for her to call me. I tried to call Mikey. We didn't talk much, not since I left home and joined the Air Force. He was in college, still living with Gabe, who Mom had finally divorced soon after I left for the Air Force. Mom had moved to Massachusetts. Mikey still had to finish college.

I hadn't talked to Gabe in years. I called the house in Texas, and Gabe answered. I didn't get the words out— "Can I talk to Mikey?"—before he hung up.

I wasn't sure until that moment that I would call

my dad. But somewhere between the click of the line
going dead and my setting the phone back into its cradle,
I knew I had to. I walked back to my dorm room and
waited for the phone to ring.

Valerie called back and gave me the number for a Family home in Sweden where she thought Dad might be.

Because Dad was still in the Family, we were never
sure where he was. I didn't know if he'd ever leave. He'd
visited a couple times since we'd left the cult when I was
fifteen. But the joy of each visit had dissolved into heated
words and tears as he defended them. His eyes damp,
he'd say, "Let's just agree to disagree." And I'd tell him,
"They told you to say that." Because they had. I'd read
the memo. But sometimes his love for me broke through
the fog of a cult member's brain. When I'd told him I
was gay, he didn't condemn me. I knew he was supposed
to. But he didn't. All he said was, "Oh, honey, that must
be so hard on you." I hoped I could break through again.

I didn't always make it easy. When I told him I'd
joined the Air Force, I told him to hurt him. He was a
pacifist who'd gone so far as joining a cult to avoid getting
his draft card. He was nineteen, hitchhiking to Mexico.
A couple cult members found him sitting out in front
of a library in Dallas. Asked him if he believed in God,
and he said, "Yeah, sure, man. I'm god, you're god, we're
all god." They took him back to the Texas Soul Clinic.
Thirty years later, on a different continent, he was still
under their sway. I knew you couldn't argue someone
out of delusion. Each hateful word would cause him to
dig in deeper. But still, I wanted my dad to come to my
court-martial. At least I knew there was no way he'd side
with the Air Force.

I called the home. I never concerned myself with time zones. I didn't care about who I woke up. They'd never been all that concerned with respecting my sleep. The guy who answered the phone pretended he didn't speak English at first. Said he didn't understand. That line, "I don't understand," is the sum total of my Swedish. I said, "I'm looking for my dad, tall guy, American. I think he's going by Joshua. Married to a little Venezuelan woman, probably goes by Esther."

He said, "Oh, he's not here?" Something close to an American accent. Hard consonants, gratingly positive inflection. They all fucking sound like that. "Listen. Can you call back in a few hours?"

I asked, "Is he not there right now, or he doesn't live there?" I had to be careful. If this guy hung up the phone, there would be no way to reach my dad.

He said, "Doesn't live here."

"Well, I can't call back. I have to find him. It's an emergency."

He said, "Okay. Call back in a half hour? I need to ask someone. God bless you."

I could hear a party gearing up in a room down the hall, loud voices, Limp Bizkit—Friday night in the dorms.

I called the number again. Three rings. Four. I was afraid he wouldn't answer. I was afraid they'd pack up the home and leave because of a phone call—not actually unheard of. All it takes is asking them if you need to pick up white sugar on the way home—universal Family code for "the police are on their way." The home will be empty in less than an hour. They're easily spooked. But on the seventh ring, the same guy picked up. "Hello?" he said.

"Were you able to find anyone?"

"Oh, yes," he said. "I'm not sure, of course. This is the number of a home in Moscow, but you'll have to look up the country code? He might be there. If not, ask for Swiss Aaron. He might know."

Moscow. The OSI was going to open an entirely new investigation into my phone bill. But I couldn't worry about that. Swiss Aaron passed me on to someone else, who passed me on to someone else. Another home in another country. In all, I went through five numbers before I called a different home in Sweden and Dad answered. Even in Swedish, I knew his voice. I said hi.

He said, "Schatzi!" He always calls me that—it's something like a German version of "sweetie." "Hey, kiddo. How are you?" I'd done the math by this point. It was five a.m., and this was how excited my dad was to hear from me. I wanted to cry. I wanted to ask him if he'd been fishing lately, anything but what I had to tell him.

"I'm in trouble, Dad."

"What? No. What's the matter?" he said.

I told him everything—started with the death threats, moved on to the car, the investigation. "Anyway, there's going to be a court-martial," I said. I knew he might be fuzzy on what that meant. "It's like a trial, Dad. It is a trial. And if they say I'm guilty, I'm going to jail. The max is ten years."

"But you didn't do anything," he said. "So there's no need to worry?" At least he didn't offer to pray with me.

I told him, "No. It looks really bad. I'm the only suspect because they never looked for who did it. And they're saying I didn't want to go to Greece."

He interrupted me then. "Why wouldn't you want to go to Greece? That's so stupid."

I said, "Fuck if I know, Dad. But they're saying I couldn't afford the car and didn't want to go to Greece, so I torched it. I don't know. It looks bad."

He asked for my number. He said he'd call me back. I figured he'd wake up the shepherds, whoever was in charge of the home. They'd pray about it and decide it wasn't in the Lord's will for my dad to care about what happened to me—story of my life. I wondered if he'd call me back at all.

My phone rang. "Hey, so when is this happening?" Dad asked. I gave him the dates. He said he was coming. I couldn't believe it. My dad, who hated that I'd even joined the military. Who I hadn't seen but a couple times since I was seven. Who stayed in the Family long after we'd left. My dad was coming to my trial. I'd fought against letting myself hope. He said he'd called his brother, a lawyer, who told him I needed a civilian lawyer. Said his mom had left him some money and he'd pay.

And so my dad got me a lawyer named Gary Myers. Gary would run the defense, but Gary said I could pick a free Air Force lawyer from a different base, and should. I might as well have both. The Air Force gave me a captain from a base in Oklahoma. I named him the Apostle because he asked if I was a Christian. When I said I'm not anymore, he wanted to pray with me. I wanted him to defend me, but if he just wanted to pray, I had Gary Myers, who was exactly as big a prick as you want defending you.

I'm serious. He yelled at me on the phone for talking

to Sheriff Horton and the investigators on base. I said, "I didn't know any better. I talked to legal and didn't talk to him after that."

He said, "Well, maybe you're not a complete fucking idiot. All right. Keep your mouth shut."

My court-martial was held in October 2000. The trial lasted four days. Mom and Dad shared a rental car from the airport and stayed in the same hotel. They showed up every morning and sat outside the courtroom. They couldn't come in, in case they were called as witnesses.

The prosecution started. (Prosecution, jury, trial—there are different words for all of these in the military. But we'll skip the lesson in military law.) They said I was a liar, bought a car I couldn't afford. I didn't tell anyone about the death threats. The first bit may have been true, but not how they meant it. And "Okay, sure, but I lie to hide who I am" isn't much of a defense.

Sergeant Peters took the stand. He'd been transferred to another base, but was back for the trial. He said, "Those dogs always bark at anything on the street, even if they're dead asleep." I thought we should all drive over to his house, play a game of touch football on his lawn to prove his dogs wouldn't bark unless someone rang the doorbell.

I wasn't surprised he'd turned on me. You may think you have friends who'll help you bury a body. But when the cops show up and flash their badges, your friends will point to bodies you've never seen to keep the cops from looking their way. There are only two sides, and when it comes down to it, even those with nothing to hide will side with those who have the power.

They put my old roommate, Eric, on the stand. He said, "She always locked her car."

If I always locked my car, no one could have filled it full of gas without setting off the alarm. What he didn't mention was that soon after I'd had the alarm installed, I'd regretted the money I'd wasted on it. The fighter jets set off every car alarm on base every time they buzzed over. We'd talked about it. He said I should have the alarm sensor recalibrated. Instead, I stopped locking my car, to keep it from going off.

He said, "Her CDs weren't in the car when it burned."

If my CDs weren't in the car, obviously I'd removed them before lighting the car on fire. Or I'd brought them into the house to listen to something or reorganize my CDs, a favorite hobby of anyone with two books full of CDs. Maybe by mood this time. I don't actually remember, and I didn't then either. I just remember the exasperation I felt as he said it. "A few days later, I saw her CD case in the house." And the prosecutor looked at the jury like he'd found the smoking gun.

Eric said, "She didn't want to go to Greece."

As my dad said, that's just stupid. I hoped my lawyers would have an argument because all I could think of was, *That's fucking stupid. I tried to go twice.*

He said, "She borrowed my gas can a few weeks before."

Okay, that did look bad. Really bad. And my explanation after the fact wouldn't help much. The last time I'd driven through Alabama, before borrowing the gas can,

I'd been jumped coming out of a gas station bathroom because a high schooler told her boyfriend and his buddies, "That's the pervert was usin' the ladies'." I was only spared serious injury when a trucker named Jimmy T saw my uniform and stepped in about the time I hit the ground. Jimmy T told me as he helped me back to my car that he didn't much care for my "lifestyle and such. But that uniform means somethin'." And "you can't come back to Jesus if yer already dead." Guess he wasn't a "once saved, always saved" sort of Christian.

To avoid a repeat of the experience during Thanksgiving that year, I was planning to only stop at busy truck stops if I could. Just in case, I borrowed Eric's gas can. But on the way back I'd given it to someone who came up to me and said he was out of gas—I figured it'd do him more good than giving him money. And then they'd found the molten remains of a gas can in my car.

This was the prosecution's big moment. And they played it up, and Eric was happy to play along. He wanted to be a state trooper when he got out and moved home to Ohio. His brother was a trooper and told Eric his association with a known felon wouldn't look good on his application.

He said, "She joked about the whole thing. She didn't seem scared at all." We'll ignore that assessment of my fear level because he didn't know. I did joke about it. That's true. My outward reaction to the entire affair didn't fit what everyone seemed to think should have been my reaction. Seemed like they'd have believed me if I'd cried in front of them. But they didn't grow up in the Family. They didn't grow up in constant fear. They hadn't learned sometimes all you can do is fucking laugh.

Sheriff Horton took the stand, after a small commotion caused when he walked into the courtroom wearing his gun and the Air Force police had to take it from him. He corroborated Eric's opinion of my unlikely affect. He said I was too calm when I talked to him. Most people, he said, "They're crying or foaming at the mouth to kill the bastard who did it. She laughed about it." See what I mean?

Gary asked him if he'd tried to find the white car the neighbor had seen speeding away, if he'd looked at anyone else.

Horton shifted in his seat and said, "Well, no. But she wouldn't take the polygraph."

"It's all circumstantial," Gary told me. "This is what happens. You'll even start to believe you're guilty. Just hang tough until it's our turn." He didn't seem the type to play cheerleader. Leading up to the trial, he'd been all business. How I was holding up wasn't any of his concern. Now he was trying to comfort me, and that scared me. I knew I wasn't guilty. But guilt or innocence had never mattered all that much in my experience. And I was learning my experience in the Family wasn't as unique as I'd believed it to be when we left.

In between testimony, Gary paced the hall and talked to himself. The Apostle prayed with Mom—turns out he was useful after all. Dad sat in a chair and looked dazed. I stood outside and smoked. And I thought about going to prison.

I'd been locked in rooms before. The Family believed problem cases like me needed to be isolated from the rest—one bad apple and all. The last time, when I was fourteen, I broke down after only two days. The walls closed in and I couldn't breathe and the world got dark. It changes you each time. You go through the first few hours in silence. Then you start talking to yourself. You time your pulse. You pick at split ends, scabs, and ingrown hairs. You sleep. And when you wake up, the room is smaller. You have to get out. Your chest tightens. You need space. Just a little breeze. You have to see the sky. One star. You tell yourself it'll be okay, they'll let you out. But you don't believe your own words. The harder you try to control your breath, the worse it gets. You start hearing voices. You start to really panic then, and you've lost. Once the panic starts, it doesn't end. You can learn to ride the waves, but every single wave is a fight for survival. And you don't come out stronger. You lose something each time. You lose faith in yourself. I wasn't doing it again.

The prosecution rested and my lawyer Gary took over. My new sergeant, the guy who replaced Peters, said, "Every airman on base is driving a car they can't afford. That's what idiot kids who've never had any money do."

A couple airmen from my squadron said, "Everyone knows she's gay and some people have a big problem with it." They'd seen the first message in Egypt, the one in the dust on my car. Shouldn't have been a surprise. The car had been parked right where everyone smoked outside the operations center. But I'd been too busy hoping no one had seen the writing to ask if anyone had.

Another roommate said, "She never always locked anything. She's a slob. Sometimes her CDs are in the house because she never sleeps and she listens to music late at night. All she ever talked about was leaving this base. Do you know how much it sucks here?"

The lab guy said, "The DNA test on the hair they found on the rag was inconclusive."

Gary said, "The results I have here say it's not a match."

"Well, yeah," the guy said. "That's what I said."

Mom took the stand and told them how many countries I'd lived in and maybe I wasn't a liar when I said I've been there. She said, "When things go really wrong, Lauren gets quiet or tries to make it a joke. If she needed money, she would've asked me. She knows she can."

It was strange watching my mom on the witness stand. She didn't look at me. But she was defending me. And I wondered then why she hadn't before, when I was younger, when I needed her to protect me. I flashed through all the times I'd been in trouble, and I couldn't remember a single time she'd spoken up. But mostly, she wasn't even there.

I did like that Mom and Dad were going to dinner together every night during the trial. They weren't fighting.

I've never seen *The Parent Trap*, but I think most kids nurse a fantasy their parents will get back together. I was no different. After Dad, Mom had married my stepdad and my stepdad was an asshole. My dad was nice. But the fun thing about being a child of divorce is you're half of both parents. And both sides of you are tired of the other's shit. My dad was forgetful and so laid back he seemed stoned. My mom's baseline anxiety level is "just saw a spider." Still, I was glad they'd have each other because I'd decided, if convicted, I wasn't going to prison.

Even before you get the verdict, the military makes

you prepare to be locked up. You have to box up your belongings for storage. You're given a list of what you're required to take—five white T-shirts, five black T-shirts, one white towel, five pairs of socks, five white sports bras, one bar of soap, and so on. So after I packed up my room, I borrowed Dad's rental car and drove to Walmart, where I bought what I needed off the list. I stopped in sporting goods and contemplated the knives. They wouldn't work—too slow. The base hospital was a five-minute walk from the courtroom.

I dropped the car at the base hotel, gave Dad the keys and a hug. He wanted me to stay there. Just have a beer at least, he said. "Your mom wants you to call her." I didn't stay for a beer and I didn't call. I knew she'd convince me to sleep in her room.

Back in my dorm room, I wrote them each a note. I didn't say much. Just told them not to blame themselves. Told them I was sorry. I hid the note behind a painting I left on the wall because my brother painted that and I wanted to look at it some more. Everything else I owned was boxed and labeled for storage. I put on my blues, made sure my ribbon rack was straight, and shoved the gun under my service jacket, under my belt at the small of my back. I checked the mirror. You couldn't tell. I took it out again and sat down to wait for the morning.

I sat there on my bare mattress all night, and all night I tried to talk myself out of it. It was only ten years. Maybe I wouldn't get the full ten. I couldn't do it in front of my mom: How do you make your mom watch you die? But what if they cuffed me right away? My dad would be there, and maybe he or someone else would know and cover her eyes. I'd have to be fast. The sentence was only ten years, and I could take ten years. I'd be thirty-three when I got out. That wasn't so old. I stared at the painting and wanted to call my brother. I wouldn't tell him. But if I did, I knew he wouldn't try to talk me out of it. He'd just talk. And say all the wrong things and all the right things that only my brother can say. I'd hang up the phone, and I wouldn't want to die more than I wanted to live in a cell. But I didn't call.

We sat in the courtroom and waited for the jury to decide my fate—my parents, my lawyers, a few of the airmen who'd testified for me—talking about nothing. The roommate who called me a slob said he was secure enough to admit Ricky Martin was damn sexy. My new sergeant said, "Your mom's got presence. Like Jackie O, with balls of steel." I appreciated that they were trying to break the tension, but all I could think of was whether or not I'd be able to do it.

When they said not guilty and my mom started crying, I cried too. And then I started laughing. I knew people were looking at me, the jurors questioning their verdict. Who laughs? Who goes through a trial and then fucking laughs? Maybe people who have grown up in cults laugh. Of course they didn't know that. But I laughed. Maybe it was just how the tension fell out of me, maybe because I'd get to live because that one time, maybe the only time in my life, my parents stood up for me.

The next week, I didn't expect to go right back to my desk. I had "won," but I knew I'd lost even the small place I'd carved out for myself at Shaw. They'd already replaced me since I was supposed to be in Greece. Besides, there was the issue of my security clearance. They gave me a new job that still wasn't my old job, but at least I wasn't handing out towels at the gym. My new job was supervising the new airmen, just out of training, who'd been assigned to maintain the dorms—changing lightbulbs, cleaning dayrooms, mowing lawns. At first it was fine. I drove around in a golf cart and made sure everything got done. But soon it became apparent how much damage the OSI had done with their little investigation.

Everyone on base knew who I was, and what I was, and it didn't take long for word to spread to the baby airmen I was supervising. Mostly it was just jokes: "Where've you guys been? You're two hours late." "Hey, don't ask, don't tell, right?" But a few of them stopped listening to me altogether. I'd assign them to clean a dayroom; they'd tell me I shouldn't be wearing a uniform, much less stripes, and there wasn't a goddamn thing I could do about it.

A month passed and new orders came, to Greece again. Somehow they still hadn't filled the position I'd been assigned a year earlier. But I only got a day to celebrate before the orders were canceled. The Greece assignment required an add-on security clearance called the Personnel Reliability Program. The PRP is supposed to ensure only qualified people have access to nuclear weapons. Mine was denied because I had a food allergy. I guess you never know when someone will bring guacamole into the office and, bam, my avocado allergy sends me into a guac-fueled rage and I hit the launch button. You just can't take that sort of risk. I knew then they were never going to welcome me back. My career was over. And that's when I finally heard from Mikey.

Because we couldn't talk on the phone much—this was long before everyone had a cell phone—we used to send books. I sent him *The Fountainhead* because I thought Rand had some great ideas. (I was nineteen.) He responded with *Of Human Bondage*. I sent *Slaughterhouse-Five*. Mikey sent *Catch-22*. I sent *Trainspotting*. A few months later, he sent me *Fight Club*. We'd underline passages we liked, sometimes write notes in the margins. And we'd been doing this ever since I left home. So when I opened my mailbox and saw his blocky handwriting on a package, I didn't open it in the mail room. I waited until the end of the day, and all day tried to guess what he'd sent me. When I got back to my dorm room and tore open the brown paper, I sat down and laughed— Oscar Wilde. I flipped through the book and found the passage he'd circled.

Society, as we have constituted it, will have no place for me, has none to offer; but Nature, whose sweet rains fall on unjust and just alike, will have clefts in the rocks where I may hide, and secret valleys in whose silence I may weep undisturbed. She will hang the night with stars so that I may walk abroad in the darkness without stumbling, and send the wind over my footprints so that none may track me to my hurt: she will cleanse me in great waters, and with bitter herbs make me whole.

My little brother had been with me through it all. We grew up together in the Family, slept in the same bed for years, had the same stepdad who would never think we were good enough to love. Mikey had seen the worst in me and still loved me because it was never a question—he was my brother. And he knew what I wanted, maybe understood more than I did why I joined the Air Force. I thought I'd find something in the military. I'd wear the same uniform as everyone else. They'd have to accept me because I was one of them. I'd find what every book I read, every movie I watched, told me I'd find: friends and maybe even a sort of family, a place where I belonged.

But all I'd done was join another cult. And they didn't want me any more than the last one had. And there was my brother telling me what I knew but hadn't been able to admit: I'd never belong. But maybe that was okay. I stayed up all night reading. And I knew what I had to do. I wrote a letter.

A few days later, I walked into Colonel Young's office for the second and last time. His secretary didn't have to remind me to report. When he said, "At ease," I handed him a piece of paper. I didn't trust myself to speak beyond the required "reports as ordered" bit. The letter said, "I'm gay. Please process my discharge." And on January 12, 2001, I was given an honorable discharge, and forty-eight hours to leave the base.

My DD 214, my service record, says, "Homosexual admission." It leaves out the other part, that the Air Force was never going to let me leave Shaw Air Force Base, that they didn't care who'd been threatening me, who'd torched my car, or what that person might do next. The paperwork doesn't say that they would never accept me, that they gave me no choice.

So I did what I'd been trained to do my entire childhood when we'd been ready to leave at a moment's notice: I packed what I needed and tossed what I could do without.

And I tried to come up with a new plan for my life.

The Slide

When I met Jay, he had a mustache and an accent like Julia Sugarbaker, if Julia Sugarbaker'd ever bragged her family owned a double-wide. He lost the mustache eventually. The accent never faded, but did help when I felt like strangling him, which was often. He's the sort of freak who wakes up in a good mood and thinks singing Bette Midler's "The Rose" at the top of his lungs will improve yours. He was raised a Pentecostal in some backwoods strip mall with a trailer park on the Georgia-Florida border. He'd never seen snow. But the strip mall had a recruiting station. So he joined the Air Force, and got stationed about fifty miles north, at Shaw Air Force Base.

The other thing about Jay is he's smarter than I am. One threat left on his truck, he didn't wait to see what caught fire. He violated Don't Ask, Don't Tell and got himself kicked out of the Air Force before the Air Force had time to fuck with him.

I ran into him at a gay bar in Columbia, South Carolina, after my own discharge. The first thing he said was, "Oh, Lord. Honey, what did you do to your hair?" The word "hair" had three syllables. I'd just shaved my head. Granted, I have the wrong-shaped head to be shaving it, but you don't know that until it's too late. I didn't give him near as much shit for his mustache.

I told him I was headed to D.C. He said Atlanta could work too—we could reach either on a tank of gas. We figured we'd have a better chance of surviving if we teamed up. I ordered a beer, and when the bartender handed me the change, I pulled a quarter out of the pile. It landed on heads. Jay headed out first. I was waiting on a final unemployment check. With that, and a couple more plasma donations at thirty dollars a pint, I figured I'd have enough to survive a few weeks.

I rolled into D.C. the summer manhole covers kept flying into the air and people told you Chandra Levy was in their ab class at the gym. Every radio station was playing "Lady Marmalade." It was the time people now refer to as "before America changed."

We thought it should be easy to find jobs in D.C. Or maybe that was just me. I somehow naively still believed the utter bullshit that anything I learned in the military would be worth something outside. I thought I could mention I'd just been kicked out under DADT and gays would hire me out of, I don't know, pity, maybe? I didn't exactly think it through.

I didn't realize no one outside the military knew gays were getting kicked out of the military at ten times the rate before Don't Ask, Don't Tell. You could argue more gays joined the military, duped into believing they'd be safe because of the law. You'd be wrong. For people like Jay and me, the military's the only chance we have of getting out of our shithole towns and our miserable destiny of maybe making middle management at the meatpacking plant or the Piggly Wiggly. We didn't have Google. We had commercials promising us college and travel, training in a high-demand field. Put "proven leader" on your résumé and rise to the top. Air Force blues were a golden ticket to success. We ended up in South Carolina, with "HOMOSEXUAL ADMISSION" stamped on the discharge papers we'd have to show anytime we applied for a job.

When we talked about moving to D.C., we talked about not having to hide who we were. We talked about living in a place where you didn't have to look both ways when you left a bar—checking for the occasional truck full of rednecks waiting to toss their empty beer bottles at a few queers. We talked about having gay friends. We talked about living.

We probably should've talked more about jobs and a place to live. I don't know how we expected to find a place to live without jobs.

With just the money I'd make selling my car, renting a single room was the only possible option. Even so, judging by the ads, the assholes I'd potentially be sharing a house with were insufferable. They all sounded the same: "No meat eaters, no vegans, gay-friendly but don't be obvious about it, down-to-earth, professional, spiritual, no drinkers, no overnight guests without permission from all roommates, no drugs, we have the most insane house parties, quiet and clean, laid back, share cooking, don't touch my fucking food, no whores, no sluts, no degenerates, no Republicans, no Democrats, no smokers, only outside smokers, 420-friendly, no drama, no atheists, cat-friendly. Cheerful. Upbeat. Positive vibes only."

They had all the power and knew it. I wished bedbugs on all of them. After days and weeks of searching, it was clear no one was renting to us without jobs. But then we didn't have a fucking phone number to write on our job applications, much less an address.

This was about the time everyone started getting cell phones. It wasn't yet weird to not have one, but phones would've helped, if only to find each other, because without a room to rent, we were living in our cars—me in a Ford Aspire, Jay in a single-cab Ranger—and we had to move them constantly to avoid being ticketed or towed.

During the day, we opted for the more residential streets of Dupont Circle and hoped the prying eyes of neighbors would keep someone from breaking a window and stealing what little we had. At night, we'd park nearer the bars on 17th, hoping someone would think we were sleeping it off.

There's no sleeping in when you're living in a car. You're up when the sun hits the windshield. A quick shower in a McDonald's bathroom sink, and it's time to find a coffee shop, share a drip coffee, and keep an eye out for an abandoned paper to check the want ads.

After a day of walking around the city, applying for

jobs I wouldn't get, I'd search the usual streets for Jay's bright yellow Ranger. Some nights I never found him. If I did, we'd do dinner.

Dinner was nachos from 7-Eleven with as much Alpo-looking chili and condiments as we could pile onto the chips. We'd sit on his tailgate, and he'd say someone told him a bar down on Capitol Hill was hiring. I'd tell him I looked at a studio. It was $1,100 a month for bunk beds, a dorm fridge, and a hot plate. Then he'd head off to the bars to see who'd buy him a drink. Sometimes I'd tag along. But I'd usually slip out long before closing.

This was where I was supposed to fit in, the gay community. But the wealthy white population of Dupont Circle, with their straight white teeth and gym tans, Abercrombie & Fitch T-shirts and J.Crew flip-flops, their therapy appointments and brunch dates, their Rehoboth vacations and weekends in New York, were so fucking happy and well-adjusted it made my skin crawl to be around them. Happy well-adjusted people don't join the military. They don't have to. Goes without saying that happy well-adjusted kids weren't common in the cult either. But both cultures—the religious cult and the white-teeth gays—share a rule about smiling. Both believe in the power of positive thinking to keep things like homelessness at bay. This way, when you fall, you have only yourself to blame. There has to be a reason because no one wants to think it could happen to them.

I used to get in trouble for not smiling. I have this weird tic that means my face generally expresses the emotion I'm feeling. "Be so happy!" is a Family order as common in communes as "positive energy" is out here.

The single stupidest thing I got in trouble for was, unsurprisingly, about the worst trouble I got into. I was ten. We lived in Osaka in this tiny apartment with two other families—one family per room, and a single person called a single in the living room. Osaka and D.C. have similar climates—brutally cold winters and swampy summers. We convinced a fan-store owner to donate a few fans to the nice Christian missionaries. But mobile hot air isn't much of an improvement.

I'd lie there on the futon I had to share with my brother and try not to scratch the heat rash on my back and belly. We couldn't shut the window to drown out the nightly fireworks in the park without suffocating in the heat. I couldn't fucking sleep.

One morning I was folding laundry for the home, and I said, "I need some coffee." A rational person might respond with "You're ten." I was not raised by rational people. After the worst beating of my life and two days of intensive prayer to figure out why I'd been walking around in the dumps (I was tired), why I hadn't smiled two days before when I'd specifically been told to smile (I was tired), and why I, a ten-year-old, didn't say "I need Jesus" or "I need the Holy Spirit" or "I need to pray more," all very normal things to say when one is tired, they figured out it had been their fault all along. I'd never received the Holy Spirit.

They laughed like they'd just found the remote control in the fridge after a thorough search of the couch cushions. It was a silly mistake. Easily rectified.

They prayed and I prayed and accepted the Holy Spirit. We waited, kneeling on the tatami-mat floor with our faces cupped in our hands, sweating. Nothing happened. So I did what anyone would do: I started speaking in tongues. I thought for sure I'd be found out. They'd know I was faking it. But the home shepherd, the big honcho of our little apartment, ordained by God, started translating my tongues into King James English. I kept my eyes shut in fear they'd see the incredulous look on my face, the *Holy shit, you guys have been faking this whole time.* Then they changed my name to Merry.

I wasn't any less tired, and I sure as fuck wasn't any happier. But I was careful to be upbeat, to make my voice sound positive, to walk around with a smile on my face like a lunatic named Merry.

One night in some Dupont bar, I had a couple too many free beers from a guy who thought Jay's accent was "just delicious," and someone told me to smile. I was being a drag. I told him I was tired, I'd been sleeping in my car. He said, "You're never going to fix your situation if you don't put out some positive vibes."

People like that are why I felt better walking around at night. I couldn't sleep anyway. My little Ford Aspire, the car my mom bought me to replace my toasted Acura, forced me to sleep sitting up or in some origami-inspired knot in the back seat. It was too hot to sleep with the windows up, but the mosquitoes found a cracked window as fast as they'd find a vein. I'd spend hours just walking around the city, waiting until the air was cool enough and I was exhausted enough to sleep.

Some nights, I'd wander down to the National Mall. I liked the Mall at night. Too dark to see the dead grass and the trash. No sweating, corn-syrup-fed tourists dragging their sunburnt kids to another monument. No delusional activists convinced if they just had a few more protesters or maybe if the corporate media would just cover the march, man. No happy couples holding hands or groups of friends throwing a Frisbee around.

The Mall at night looks like West Texas, dark and lonely, but instead of a grain elevator glowing in the distance, it's granite monuments. And homeless veterans. One of them had a dog who was licking hotdog remains off the marble steps of the Lincoln Memorial.

I told the old vet it was strange, that this is where people in movies eat ice cream during their clandestine rendezvous. I didn't mean to tell him. I'd started talking to myself. I'd think something, often just a word, and realize I'd said it aloud and look around for witnesses like I'd tripped on the sidewalk. And to me, it was strange to sit on the steps looking out at the reflecting pool like a movie character. It looks different in the movies. It looks bigger. It looks real.

He said, "The ice cream vendors charge too much." He was sitting on the steps and asked if I had a spare cigarette. I dug my pack out of my pocket, trying to pull out just the pack and not the few dollars I had folded there. I asked if I could pet his dog and he nodded and said, "Sure thing. That's Sergeant." Then he added, "She's a girl, though."

The dog, just a puppy, a brown mutt with white patches, rolled over and let me pet her belly. Then she darted back over to the guy, so I sat on the steps, hoping the puppy would let me pet her again. We talked about his dog for a minute. I asked why "Sergeant," and he said, "She keeps me in line."

I kept thinking I should've just given him a dollar with the cigarette. Seemed rude to hand him one while we were talking, like I'd be interrupting a moment of normalcy to remind him of his circumstances. So I waited until he stood and lifted his backpack.

Then I handed him a dollar. He took the dollar and stuck out his hand as if to shake mine. So we shook. But then he turned my hand over, gently, and placed the dollar in my palm. He said, "You just try to find your way back before it's too late."

I said, "I will," hoping to end this scene.

He didn't release my hand. His damp eyes bored into mine. And he said, "Listen to me. Don't wait until you hit the slide." I thought I knew what he meant. This was getting weird. I wasn't scared of him. He had a dog. But I wasn't exactly comfortable holding hands either.

I said, "I will. Really," with a conviction I was quickly losing.

He shook his head slowly like I was a dumb kid who wasn't listening. He told me the slide's when you start looking homeless. "Like me. See this beard? My clothes? The way I smell? You lose too much. You run out of toiletries. Your shoes wear down. Your clothes start looking like shit. Then they won't even let you into a bathroom to try and clean up. You don't come back from this." Then he whistled his dog back over to him and he was gone.

I just stood there a minute and thought, *Well, fuck.*

Then realized I'd said it aloud. I wondered whether, if I'd been someone else, he'd have just thanked me for the dollar, told me things were looking up, projected positivity, the can-do attitude we demand from the poor.

What scared me is he knew I was homeless. What scared me more is he gave the dollar back. I don't think I slept at all that night. I'd been trying to think of anything but how close I was to what he called the slide. But he knew how close I was. I refused to give it a name for fear I'd call it something like They Were Right.

One of the less pleasant hang-ups from growing up in a cult—and none are pleasant—is the gnawing thought at the back of your mind that they might've been right. Anytime they wanted to scare the shit out of us, they used these stories they called Traumatic Testimonies. They had a whole series of them. The plot was always the same. Someone left the Family, turned his back on God, rejected our prophet, and returned to the System. Bad things happened. He ended up using drugs, marrying a godless woman, rejoining Fleetwood Mac. Either way, the fool who'd left the Family would soon spin into suicidal depression or profound sadness. He'd realize he'd been selfish and proud. And he'd come back to the Family, where all his problems would go away because Jesus still loved him.

I was living the plot of one of those Traumatic Testimonies. Of course the guy who ended up homeless in that story wasn't homeless anymore once he moved back into a Family home. So I don't know if he learned his lesson so much as made a desperate decision.

Either way, this was the threat they worded as

prophecy—if I left, I'd end up homeless on the streets of New York. Eventually I'd turn to prostitution. They weren't all that creative. But it stuck. That I couldn't afford a bus ticket to New York wasn't much comfort. I'd fucked up my life so completely I was proving them right. And I sure as fuck wasn't planning on rejoining the Family to complete the cycle.

The next night, I followed Jay to the bar. No more wandering off alone to talk to weird homeless guys who knew too much. And somehow, we ended up at the one bar that was hiring.

I don't remember the ad in the *Blade*. I only remember that Jay and I agreed it seemed "sketchy." We also agreed that no matter what we found at 444 M Street, we were taking the room. We were out of money, couldn't even afford the metro from Dupont.

The neighborhood was in fact sketchy, down by what would become the convention center, which back then was just a hole in the ground. The sort of neighborhood you'd head to if you needed a blow job or rock. But I didn't mind the neighborhood. At least no one in the hood tells you to smile. (Okay, one guy did. He'd just tried to mug me. I say "tried" not because I did a Bourne-style slap-and-grab and turned the gun on him. I don't know karate. He kept the gun. I told him I had three dollars and was headed to the store to steal tampons if he wanted to hit me on the way back. He stared at me a moment. Then he shoved his gun back into his pocket, grinned, and said, "Smile. You're white enough, you don't need a gun." I smiled. But that was later on.)

When Carl answered the door in a flowing caftan, the memories of his hair tied in a low ponytail, our suspicions were confirmed. Sketchy. Carl said he was an Episcopalian priest. He asked our birth dates and offered to do our charts, for fifty bucks, a discount. If he'd dreamed bigger, he could've been a cult leader. He said I had a good aura, but he said it like he'd just noticed an unpleasant smell in his mustache. I hated him.

The main level of the house was littered with crucifixes but also Shivas and voodoo idols and Buddhas, the skinny Southeast Asian variety, not the fat, grinning Buddha I remembered from Japan. It looked like a fusion church for the insane. There was an English basement he said was off-limits as he padded up the stairs in pink jelly sandals. We later found out the basement held a meth lab. We didn't recognize the smell then. We've never forgotten it.

Carl said he didn't need the money; he just liked the company that he found in his renters. The renters shared the third floor. Three rooms. One bathroom. There was Tony, whose name wasn't Tony, but he was from Jersey (I'd watched a few episodes of *The Sopranos*), and Alanna, the Capitol Hill intern who'd turn me on to Billy Bragg. And there was the alcove with a door that was meant to be our room, or my room really.

The room, a ten-by-six closet, was for one. Carl was adamant about that. An extra person would be charged ten dollars per night after seven nights. I looked at Jay. He was looking at the twin bed. With the twin bed shoved against the front window, there wasn't much room left. I assured Carl it would only be me. Jay had a place. He might stay a couple nights. No big deal.

Carl wanted first, last, and deposit, $1,500. I told him we'd be back with the money. Sorry, *I* would be back with the money. No, Jay definitely has his own place. We shook on it.

That was Sunday. On Monday, CarMax gave me $1,650 for the Ford Aspire. The check came with a twenty-four-hour hold.

We just had to make it one last night.

It'd been weeks since I checked my email. The upside of all this happening when it did: social media didn't exist. I didn't have to post hopeful updates on Facebook about feeling really good about the fifty-seven job applications I'd sent out. *Send positive vibes, guys.* I didn't have to decorate the Aspire with stenciled aspirational quotes about stopping to smell the flowers. No one saw a picture of our Alpo nachos on Instagram. But with a room and jobs in our near future—#FingersCrossed—I decided to blow a couple dollars on the coffee shop computer.

I found a message (Hotmail) from a guy I'd known at Shaw. He was stationed at the Pentagon now. He said we should get a beer. I shot a message back asking if he'd mind if I crashed at his place for a night. I didn't tell him I'd be bringing a friend. I hit refresh a few times. Let Jay check his email. And when I pulled mine up, I had a reply. He said he had to work. But he could leave his keys on the wheel of his truck in the Pentagon parking lot. This sounded like a simple plan.

We had a couple drinks first to celebrate. So by the time we got to the Pentagon, it was nearly two a.m. I don't know why no one stopped us, driving around in that fucking banana-yellow truck. I'd never been to the

Pentagon and didn't know I had about as much chance of breaking into the Pentagon as I had of finding a gray Chevy in the parking lot. A parking lot that, by the way, is bigger than most Midwestern towns. Every fucking truck was silver or gray. I started blaming the trucks. I started yelling about the fucking military. I started crying.

All this time sleeping in my car, watching my cash dwindle to nothing. Applying for jobs I'd never get. Showering in bathroom sinks. Worrying about parking tickets. Worrying about being seen. Worrying about the little things I could fix because I couldn't fix the big thing: that the Family had been right. I was fucking terrified I'd wake up on Tuesday and we'd lose the room or the job or the check would bounce.

Not finding my friend's truck seemed like a bad sign, a very bad sign. If I were someone who believed in signs, who believed in having a bad feeling about this, I'd say I knew what was coming. I'd be full of shit.

Jay handled my freak-out well. It was only fair. I'd dealt with his snot-crying over a broken cigarette—it's always the fucking little things—only a few days before this.

He slammed the brakes somewhere between a row of gray trucks and row of silver trucks, and in his ridiculous accent told me, "Honey, fuck this. We're gonna get some food in you. It's one dang night." (Southern gays can swallow cock, but they draw the line at taking the Lord's name.)

I don't remember my dreams as a rule. But that night I dreamed of drowning in a vat of Alpo. When I woke up,

I realized the pillow Jay'd lent me to sleep in the bed of his truck was resting on the remains of our nachos.

We were drinking coffee—why not spend our last five dollars?—at a place on Connecticut Avenue when someone ran out onto the patio and said a plane had hit the Twin Towers. When the plane hit the Pentagon, I remember Jay looked at me and his mouth opened. But he never said anything.

I don't remember much of that day everyone seems to remember. People talk now about how united everyone was. Maybe they were. I remember leaving a bar when the crowd, a crowd of gay men old enough to remember the plague, broke into singing "God Bless America." I didn't want anyone to see that I didn't know the words. When did everyone learn the words? I never even heard that song in the Air Force. I remember a man outside fell into me, sobbing, because he couldn't reach his boyfriend, who was in one of the Towers. He was missing a flip-flop like he'd been running. I walked him home. He asked if I needed to call anyone. I called my mom and got through. I told her I loved her. But there was nothing else to talk about without lying. And I didn't want to tie up his phone.

There was an edge to the mourning, jagged and sharp. In the days and weeks to follow, when people talked about America being attacked, I felt like we were thinking of different times. Pearl Harbor maybe. That morning, I thought people had been attacked, just people. They said it had never happened before. Which is a strangely

American way of looking at things. I remember the curfews, the smell of tear gas, and soldiers with machine guns on street corners in Chile when I was a kid. But even in the United States, Tim McVeigh bombed a federal building in Oklahoma City when I was in high school. Hadn't been all that long ago.

I'd spent a long time trying to feel like an American, like I belonged. Funny thing is, I felt more American in the cult than I ever did out of it. Back in the cult, being American was part of my identity. I had what the other kids told me was an American accent. I had an American passport. My grandparents and aunts and uncles and cousins lived in America. My parents were American. And so, from the time we landed back in Texas when I was fifteen, desperate for any identity, I tried to be what I thought was American, the way I understood it, which was not at all.

I said the Pledge of Allegiance in school. I listened to country music. I ate junk food and drank more soda and milk than water. I smoked Marlboros. I tried to love football and pretend I found soccer painfully boring. I joined the military and took an oath to defend the Constitution. I actually read the Constitution. I hung an American flag on my wall. I bought a gun. I was like an inept spy pretending to be American based on movies I'd watched and books I'd read. None of it worked. I felt nothing. And I couldn't understand what I was supposed to feel.

I didn't feel American. In the Air Force, every morning I put on that uniform, I felt like I was playing dressup. America was to me what it had always been: a place to visit family on the way to another country, where I still wouldn't feel at home. I'd just been here a little longer than usual. And now I was watching this event, a shared experience, but I wasn't a part of it at all.

No one felt safe anymore. They kept saying that: "We're not safe anymore." Every time I heard it, it shook me again. There were people all around me who had felt safe. They'd felt safe so long, the loss of that perceived safety shocked them, traumatized them. They'd spent their lives feeling safe. They woke up and went to work and came home, and every step of the way, they'd felt safe. They'd felt safe enough to smile. Safe enough to demand smiles and positive thinking from others.

When everyone cheered because the president stood on the rubble and said they'd hear us, I didn't know who "us" meant. The military? They'd just thrown me out. The country? I felt I had more in common with the Muslims praying in Dupont Circle than I did with the gay liberals surrounding me who were screaming for blood because for the first time in their lives, they felt fear.

I felt like I was trapped in some horror version of a high school pep rally, watching the football players flex and strut and shout about ripping those sandies' throats out and wondering if school spirit was all that fucking different from the Holy Spirit.

I reacted to the universal feeling I didn't feel in the same way I always reacted: I tried to disappear.

By the time we switched back to regular programing, once we grew numb to the sight of the Towers falling—and we did switch back because even a terrorist attack can't damage our national religion of optimism at gunpoint—I'd crawled so deep inside my own head, I didn't care that my landlord was a creep and my roommate was fucking a go-go boy a foot away.

Those first nights, after we secured the room at Carl's, I slept like I'd been awake for months. All I cared about was that we had a door and a roof, a bathroom. I wouldn't come home and find my home and the last few things I owned towed to a lot where I could never afford to buy their freedom. I had a home. It was hard at first to focus on anything but that relief. But you can't share a twin bed past the age of ten unless you're related or fucking. Jay's an aggressive cuddler. I'm an unrepentant snorer. There wasn't even room to build a pillow wall between us. So after a few sleepless nights of his telling me to roll over and my trying to shove him just hard enough to get him away from me without throwing him onto the floor and slapping at his legs because I thought his hair was a mosquito, we headed to Walmart. The cheapest air mattress was $19.99. But in what we thought was a stroke of genius, we found a five-dollar inflatable pool raft in the clearance section of sporting goods. It's probably a good thing we bought it. Anyone hoping to stay afloat in a pool would've drowned.

Since Jay usually got home from the bar first, I ended up on the raft. We'd listen to the Top 40 station with the relentlessly cheerful DJ who read off the weather report and traffic fatalities with the same upbeat giggling voice she used to gush about Britney Spears and Justin's perfect romance and how they'd have the most adorable babies. When Jay fell asleep, I'd shut it off and listen to my raft deflate, unless he brought someone home, which was often.

After the night Jay's shockingly hairy ass landed on my face, I learned to sleep with my head to the door. It only took a couple weeks to start missing the solitude of living in my car. Not enough that I wanted to live in a car again, but enough that I started taking the long way home.

I'd walk down P Street, take a left at Dupont Circle, and head up to Church Street. I liked Church Street. There was a church, as there should be. Some ancient stone building that looked too old for this continent, with a little garden where I used to sit and work the crossword puzzle from a stolen paper, back before I had a room. One of those things homeless people can get away with until the slide engulfs them completely and they actually look homeless.

When I lived in my car and spent my days wandering around Dupont, I'd never parked on Church. If I'd found a spot, I'd have passed it. Seemed like the kind of road where neighbors rap on your window and tell you you can't sleep here. Streets need to be a little wider to get away with sleeping—R Street was good, past 17th, where dive bars still outnumbered the fifteen-dollars-for-a-vodka-soda places. But Church Street was a quiet place to spend time when I didn't want to walk anymore, when I couldn't bear the sight of plates of barely touched food abandoned on a restaurant patio.

I had a room now, but I missed those perfect houses where the privileged blew money on things like retro iron doorknobs. Church Street was too quiet at night. So I'd swing up to T Street before I cut down to Logan. The pink house with the forest green door where they always seemed to be throwing a party. The brown house with the black door with the old dog watching the street. He never did bark at me. Sometimes I'd watch to make sure he was still breathing. The Caribbean-blue house with the white door and the couple who sat at a table and never looked at one another. They looked like that Hopper painting. But the man in this window read his laptop screen instead of a newspaper. The woman wrote in a notebook. In the painting, she's hitting a key on the piano. Not playing it. Just hitting a key as if to annoy him, to get his attention. The painting captures the instant before he explodes. The next time I'd walk by, they'd be watching TV.

I'd walk past these houses and watch through the windows. Not long. I told myself it wasn't creepy as fuck because I didn't stop walking to look. But I looked. And I wondered what their lives were like. The parts I didn't see. I wondered what they were writing on those laptops. I wondered what they were fighting about. I wondered what they were talking about at the dinner table that had them so excited they were all talking at once. I wondered what they were reading, if it took them someplace else. I wondered if they were lonely like me. In the wee hours, walking home from work, I didn't see them so often. I didn't miss all of them. The guy on R Street who jerked his little terrier's collar so hard I thought for sure he'd snap the dog's neck, I stole his paper for weeks. The asshole on Swann Street who called me a loser for the sin of being poor. Sometimes I'd watch a parent sleepwalking a crying infant. An insomniac like me curled up with a pillow on the couch, a movie lighting their face.

There never was much to see through our living room windows. But if the lights were off, Carl had gone to bed, and I could usually make it to our room without questions about rent, or horoscopes.

I dreaded taking those stairs in the dark. Every floor of that fucking house tilted another direction. The stairs, each step was a crapshoot—left, right, back, forward. Never occurred to me to throw myself down a flight and hire a lawyer. But the streetlights helped. And the streetlights in the window once I made it up the stairs lit Jay's face just enough to see that something was wrong. He was wet like he'd stepped right out of the shower into bed. He whispered "strep" like everyone does when they have a sore throat. I used the little penlight on my key chain to prove him wrong. But his throat looked like hamburger with acne. He'd been to the VA, showed me a bottle of meds.

This is how I found out I could use VA hospitals. You miss all those briefings when they kick you out. Jay found out about the VA when he asked Carl for a ride to a clinic. (He'd brought his yellow truck back to his mom's in Carolina so the bank could repossess it and taken the bus back to D.C. His poor Pentecostal mother—he'd left a porn tape behind the seat, *Balls to the Wall 4*.) Carl told him the VA hospital was a couple blocks up. "A couple" meant about thirty. But I could yell at Carl later. Jay said Carl put oil on his forehead. I swear to Christ. Oil. I muttered something under my breath, a joke I'd been workshopping since I was ten about olive oil for colds, motor oil for flu. (I'm still working on it.)

I asked Jay if he'd eaten anything. He said fruit salad. "Fruit salad" is what you call garnish and people who work in bars who can't afford or don't have time for a meal call dinner. He'd been living off olives. So had I, but I wasn't sick. I thought about checking the cabinets for a can of soup and hoping no one missed it. But it's hard to steal from people you know. Even if they're assholes, it can get awkward fast.

I lit a cigarette. I already knew what I was going to do. I just wanted to sit for a minute in the half-light and think. I figured I owed it to myself to play out the possible outcomes, something I'd been trying recently. Think like a chess player. Stop making every decision based on what I needed to survive right at that moment. But my brain wouldn't play along.

Our situation was so tenuous that a couple days out of work, an infected throat, one misstep, and we'd slide, no bumpers to stop us this time. I didn't know how long he'd been sick. Jobs like we had, you don't call in sick. You work. You may infect everyone else, but you fucking work. A doctor's note won't save you. Not that anyone has insurance. They'll hire your replacement before you realize you've been shitcanned.

Carl was already hounding us. We were late on rent, and he'd been demanding extra money for Jay living with me. He'd never get it. But he didn't need much of an excuse to throw us out. This time, we wouldn't have cars to sleep in. But then, every time I stole—tampons, socks,

Advil, those little processed lunch-meat packets that are easy to hide—I was risking jail. Same outcome. Same free fall, bonus criminal record and chance of jail. But none of that mattered because Jay was sick and getting worse.

Jay patted my hand and said he wasn't bored, like that was why I was worried. He said he'd been watching *Jerry Springer.* Skinny guys who date fat girls. I stared at him a moment, but he kept his eyes closed. We didn't have a television.

I told him I'd be back in a minute. He asked if I could pick up juice, and I knew he was fucking delirious.

I was too dumb to be scared of walking around the hood, didn't even know those buildings between me and the all-night grocery store were projects. I just trudged up 5th staring at the ground, thinking maybe I could buy a couple packs of ramen. I had four dollars and some change. I could steal dried-soup packets and tea. Flat objects fit well into pockets. No one was getting any juice. Maybe Kool-Aid. A few cop cars had collected on the next corner with their lights flashing. I looked down again, and like some ghetto miracle, I saw a roll of cash on the sidewalk. There was no one around.

The cops up the street would never find what they were looking for because what they were looking for, seventy-six dollars and a couple rocks, I shoved in my sock, and shoved my hands back into my pockets. Kept on walking, even nodded to one of the cops like I appreciated their keeping the neighborhood safe.

I came home with a sackful of groceries—canned soup, ramen, apple sauce. And juice. And a few rocks of crack to throw in with our rent. Carl's boyfriend, a tweaker with a handlebar mustache, had already made it clear he was happy with the barter system. The rocks bought us a couple weeks. In the meantime, I'd walk past the doorways and look through windows and wonder if they could see me at all.

Badlands

I was twenty-three years old when I got a job at Badlands, a gay club on the western edge of Dupont. This was back when Dupont was still a gay neighborhood, but it was already changing fast as rents climbed and million-dollar lofts sprouted from vacant lots and smothered gay video stores. "Gentrification" wasn't a word really used yet, but we saw it. A few Pride flags hung on the porches of row houses as the gayborhood moved east, creeping into Logan from Dupont, renovations underway, a pile of drywall scraps and stained carpet ready to haul to the dump. The new walls painted a tasteful gray. The gays move in, renovate, rents go up, gays move east, to Logan Circle, then Shaw, whatever the neighborhoods are called in your city. The working class hadn't yet been priced out of the District. I don't know if everyone recognized yet that a Pride flag in a disadvantaged neighborhood signaled an invasion already underway. I didn't give a shit. I wasn't even working class.

Rumor was the Badlands building used to be an auto-repair shop and before that a carriage house. Seven bars, two floors, five rooms, and a massive dance floor. I truly believed I'd been hired for my military experience, or because I'm tall and had a crew cut and a walk like I might be able to fight. Truth is more likely that I spelled my name right on the application and showed up on time. Still, I was to be a bouncer.

My manager at the club was a guy named Joey— pirate shirts and skater shoes. Stubbled head where he'd shaved what hair he had left. You might've called him "rugged" until he opened his mouth and his purse fell out. When he interviewed me, Joey said, "We're a family here." Translation: *We'll underpay you and overwork you and treat you like shit, but expect you to stay, expect you to smile, expect you to eat shit, out of some misplaced sense of loyalty.* If you hear that "family" line at a job interview, the smart thing to do is walk the fuck out. I didn't know that then. But it's not like I had a choice. You don't end up bouncing at a club if you have other options. I wasn't all that concerned with what "family" meant to him. I just didn't like the word. This is the sort of weird hang-up you're left with when you were raised in a cult called the Family.

I was barely speaking to my own family. It wasn't out of acrimony. For a while, it was mostly shame—about getting kicked out of the Air Force, about living in my car, about selling the car my mom had put on a credit card so I could rent a shithole off New York Avenue. My brother was still living with my stepdad, Gabe, in Amarillo. My mom had moved up to New England to be near my sister. I was in D.C. And I couldn't remember why.

I had strong feelings about the word "family" when it

didn't apply to my own literal family. The word was bad enough in the South. When someone wanted to know if I was gay, they'd ask if I was family. Entirely possible I'd have made more friends were it not for my visceral reaction to the word, and the knee-jerk denial. Though I hadn't chosen to join the cult, I had chosen to join the Air Force. Neither wanted me. I was fucking done joining.

Dictional problems aside, I was out of options. I took the job and figured I'd keep my mouth shut and collect a paycheck, like any other job. I could play the role. Nothing new. I'd spent my entire life having to play a role.

In the cult, the smallest sigh, you'd think I'd shouted "Hail Satan" the way they reacted. Every job I'd had— fast-food cashier, waitress, hostess, pizza delivery—they all required the same act, happy to eat shit so that customers and managers would feel better about serving it. *You're absolutely right, sir. Appreciate the opportunity to satisfy your pathetic need to feel superior. I'll be anything you want me to be.*

The Air Force was easy comparatively. Military bearing was just the sum of what I'd practiced as a child: hide all emotion, fake the correct emotion, don't make eye contact, don't volunteer.

As a manager, Joey would be easy to keep happy. Bouncing is 80 percent cleaning and 20 percent convincing drunk or drug-addled adults with fragile egos that they'd rather not hit you, they like you actually, you listen, you're on their side. Any child of narcissists, addicts, or rage junkies is an expert at de-escalation. And like I said, I grew up in a cult. Mopping up puke and cleaning bathrooms would never smell as bad as washing twenty toddlers' cloth diapers in a bathtub.

The thing about Joey was he didn't expect me to be happy about any of it. He didn't expect me to watch my language or tone. I realized that the first night someone grabbed my crotch.

I'd served five years in the Air Force, surrounded by all the toxic masculinity the military attracts and breeds in men. Never mind the Air Force, the Family was a fucking sex cult, and I'd never had a man grab at my crotch, but it happened a lot at Badlands. Gay men aren't immune to misogyny. It's often worse because they think they have an excuse. Not a night went by that some asshole didn't make a comment about my vagina. But the first time someone grabbed me, I froze.

I'd told him to leave. He was too drunk, screaming at one of the bartenders about the ice-to-booze ratio in his drink. Which, for the record, is fucking stupid. You get the same amount of liquor. The ice means you get less of whatever mixer you've ordered. Anyway, I walked him to the door. He was shouting the whole time about how he knew the manager. He could have me fired. He was a paying customer. The universal script. I got him to the door and then it happened. He'd turned to leave, and I'd relaxed. That's when he spun around, grabbed my crotch, and jumped back. Maybe he said something. Maybe he laughed. Couldn't tell you. Couldn't even tell you if he was young or old. Short or tall. No idea. I just fucking stood there, waiting for it to be over, not realizing it already was.

I ended up in Joey's office, my eyes wet but my jaw tight. Some part of me, the part that wanted to fight, wanted to scream at the part of me that had learned better long ago. Men grab crotches, boobs, ass, anything else they feel like grabbing to show you they can. It's humiliating enough without your breaking down and proving their point. I was shaking with the effort of holding myself together.

Joey poured me a shot of whiskey and asked why I didn't kill the guy. My brain sort of glitched there. I was expecting praise for self-control, praise that would've tasted like acid because I hated that I'd frozen. I said, "Fuck you," and downed the shot. I thought that was it. I'd be fired. And in that moment, I didn't fucking care. Instead he said, "Sorry." Then, "Don't let anyone touch you again. I don't pay you enough for all that."

It took a minute for the rest of it to sink in. I was still stuck on how good it felt to tell someone with authority to go fuck himself. Over the next few years, I made a habit of it. I probably went a little overboard at first. I still did my job. But if he bitched about a vomit pool I'd left too long on the dance floor, I'd tell him to suck my dick before I cleaned it. And he'd laugh. I'd tell customers to fuck off when they got out of line, and the crazy thing was, they usually loved it. But I didn't stop there.

There's a way of speaking in the Family, and I don't just mean the vaguely continental inflection, the hard consonants, the rising intonation at the end of sentences, or the overreliance on "super" as a qualifier, though all that is super annoying. I'd covered most of that with a slight Texas accent. What drove needles into my ears was that they always sounded like they were explaining bedtime to a toddler. I mean, like you would explain it. They'd just hit the kid if she got up again. But their voices, didn't matter if they were praising or cursing you, or sending you to clean the herpes bathroom (their attempt at containing one of the sexier benefits of a sex cult) because you'd sounded too harsh when you'd said "Pass the salt, please." Every word out of their mouths sounded sweet and slippery as a Southern bon vivant describing the drapes.

It's entirely possible the way I speak, and, by extension, the way I write, developed in rebellion to Family-speak. And being able to sound like me, truly like me, without worrying about losing my job or even getting in trouble for what I said, or didn't say, is how I found my own voice.

It was like I finally learned to inhabit my six-foot-tall body and the voice that came with it. Almost. I'd spent my childhood and most of my young adult life building layers of filters to avoid punishment and humiliation and pain and rejection, a constant effort to be a little less of who I was because I'd been taught who I was was wrong. It was going to take some time to figure that out, pull off each filter, one at a time, and discover who was underneath. I couldn't even begin until I felt safe enough. Maybe a busy nightclub is an odd place to feel safe. But my boss gave me permission. That I could be an asshole was a revelation, but it wasn't necessarily unhelpful.

The next time a guy grabbed my crotch, I froze again, at first. Then I swung, with my eyes closed, of course. These things take practice. But I caught him on his mouth. Before I realized what was happening, one of the other bouncers hit him with a walkie-talkie. Then there were more bouncers, and Joey, who never asked who'd started what. He didn't care. To Joey, to the other bouncers, they were there to protect their own, us vs. them—made fuck-all difference who was right or wrong.

I don't have words for that feeling—to know someone's on your side no matter what. It felt good. It felt like safety. Maybe it felt something like family, though I don't use that term.

On any given Friday or Saturday night, we'd be invaded by six to eight hundred shirtless gay men to whom we were mostly invisible unless we were taking their money, taking their drinks, or kicking them out. I learned to weave my way through them, tapping their heads with a case of beer if they didn't feel like moving, carrying them outside for a cab or an ambulance when they'd had too much, breaking up their generally half-assed attempts at fighting, and they never saw us unless we pissed them off, or god forbid they suffered the indignity of a poor person hitting on them. I once heard a Hill staffer tell one of my favorite bouncers, "Honey, I don't date the help." The Hill staffer overpaid for a gram of Equal every weekend for months. I wasn't a dealer, but he wasn't that bright.

The only nights I don't remember a line outside the door to get in were during those three weeks of the sniper attacks in '02. We stopped checking IDs, stopped charging admission so no one would have to stand outside like an easy target. But a lot of people stayed home. Any other night, four hundred through the door was considered slow.

I'm not guessing at the number. I'd work the cash

box often enough. I must've seemed like the trustworthy type Joey could stick in the little closet by the entrance. I felt like a fucking goldfish behind that mirror. All the closet held was a stool, a cash drawer, and a surveillance camera. That my drawer was never short was taken as proof of my trustworthiness.

The way it worked was, a patron of our fine establishment slid a twenty through the window—the entry fee varied, but let's go with twenty. I'd slide a ticket through the window slot, which the patron then handed to my buddy Kenny or whoever was working stamps. Kenny would stamp the patron's hand. And he was supposed to drop the ticket into a little box.

End of the night, if the ticket count matched the drawer count, we were deemed good and honest employees of Badlands. The system was nearly thief-proof, nearly. The only way to steal was to work together and avoid the cameras. The cameras were easy enough. I'd lean up to the glass and scream at Joey to let me out of the fucking aquarium, I don't deserve this shit, god, I'm so fucking bored. And I'd grab a few twenties while my body blocked the overhead camera. Kenny'd palm a few tickets, enough to cover the loss. And I'd sell those tickets to the next customer.

I know; stealing is wrong. But I wasn't stealing from Joey—he was the manager, not the owner. And your morals get a little flexible when you don't make enough to cover your rent, let alone food; when, at the end of the night, your boss sends you and a buddy across the parking lot with thirty to fifty grand in a backpack to store in the safe at the other club owned by some fat guy in

Rehoboth, who you'll see exactly once in four years and he yells at you for not knowing that he owns you. There was always talk of a backpack heist. Far as I know, no one ever pulled it off.

It's not like I was new to embezzling from my employer. I spent years of my life walking a bridge in Namba, Osaka, or a town square in Zurich, or Lucerne, or Munich, a shopping alley in Bern, on sweltering days that made heat rash blossom on my thighs and frozen days when the wind pierced something inside my ears, through slush that seeped through broken shoes to turn my toes blue, handing posters to pedestrians, quoting the lines in Japanese, German, French: "Hi. This is for you." (It wasn't. We'd take it back if they didn't donate.) "We're Christian missionaries. Would you like to donate to our work?"

You think I didn't pocket a few coins? You think I was the only one? Here's an exercise in moral relativism: Which is worse—forcing kids to beg to support a cult by soliciting donations under the guise of missionary work, paying someone below a living wage, or stealing from those who do? Were the bouncers any worse than the bartenders known for pouring the heaviest glasses of water in D.C.? I've put a lot of thought into this and come up with the same answer every time: I'll do what I need to do to survive.

The other bouncers at the club were not what you picture when you hear the word "bouncer." I don't know if Joey had any hiring criteria other than "desperate enough to take the job." They were twinks, gutter punks, vogue queens, and tweakers. They were tattooed and pierced and wore jeans the size of hoop skirts and skater shoes with the brand emblems worn off. They came from shitty small towns in West Virginia, South Jersey, and Pennsylvania, the Maryland and Virginia suburbs and exurbs, towns country singers don't bother writing shitty songs bragging about, towns where, growing up, queer kids live the stories they won't tell their friends, even in the dark, even on the drugs they use to feel something that doesn't hurt. You can pretend to be concerned about casual drug use. I'll tell you that you're the reason we casually used drugs.

They'd drop a headline about their pasts here or there. The sort of hints at a story that would make anyone want to know the story. But ask a follow-up question and all they'd say was "Shows, honey. Just shows." Far as I can tell, it means something between "drama" and "you're an idiot." Not everything gay translates directly. What it meant in this case was "You should know better than to ask." What was left was tragedy by buckshot: "Girl, I lost my virginity to the counselor at the camp they sent me to to pray the gay out." "I fucked a Republican once. I was fourteen, though." "My daddy's the only one who gets to call me a faggot."

There was this kid we called Lil' Joey, because the boss was Joey. If that sounds confusing, at one point, we had four bartenders named Mike serving cosmos to a never-ending stream of Kyles. Anyway, Lil' Joey was a twink, weighed about ninety pounds if you put a case of beer in his stick arms. He was blond, but for the life of me, I couldn't tell you the color of his eyes. He always looked like he was staring at the sun. He started as a bouncer but worked barback some nights. He'd come in on barbacking nights and hand you a photo of Whitney

Houston and tell you she'd be helping you out tonight. I don't know if he believed he was Whitney, but it's possible, likely even.

The thing about Lil' Joey was, he'd pick fights. That's not entirely fair. But the idea of backing down when some Abercrombie queen didn't recognize Lil' Joey's authority, vested in him by Whitney herself, was unthinkable. I never knew what happened before he screamed my name. I'd crash through the crowd, hop over the bar, whatever it took to get to him. He called me his big butch brother. I liked playing the hero. But more than that, it turns out I liked fighting.

I liked being able to hit back. It was a new feeling for me. I didn't care how hard they hit. I didn't care if they won—the other bouncers would show up sooner or later anyway. I only cared that I could hit back. I liked that my size, my reputation, the look on my face when I was in the club, made me feel safe.

I was angry. I was tired of feeling sorry for myself. Which is really the same thing, but anger provides a comforting lie: that you're safe, that you have self-respect.

I'd been hit as long as I could remember, by more adults than I could count. That I know a flyswatter hurts more than a belt is hardly unique to my upbringing. There are few codes held more deeply among the poor, the religious, and the uneducated than that it is good and healthy and wholesome parenting to hit your kids. That their kids grow up with anger-management issues, who like hitting almost as much as they like getting hit, is not taken as evidence that maybe they're wrong here. It's right there in the Bible: "Spare the rod, and spoil the child." The Bible also says, "Violence begets violence." But the Bible says a lot of dumb shit.

It may not be as visible a mark of your class as bad teeth, but a history of violence being acted upon you by those you love is just as effective at keeping you from climbing too high. Violence isn't so much a belief system as it is a symptom. The Bible only serves to provide a necessary excuse, because the truth is, you can't afford the cure for the disease you inherited. It was passed down from your parents who still don't believe in therapy. They inherited it from their dads who came back from France with shattered nerves and screamed at night, sucked it up and went to work. So what if a man hit his wife when she stepped out of line. Just the way things were. She didn't leave because she couldn't get a fucking job. Go back one more generation, if that, and the only wedding gift that might've done any good was a rape whistle. But no one would've answered. We barely care now. The good ol' days of battered wives and children didn't change all that much, not for those whose only inheritance was anger.

It wasn't only our stepdads. When our moms were working long past exhaustion, just to get by, no chance of getting ahead unless they met a good man, always one slipup, one cruel act of God away from disaster, and their fucking kid broke her glasses, lost a jacket, forgot to return a library book, is it really so shocking they lost their shit? Throw in a little addiction, plenty of mental illness, and a justifiable anxiety level that would kill you if you could afford the funeral, you end up with what we call "anger-management issues," because goddamn if we don't believe in personal responsibility.

A lesson I retained better than most: violence is, if not the answer, always worth a shot. When adults were angry, frustrated, scared, when the stress got to be too much, they hit me. The stress and fear for me were near constant. Being hit will have that effect on a kid. I'd hold it all in until I exploded in panic, and I expressed that panic exactly as I'd been taught: I hit someone smaller than me, usually my brother. I'd see the fucking terror in his eyes. And I'd fucking hate myself. But I couldn't fucking stop. Until one day he got big enough to hit me back. With no one else to hurt, I found another target for my rage: me. That is, until Badlands.

Maybe it felt good to protect someone else, a younger, smaller boy. I could fix it. I could make it better. I could protect him. Maybe it helped that I knew he'd been bullied, though he never said as much. Sometimes it was clear just from the fights he'd choose.

One of those times, Lil' Joey managed to piss off a guy who looked like he'd played some ball in high school and was now working on getting fat enough for his future as an assistant coach. He had Lil' Joey by the front collar, screaming spittle and threats. I got in between them. And the future coach tried to reason with me, assuming I had any more authority. Lil' Joey had thrown his drink away. It wasn't fair. He was a paying customer. The usual. I was thinking I could walk him outside to talk and shut the door after him. Problem solved. But Lil' Joey wasn't having it, kept calling the coach a bitch, taunting him. The coach took a swing. And like I said, I liked fighting.

Most bar fights don't last long anyway. Most of the time, they'd rather you break it up before they hurt themselves. When a fight does break out, no one has to deliver a knockout blow to the chin. One drunk will swing and fall. Or the other drunk will trip and fall. And everything happens in slow motion because everyone's drunk or high. If someone does land a punch, they're more likely to break their hand than anything else. But I started remembering all those moves bored marines taught me way back when, mostly how to put someone on the ground and not risk breaking a hand. And god-damn if it's not fucking satisfying.

Our head bartender, if not by title, then by age, was a woman I'll call Amy. And god help me, she was proba-bly only thirty-five. She wore black vests, sans shirt, and black eyeliner and kept her boyfriend, who worked the light show, a casual footnote to those who didn't need to know she was straight. Sort of straight anyway. But since she kissed like she was auditioning for a threesome in a Showtime soft-core and her boyfriend expected to join, her orientation was irrelevant to me.

Amy was living, breathing proof of something I'd known since I was a kid begging for change on the street: that is, that the only people who will ever help someone and expect nothing are those who've been poor.

Amy was the one who'd make you hot tea if you were working sick. And we were always working sick. No health insurance. No sick days. We diagnosed ourselves with "bar flu," threw up in trash cans, napped in the coat closet, and hit another line of coke to make it through the shift. But Amy always had off-brand Theraflu. She was the one who always had a tampon and ibuprofen stashed under her bar. The one who'd listen to my girl-friend drama and usually manage to not tell me, "Jesus, just fucking break up with her already." Anytime I was ready to lose my shit, Amy would happily sneak me a shot of Grandma, Grand Marnier. Tastes like sucking on a rotten orange, but it does the job. Without realizing it or putting a word to it, I started relating to her like she was a big sister. Someone I could tell my problems to, someone to call me on my shit, someone who looked out for me.

Every so often, Amy would stuff the trunk of her piece-of-shit Toyota with day-old bread from the bakery near her apartment to pass out to the hungry, broke bouncers who were paid like family, next to nothing. I mean, who needs to pay family?

I'd only been working there a couple weeks the first time she did it. We always left as a group, bar staff being prime targets for mugging. She told everyone to meet out by her car. The other bouncers were happily grabbing bags of bread and stuffing them in their backpacks. I just stood there with my hands deep in my pockets.

The way people look at you when you're poor, the shame they need you to feel, it changes you, makes it hard to accept anything that feels like a handout. We fetishize poverty as though it makes you a better person. The truth is, all it does is make you mean. The constant stress of it. The never-ending fucking shame of it. It makes you angry and hateful. You're not jealous of those who have more. You're just exhausted by the fucking humiliation they will not hesitate to throw at you. There's a world of opportunity you'll never reach. College. Jobs. A network of contacts. There's no loan from Mom and Dad for a down payment. People say "broke" when they have to tap savings, run up a credit card. There's an entire society of people who don't have checking accounts. The shame of it means the only people you can risk empathizing with are those who've been there, who won't humiliate you.

Once you've been hungry, the sort of hungry that feels like your body devouring itself as you fall asleep, you're never really comfortable around people who haven't felt the same gnawing under their rib cage. I hadn't been comfortable around people in a long time. And there's always someone who will say, "I don't eat leftovers. I'm not homeless."

I don't think most Americans realize how fucking insane it is to the rest of us how much food is wasted here. We don't even finish a fucking apple, or you don't. I do if no one's looking. Never mind the portion sizes at restaurants that make it impossible to finish a meal, laws are written to make damn sure no one else can eat it either. The food wasted at office parties and company meetings hurts. It hurts like the hole in my belly I can still feel like a phantom limb. We toss food in dumpsters and mock those desperate enough to dive for it. Restaurants pour bleach on the garbage bags to make sure their castoffs don't attract the hungry.

I never got past survival mode with food. When you live on what's pulled from grocery store dumpsters, you never feel secure unless you have enough food to get you through a week. But I learned pretty fast that finishing an apple or eating bread crusts or canned sardines or chopping the rotten part off a vegetable or eating green peppers or cutting mold off cheese or sniffing meat to check if it's spoiled or not being able to name a food I won't eat is considered weird.

So my first instinct upon seeing a trunkful of expired bread was to shrug and look away rather than risk the humiliation of looking hungry.

My new coworkers were unconcerned with looking hungry. They already knew they were among their kind. They grabbed loaves and traded bagels for English muffins and didn't give a shit that everyone knew they were poor.

One of them was a guy I'll call Kyle because there are always Kyles, so many Kyles. Kyle was covered in tattoos of varying quality on skin like mayonnaise left on the counter too long. He told me once that after his dad went to prison, the county sheriff used to call his mom if he found a fresh deer on the road. They'd have meat for weeks.

He told me that random detail one night as we walked home together. I was renting a room at the time from an old Turkish lady who wanted me to marry her son for a green card. I could've used the money, but I didn't think INS would've bought that Jesus healed the gay in me so I could fall in love with a five-foot-four Turkish dude who didn't speak English.

We were eating some of Amy's bagels as we walked up Connecticut, and Kyle's bagel bag ripped open, bagels rolling down the fucking street, inevitably landing in puddles. He punched a bicycle that was strung off a balcony and nearly broke his hand. Then he just fucking started crying. And he told me about road kill. We split my sack of bagels. Neither of us ever mentioned it again.

That first time I hesitated in front of Amy's trunk, it was Kyle who said, "Wait. You get any?"

I said, "It's okay," because I'm an idiot.

He said, "It's still good." Like he was warming up to explain expiration dates to the dipshit rich kid. I wanted to tell him, "Oh, honey. I know all about expiration dates." Instead I took the sack of bagels he held out and nearly fucking cried. He looked at the two loaves he had left and said, "Sorry if you don't like raisins." One of the others said he didn't mind raisins so much. I could have his pumpernickel. And I just fucking started laughing and hugged my sack of bagels to my chest. You don't survive the Family with an aversion to raisins. I was sure they'd think I was nuts. And maybe they did. But they weren't going to judge.

The only people we did judge were the customers: *them.* Helped that I already wasn't a big fan of *them.* Them, being the mostly affluent, white gay men of the D.C. area. They weren't fans of me either. Most of them barely tolerated women. It was a little better as a bartender. The shittier I treated them, the better they tipped. Everyone loves a surly bartender. But especially as a bouncer, when I didn't recognize their superiority, their first instinct was to act like men will whenever a woman doesn't obey them. Because I had no status, not to them. It didn't even matter that I looked like them, at least dressed like them.

Gladys, the old drag queen who ran the coat check as some form of a drag queen retirement plan, was my unofficial stylist. She looked like a Baptist preacher's wife. I liked her immediately. She punctuated stories the same way my grandma used to tell us about her neighborhood: "That was when Miss Ambrosia, she's dead now, was living with us over that video store on 17th with Aaron, who passed about a year or so later. There was a boy named Felix. Girl, she was the statue of David come to life. Lovely boy, passed in '89, I think."

She'd let us raid the coat check for left-behind clothes. If she hadn't, we'd have pilfered what we needed anyway, but it helped that she often examined my selections and said, "Honey. No." Our customers checked everything, not just jackets; they'd check their pants, shirts, and sometimes bags of work or gym clothes. For years, my entire wardrobe came from the Badlands coat check— lots of Abercrombie and Banana Republic. Old Navy I had to buy myself, or else show up to my other job, whatever that was, in shirts that cost more than I made in a day.

Badlands wasn't my only job most of the time. It was the only job I couldn't sabotage. I'd been fired twice, quit once. Every time, Joey took me back. Badlands was where I felt safe. Where I felt at home. Where I could hide. Where the music and lights and drugs made the world outside and all the pain that came with it disappear. I could stand behind the bar and pour drinks and the world came to me, but not too close. I didn't need to fit in. Didn't have to worry about saying the right thing. Didn't need to be accepted by anyone outside the club. Didn't matter that I couldn't go home for Thanksgiving. Someone from the club always took in the strays.

I didn't need a social life. I had a job at a club. The hours don't really allow for a social life anyway. It doesn't take long working bar shifts—seven p.m. to three, four, often five a.m.—before you become entirely nocturnal. The first week or so, you fall asleep right away, or something like it, your eardrums still thumping from the house music. Then one night you hit the after-party with the others. Sit in a hot tub and sip Grand Marnier because, while it really does taste like sugared ass, that's what everyone drinks. You go for pancakes after the after-party. Why not. Even if you save your entire check, you won't make rent. Eventually, you need an hour of TV before you can sleep. It helps with the goddamn thumping in your ears. When you no longer go to bed until the sun comes up, it's over. You're on the night shift now. The 7-Eleven clerk knows your name. You ask about his kids. The prostitutes in the park warn you about the guys around the corner. Better if you stay on Rhode Island. Lunch is bar olives at ten p.m. while you fill in a crossword. My only friends were similarly sleep-deprived bartenders and bouncers, sex workers, servers and cooks from restaurants around the neighborhood who hadn't seen the sun in a week.

When that job doesn't pay enough, and it never does, you take second jobs—shuttling lobbyists from K Street to the Old Ebbitt Grill and back in a town car while they yell at their cell phones. Slinging coffee at Starbucks to anorexic housewives in Georgetown. Grooming anxious labradoodles in Dupont. The second jobs don't last long. Fall asleep in the town car and miss the phone call and a senator has to wait an extra ten minutes for a ride. The manager at Starbucks calls a kid a retard when he asks for an application, and you drop the green apron on your way out, tell yourself it was a moral stand. But really, you could use some sleep. You call an asshole an asshole for his dog's freshly cropped ears.

It didn't matter. I had the club. And Joey always let me come home.

When I was a kid, when we were living in Switzerland in this run-down chalet outside Zurich, I kept a radio stashed in a hole I'd carved into my foam mattress up on the top bunk of these three-decker bunk beds they always built to shelve us. At night, I'd lie up in my shelf and listen to Systemite music circa 1990—heavy on Madonna, Sinéad O'Connor, Roxette, and the Cure, for my angsty preteen heart. I'd listen to that shit, and I'd picture my life as an adult.

I'd imagine I wasn't in the Family. The Antichrist hadn't come. I'd gotten out, somehow. I'd gone to college. Had a career. I was always a little fuzzy on the details. What was perfectly clear was I'd live in a city where I'd have friends like I'd seen in movies. We'd sit outside on restaurant patios, on the stoops of our funky apartments, in tiny backyards of brownstone town houses, on the beach in the winter where we'd road-trip on vacation—I liked mixing up the locations. We'd sip wine and beer and fancy cocktails or brown liquor in clear glasses. And we'd talk. We would talk about everything—our relationships, our dogs, our jobs. We'd debate religion and politics, and someone would bring up something they'd read in, say, *The New Yorker*. (*The New Yorker* was the only publication I could name, thanks to my grandmother's stockpile of back issues.) We'd talk about books and music. We'd know the band's name and the lyrics. We'd be witty. We'd tease and flirt and joke. We'd have inside jokes. We'd smoke cigarettes. We might experiment with drugs. We'd be fun. We'd be interesting. We'd talk.

Thirteen-some-odd years later, I still didn't have any college, a career, or vacations. But sometimes, Joey would make us dinner, or we'd head to Amy's to play with her ferrets and drink and talk about books, or we'd end up sitting out back behind a shared town house, one of the Mikes' or Kyles', trying out cocktails we created from whatever booze was available, trading drugs from the club and feasting on food pilfered from the kitchens by the servers and cooks, talking well into the night, until the sun came up and the daylight chased us inside, talking about everything and nothing.

So I got some details wrong, but damn, if I wasn't living in a city, drinking on a back patio, ingesting drugs, listening to friends talk. Slowly, I started to learn how to be accepted into something like a family that I didn't have to join.

Speaking in Tongues

There was this day in Air Force basic training where they tried to make us feel like we were really in the military. The night before, they kept us up until the wee hours working in the kitchen. At dawn, we marched a few miles carrying our duffel bags, singing jodies to keep cadence.

We shot the M16 for a couple hours. Then sat in the dirt and picked through MREs for lunch. Airman Eudy, who watched all the right movies, told everyone else to avoid the Lucky Charms—they're bad luck. And because we'd never eaten an MRE, we enjoyed the plastic food. Then they marched us back, into an auditorium.

We filed in without speaking. We'd been in basic training six weeks now; no one had to tell us not to speak. The lights went out, and there, on the stage, a single spotlight popped on to show a guy, one of the instructors, tied to a chair. The bad guy entered, stage right. We knew he was the bad guy because he was wearing a towel on his head. The bad guy slapped the good airman around a little. But the good airman wouldn't give up the mission plan. Just name, rank, serial number—which is really your social security number. The bad guy pulled a gun. Shot the airman dead. And the lights went out again. Then, I shit you not, Lee Greenwood's "Proud to Be an American" kicked on.

At that point I looked around. Everyone was weeping, shouting the words. Some of the kids fell back on their evangelical upbringings and waved their hands in the air in the universal gesture of *I, a spiritual person, am feeling this shit.* I knew I was supposed to feel something. I did. I felt revulsion. Because I'd been through this before. All of it. The sleep deprivation, the fun outdoors preparing for war, the playacting interrogation by the bad guys, and the singing. Always the singing.

When I was in the Family, that whole scene was a weekly occurrence. The light version anyway. Sing a few songs we all knew. Here's an old one we haven't done in a while. Stand up and do the motions.

> I may never march in the infantry (*Everyone stand and march*)
> Ride in the cavalry (*Hands in front like you're holding the reins; gallop, like that makes sense*)
> Shoot in the artillery (*Gun hands*)
> (An old Salvation Army song they co-opted.)

Inevitably some kid would think they were too cool to do the motions. Then the guitar players at the front of the room, and there were always a couple at least, would rest their arms on their guitars while a shepherd stood to lead us all in prayer. Short prayer at first. If your shepherds weren't dicks, they'd let the younger kids go off to bed after that. The shepherd would read something from the Bible, or Family literature. Or, surprise, someone would do a skit, sort of like that Air Force skit but passive-aggressive. Maybe they'd do one about kids who won't do the hand motions during songs. Then the Antichrist soldiers raid the home and murder everybody. (This was an actual skit.) Cut to the non-motion kid sobbing over the dead bodies of his little sisters. Bet he fucking regrets not doing the hand motions now. He won't make that mistake again for years.

Then we'd pray, chanting "thankyoujesusthankyoulord" over and over again. Until, by some unspoken agreement, the chanting died down, and the shepherd would thank Jesus for a few things, then ask him for a few things. You have to butter Jesus up first. The chanting again. And off to bed we went after a few announcements.

These were maintenance doses for the real thing. And the real thing happened once a month, or every few months, depending on how things were going. If we were raking in money, local authorities weren't paying attention to us, the kids weren't committing any serious sins like being sad or wearing hair product, we might not need a dose between scheduled meetings. When we did need a dose, several homes would usually meet for these fellowships, which could last an afternoon or days. Usually, they'd make us fast first, anyone over the age the shepherds deemed the cutoff for making it a day without food.

Fasting and sleep deprivation are useful if you want to brainwash someone. After a while, you stop feeling hungry and start getting high. Of course, during any fast, the commune black market kicked into full gear. You could get anything from a hard-boiled egg to a baggie of raw oats if you knew who to ask.

Once the meeting started, all you could chew was your cheek. We'd sing for hours, sometimes hundreds of us in a room. The air would curdle with the smell of our body odor and breath. The spiritual, or those who needed to appear spiritual because they'd recently been in trouble for not being spiritual, would lift their hands in the air and weep. A Family favorite, or, as I know it, the worst fucking song in the Family, was called "My Family, My Family." It's a love song about the Family. Anyway, during that song, the tradition was to drape your arms over the person next to you, and rock back and forth to the music. (I can sing it now as I type. It smells like armpits.)

Then, more skits. Here's another: There's a kid who's rebellious, always complaining. One day, she's out selling posters to the heathens. The posters had a picture on the front, a favorite being a cartoon caricature of random cultures—an Asian with a pointed hat, a cowboy, an Arab in a robe—holding hands around a globe. There'd be a message on the back, something about Jesus and the Family. I don't know. I never read one. The point is they called it witnessing, because of the message, but it felt an awful lot like begging. Because it was.

Anyway, in the skit the rebellious kid doesn't want to sell posters anymore. She complains. A demon hears her complaining, because demons are everywhere. And he piggybacks on her, right into the home. Now there's a demon in the home. Scary shit. Everyone's bickering and complaining. There's a cool kitchen scene where the kids are all laughing at a dumb joke—being foolish—and the stove catches fire. It's fucking chaos. So they hold a fellowship, figure out which little brat brought the demon home, and perform an exorcism.

When I first saw this skit, it was particularly timely because it was performed right after one of my own exorcisms, for being gay. But the skit was the PG version. None of the beating and screaming. And for dramatic effect, they cut the exorcism down to a couple minutes. A real exorcism could last days. Depended, really, on how long it took a kid to break. Someone holding you down, sometimes sitting on your head so that you could hardly breathe. Someone hitting you with a belt, flyswatter, paddle, whatever. The whole time screaming and cursing at you, I mean at the demon to come out of you.

But it felt a lot like they were screaming at me. Funny what you can do to a kid when you tell yourself it's for their own good, you're saving their soul, when you tell yourself you're serving God. They'd give me something to read. Make me write something about what I'd read. Pray about that and hope I'd shown sufficient contrition. I don't remember much about the exorcisms. I learned to shut off my mind, crawl inside the dark, and I wondered, *Is this how you go crazy?* But they didn't show any of that in the skit version. Just prayed and shouted a little at the demon. And hallelujah, the home was saved. Let us pray.

Kneeling, ass on my ankles, face in my hands—the desperate prayer pose, more effective than passive prayer, hand-holding prayer, casual prayer. My legs would go numb. Sometimes I'd doze off, but never for long. My knees would burn. My elbows and forearms would start to lose feeling. And we would chant.

The chanting could last for minutes or hours during a fellowship. We'd kneel with our faces on our hands, until someone spoke in tongues. Soon everyone would join in. Tongues sound like gibberish because it's gibberish. I had to fake it because it's bullshit. But according to the Family's interpretation of the book of Acts, tongues are the spirit speaking through you. Or Jesus, who speaks in King James English. I know this because another person in the room would shout out the interpretation of someone else's gibberish prophecy. Usually some Bible verse or "I have heard my people beseeching me and will bestow my blessing upon them"–type shit.

Here's the thing, these people weren't faking it. It was real. The Holy Spirit. The gift of tongues. All of it. It was fucking gibberish, but this wasn't something they believed. They knew. They knew the sputtering syllable salad coming from their mouths was the Holy Spirit possessing them, speaking through them, finger-banging them into fucking ecstasy.

They all knew it, felt it. And they all understood it. I know it was real because I watched it happen for years. There would sometimes be another kid I could make eye contact with, but we'd always look away, afraid to be known, even to one another, as not having the Holy Spirit. You never did know who'd catch it next. But those who caught it, those who could feel it, those whose brains were wired to catch a mass delusion, to flood their senses with oxytocin, they were fucking levitating.

The prophecies continued, the tongues, the chanting when those faded, "hallelujahthankyoujesuspraiseyoulord," until the Spirit returned and taught us the language of angels. We wept openly. We laid hands on those of us who spoke in tongues, those who got the prophecy. Someone would end the prayer with an amen, and shout "Revolution." We'd respond with "For Jesus" and a three-finger salute, again and again. Until finally, we'd sing "My Family, My Family" again. Not a dry eye in the room. Including mine. It wasn't hard to make the tears come. All I had to think about was what would happen if they knew.

For weeks after a fellowship, the home would run like a machine—record fundraising, new contacts for food and supplies, new trips planned to go preach the Gospel (and sell shitty posters and tapes), dazed adults who'd stop you in the hall for a hug and to tell you they loved you, kids happily scrubbing even behind the toilet bowl. Most of the kids anyway. I rarely felt so alone as I did in the aftermath of a spiritual awakening. I'd live in terror I'd be found out. I'd pretend. But I knew I was as obvious as a fucking cop in a Phish T-shirt at a rave. I was terrified that at any moment, someone would point to me and shout, "Systemite!" For the rest of the home, the catharsis, the bonding, the high they'd felt, was indisputable proof of their belonging.

This is the point of the fasting, the singing of familiar songs with known motions, the sweating and physical contact, the marching, the singing of jodies, the chanting. Our brains are made of meat, just animal instinct defended by cognitive dissonance. These communal rituals are meant to shut down rational thought and reduce us to those instincts. And among our most basic instincts is the need to identify with a group. Groups are safer when you're dealing with woolly mammoths and there's only one guy who knows how to make fire and Og found a sweet rock that's pretty sharp. But if you want to use Og's sweet rock to cut the fur off the meat, you have to be in the group. You have to fit in. So you mimic the group. And because the shit you're doing, whether it's crying to a song or speaking in tongues, is so fucking ridiculous, your brain tells you it's real. So it is real. You felt it. You've lost something of your own, buried part of who you are, you've humiliated yourself to become a part of something, but now you fit in, and the group is stronger.

If you've ever chanted in yoga class, sung your team's fight song at full volume in a stadium, shouted "USA," or wept to Lee Greenwood, you've likely felt the same high. Maybe it's lower grade, but it works the same. Corporations caught on to the effect, and now the employees of your local big-box store chant every morning. Your cable guys do it during the monthly employee meeting. Doesn't work quite as well. But a half-assed attempt at inspiring group loyalty is cheaper than paying people.

I can't tell you why I didn't feel it. Not with any certainty. Might be that I was rejected from the group because of who I was, even then. They knew I was different. I knew, long before I put a name to it. Might be as simple as that the traits the cult saw as faults—my stubbornness, my rebelliousness, my questions and doubts—made me a shitty cult member. Maybe that's why they tried so hard to torture those traits, that I secretly believed to be virtues, out of me.

Don't get me wrong. There were times when I broke, when I desperately tried to feel what they said was true. I wanted to feel it. I wanted to belong, even for just a moment, to feel a part of something. But I couldn't feel it. Sometimes, often, I believed just enough to know there was something very wrong with me. But I couldn't change it. In the end, lying on my futon in a row of futons, my brother grinding his teeth beside me, I'd always come to the same thought: it wasn't real.

When I saw it again in the Air Force, that rush of euphoria, the absolute certainty of belonging, I thought, maybe it is real. Maybe I'm just broken, defective, the one the group has to reject—the lame, the blind, the other.

Maybe it's not surprising, then, that the only time I did feel part of a group was working in the service industry. Anthony Bourdain could wax poetic about the criminals and outcasts, the pirates who gladly sacrifice their bodies in a sweltering kitchen. I'd done my time in kitchens as a kid. I signed up for another group: the nightclub staff at Badlands. The pay was criminal. But the benefits weren't all bad—free drinks, free entrance to any other club in D.C., and occasionally, often, free drugs.

The entirety of my drug experience at twenty-three, when I started working at Badlands, was that I'd smoked pot a few times. I liked it. I would've done more. I would've tried just about anything. But in high school, I didn't even know who to ask. The Air Force was too risky; they'll fucking lock you up for thinking about marijuana. By the time I started experimenting for real, I was dealing with adults who were generally pretty responsible about their drug use, who knew about dosages and what not to mix, who made sure everyone stayed hydrated.

There was always someone who could take one look at any pill and say, with absolute authority, "Yeah. That's gonna be a clonazepam, one milligram. Generic Klonopin."

When nights at Badlands finally came to a close, Lil' Joey would grab one of the buckets we used to collect glasses and scuttle around the bars, the bathrooms, the couches upstairs and collect the drugs people had dropped. But the bigger haul was the dance floor. You want to do drugs in a club without getting caught, the dance floor, with a dancing mob for cover, seems as good a place as any. It's a terrible idea. You don't realize how much you're being bumped around until you try to stand still. Once your vial or baggie hits the floor, it's gone forever, or until the bouncers sweep after the lights go on. Every night, while the tills were counted, we'd sit around at the entrance, smoking, mostly too tired to talk, but not too tired to hold a swap meet of soggy pills and powders and glass vials of clear liquid.

There was a time, before they razed the Navy Yard in 2007 to build the baseball stadium, when the only place to be on Saturday nights was Nation, a massive warehouse painted matte black, converted into a club that brought in DJs like Paul Oakenfold, Tiësto, Chemical Brothers, Paul van Dyk, Junior Vasquez. We couldn't compete.

Eventually, Badlands started a lesbian party to fill the club. But late '01 and most of '02, any given Saturday night, we'd be left with a few out-of-towners wondering why there were no homosexuals left in Dupont. So we'd often close the bar early, cram into cars and taxis, and head across town to Nation.

The Navy Yard was a neighborhood just south of the Capitol, a part of D.C. tourists never saw unless they were extraordinarily unlucky or hopelessly lost, and shitting themselves about it. The bouncers at Nation were direct from central casting. Two guys with beefy arms and neck tattoos let us pass with a nod and a hug from one of our bouncers. No ID checks and no fifty-dollar cover charge. The first time it happened, I thought this was what it must feel like to be cool.

I could feel the music before I heard it, but then we passed through the double doors into the main room and I couldn't hear anything else.

The guys I came in with crowded around the bar to get their customary courtesy drinks. (Those bar years drinking for free did a number on my head. Twenty years later, I'm still surprised at the price of a cocktail, and that I have to pay it.) I was on a mission, though. I'd seen this on TV, back in Amarillo—*Jerry Springer* or *Dateline* maybe. These massive warehouse clubs with the light shows and club kids. Drugs. Drugs that kill you. Drugs that turn you into a zombie. Drugs that cause promiscuous sex. Drugs that cause platform shoes and angel wings and black eyeliner and body piercings. Drugs that cause satanism and dead bodies in bathtubs. They were all full of shit, and I knew it the same way anyone does. They said all the same shit about weed, and all that caused was dry mouth and enjoyment of *Tommy Boy*. On *90210*, they had to trade an egg for directions to the rave. A guy in a basketball jersey with the number 4 on it sold Emily Valentine "U4EA," and she drugged Brandon. I headed off to find his real-life counterpart.

Strange how no one had to tell me where to look. I followed the crowd by some instinct and found myself in the hallway leading to the bathrooms. And there was the guy. Of course he was the guy, surrounded by a small entourage, happy to see everyone who approached, big hug, backslap, no actual conversation. It was quieter over by the bathrooms. Good place to open shop. Looks like you're just waiting your turn.

I'd seen the same guy at our club. One of the bouncers pointed him out as "sort of our friend. Like, don't bounce him. He takes care of us."

I waited my turn, and when I got to him, I leaned in and asked how much for a pill. He wrapped me in a hug and said, "Girl, don't be all business. We're friends." I'd clearly been dismissed as he took money from the next guy and they were now hugging.

I couldn't figure out what I'd done wrong. I'd never tried ecstasy. I really fucking wanted to try ecstasy. But it looked like I never would if I couldn't figure out how to get a pill. Who fucks up buying drugs? Goddamnit.

I found the twinks back by the bar. Told them I'd struck out, or told one, who shouted it at the next twink, who shouted it at our bartender, each cracking up at my failure to procure free drugs. I thought. Finally one of them said, "Honey, check your pocket."

The guy had given me two, so I shared. Someone handed me a Gatorade—Nation wasn't even pretending they didn't cater to the ecstasy crowd. I swallowed the pill. And nothing happened.

I asked, "How long is this supposed to take?" I had to yell the question twice before anyone understood.

" 'Bout twenty minutes. Here." Someone handed me a lit Newport, said, "Menthol helps." I thought, this was how I wanted people to be—everyone helpful and sharing what they had. Anything you need to enjoy yourself.

He was five minutes short on the estimate. I ran through the crowd to the bathrooms. Two guys were fucking in the stall next to me and there was no door. I didn't want to puke. I didn't want to lose my pill. Then I looked at the shit-and-puke-covered toilet and lost it. As soon as the vomit left my throat, the ecstasy hit me. The toilet was a fucking masterpiece—the color scheme, the juxtaposition of my wet, red Gatorade vomit splattered over the dried blackened shit, over a layer of what must have been the remains of chopped salad. The shocking blue water in the bowl. My puke slowly swirling around a used-condom jellyfish. The Family believes you can puke out an evil spirit. My evil spirit belonged up the street in the Smithsonian.

I chugged my Gatorade and was handed another by a benevolent spirit in a gold latex unitard. Then I bumped my way through the sea of glitter-breasted gays and moved with the surging crowd out onto the dance floor. Our light tech found me. He was spinning glow sticks in his hands, and the light trails were the first miracle I'd ever seen. I finally understood the light show and the smoke. I wished I had glow sticks, but that seemed like a lot of work. I was happy everyone else seemed willing to

do the spinning thing for me. And they did. All I had to
do was smile at someone with glow sticks and they'd put
on a little show just for me, send me right out into space.

We were in this together, all of us. The DJ was our
leader, and he took us to a new world, a world full of
love and hope, and we felt everything and everything felt
like love. This is what people join cults to feel. I'd prayed
and waited and prayed with the Family, and the feeling
never came—not this calm, not this unbridled joy. Shirtless guys walked up to me and smiled and our eyes met
and we knew we had found the same god and we hugged
and then danced and then danced away to meet more of
our kind.

I'd found the Holy Spirit. I thought about calling my
stepdad and telling him. I wanted to tell him I'd finally
gotten rid of my demon. I laughed and someone hugged
me in this space wherein a man could hug me and take
nothing away. I knew then what love meant.

I felt someone dancing behind me. Close. Her arms
were around me and I turned and she smiled so I put
my arms around her. Then she took my hand and led
me up the stairs to a couch on the balcony overlooking
the dance floor. She straddled me and rubbed my shoulders and kissed me like she knew how, like this was
how we'd always kissed. She was wearing a skirt and her
panties were wet and she started grinding her crotch on
my forearm because that's what you do when you love
someone. The sex, if you could call it that, fell short of
mind-blowing. She whispered thanks and disappeared.
I realized I was sitting in something wet. I needed to
find someone I knew before the pill wore off. I needed

to wash my arm. But more than anything, I needed to be back on the dance floor with my people.

Nothing else mattered, only love and my family, those in the room who felt the music and knew God. And I thought, *Oh.*

Boys on the Side

The first time I went to a gay bar was the night I turned twenty-one. The bar was in Florence, South Carolina, a forty-five-minute drive from Shaw Air Force Base, where I was just stationed. It took a while to find a gay bar. This was 1998. Couldn't google "gay bars." Google was still in beta back then. Couldn't ask around unless I was absolutely sure of who I was asking. I was pretty sure about the nose-pierced waiter with the shag cut at a house party when he stood on the coffee table and announced to a room full of airmen that if they didn't change the music from Creed to Destiny's Child, he was going to start breaking shit. Then he apologized for standing on the coffee table. He gave all right directions considering how drunk he was.

The bouncer asked me if I had a membership. I wasn't expecting that question. But South Carolina blue laws only allowed private clubs to serve liquor on Sundays. So every bar in South Carolina called itself a private club. I was expecting to have to show my driver's license. But I didn't want anyone to notice it was my birthday, least of all this bouncer with bad skin and frosted tips that made him look like a youth minister.

I told him I was not a member. "Well, you gotta sign up here. Fill this out." The bouncer handed me a card. Name. Address. Driver's license number.

"I can't fill that out," I said. "I'm military. I can't be on a list at a gay bar." My paranoia wasn't unfounded. I'd heard rumors of witch hunts at other bases, though so far, it seemed no one suspected me.

There's an oft-repeated maxim about women in the military: you're either a whore a dyke. You hear it first from your recruiter, as a warning. You hear it thereafter as an accusation—sometimes it's meant to be a joke. But even so, if there's a useful side effect to homophobia, it's that most people who find gays abhorrent find it rude to assume someone's gay, despite all obvious signs. Which is why any gay person could have told you Ricky Martin was as queer as come on a mustache. And yet people were shocked. It's not gaydar. It's the ability to see reality without the constraints of judgment.

On base, all it would take was one person, the wrong person, the wrong grudge, the wrong rumor, and my career was over. I was still new to the Air Force, where most of the training is intended to make you paranoid. Operations Security, OPSEC—you never know who's listening. A name tag left out, a penny wedged under a table leg, a class schedule—anything could be a security violation. They had us keep a list of the serial number to every goddamn bill in our wallets. I wasn't taking risks.

And I sure as fuck wasn't putting my name on a list at a gay bar.

The bouncer said, "Honey, I don't care what you write on the card." His voice sounded like he'd smoked a pack of road flares. "You put a name down there, and when you come in next time, that name will be on this list. You point to what you wrote. And I put a little check mark by it. I don't give a shit if it's the name your mama gave you." He coughed. Swallowed something large. "Look, babe," he said and pointed to the list. "We got Mary Jane, Trent Reznor, Anita Dick, Cherilyn Sarkisian, Sam Iam, and that's just the obvious ones. You sure as shit ain't the first military we got."

I stood there trying to make up my mind. Trying not to ask if Cherilyn was Cher's real name, afraid he'd laugh at me. Part of me wanted to run back to my car, drive back to base, and forget about gay bars. I'd sat in my car listening to the radio for a good ten minutes just trying to build up the courage to walk in the door. I'd been waiting months, for my birthday, just to come here.

Even if I gave up now and turned around, it's not like I felt any more at ease on base. Sumter, the town nearest to Shaw, was a scattered tableau of churches, trailer parks, and used-car dealerships—"No Credit, No Problem (32% APR)." I didn't bother trying to find a gay bar in town. Even if there were, I'd have been too afraid someone would see my car, or worse, I might be seen by some airman who liked the music and the drugs, and would sell me out to save his ass when he was popped on a piss test.

At work, I tried to stay invisible. Sometime around

ten, Major Coffindaffer would hand me the half-filled-in crossword from the *USA Today* he bought on the way to work. He'd switch his radio from the John Boy and Billy show to the right-wing AM channel.

The guys in my office loved John Boy and Billy. There was this clip they'd play for anyone who hadn't heard it. Sergeant Peters played the clip for me my first day— some guy from the radio show, their serious news guy, reading what was supposedly a news story about queers and a gerbil. I got grossed out, made a gagging face, asked which desk was mine. But Peters blocked my path and said, "No, wait, this is the best part." I'll spare you the "best part" (there was an airborne flaming gerbil). The guys were all looking at me, waiting for a reaction. I smiled and tried to force a laugh. I wasn't angry. I was just sad. It's easy to hate what you don't understand.

Funny thing about Air Force officers is they're basically an evangelical cult—something to do with the Air Force Academy being next door to Focus on the Family headquarters. The result is an officer corps that trends more religious and more conservative than any other branch.

All day long, I'd listen to Rush Limbaugh and friends debate the president's latest treason and gay scout leaders and gays in the military. Major Coffindaffer would mutter about how we should just go ahead and hold public hangings like back in the good ol' days. And I'd fill in the crossword.

One fear never left my mind, that at any moment, any one of them would look at me and recognize what they hated. But the good thing about the little office where I worked was that the officers like Coffindaffer mostly ignored me. So that Friday, no one knew or cared that it was my birthday. No one had to know I was going to check out a gay bar.

Standing outside the bar, I told myself, *Just walk in, don't be obvious, get a drink, look around. Then you can go home.* I wondered if I'd worn the right clothes.

Someone came up behind me and asked what was going on. I turned around. He was about my age. Just a kid. Military haircut, the unmistakable ill-advised mustache that, following military regulation, always rests one shaving mishap away from Hitler lip. He lived in the same dorms I did. Not my floor, or I'd know his name. But I'd seen him in the laundry room. I felt better seeing him until I realized this meant I might see others from the base. They might see me. I hadn't considered this. I'd driven thirty miles to have a drink where no one would see me. I told him I didn't want to put my name on a list.

"Why? I'm on the list," he said. The bouncer handed him the clipboard. "Right here, Truvy Jones."

"Steel Magnolias," I said. He clapped like I'd learned to roll over. And I realized then he had just as much to lose as I did. But he didn't seem at all scared. I put down Ouiser Boudreaux on the card, filled out the address for the local carpet company with the annoying radio jingle, and Papa John's phone number on the line for driver's license.

I sat at the bar waiting for the bartender to finish wrestling with the little airplane bottle of Jack—another oddity of South Carolina's liquor laws. And I watched the room through the mirror behind the glasses. Truvy was nowhere to be seen. I'd hoped he'd come get a drink. We'd talk about *Steel Magnolias.* He'd be impressed with my vast knowledge of Dolly Parton trivia. We'd bond and maybe become friends.

We did, eventually. This was Jay, who'd become my best friend. I'd learn he loved Reba more than Dolly, and we'd fight about it. But I'd forgive him because he could quote *9 to 5* by heart. I'd learn he'd been raised by Pentecostal nutjobs who prayed in tongues over the phone when he told them he was gay. I'd learn he wasn't all that different from me. But that wouldn't happen for another year—some of it would take a lot longer.

Seemed like everyone at the bar knew everyone else. Everyone was divided into factions. The younger lesbians owned the pool table; the older lesbians occupied the tables outside. As I walked by, they all stared like I'd walked into their private house party and changed the music. A few older gay men took turns on the poker machines. The gay boys held the dance floor. I didn't belong here. That I was used to the feeling didn't make it any more comfortable.

I left early that first night, feeling defeated. But I kept going back every weekend after that. Each time I went, I felt no less out of place than the first time. I didn't know how to talk to anyone, much less flirt with a woman. If I'd planned this better, I'd have worked off a list. Step 1 would've been learning how to socialize and make friends. Step 47 would've been flirting and getting laid. Instead, I approached gay bars with all the social awareness of a homeschooler. Offering to buy someone a drink seemed like something people only did in movies. Introducing myself seemed awkward and left me way too open for rejection. I'd been trying the method I'd later watch from behind the bar—stand against a wall, avoid eye contact, focus on peeling the label from my beer bottle. The bartender could've helped me out, but he didn't.

So I'd have a couple drinks, then drive back to Sumter and sit on the hood of my car facing the highway. Just past the highway stood the fence surrounding the base, and just past that, the runway. The runway lights never went out, but no one was flying on weekends. I'd lean back against my windshield to see the sky. I'd always search the sky when I felt alone. I'd look for the constellations my mom taught us when we were little. I don't remember the stories she told about Cassiopeia or Andromeda. I only remember how to find them. But in the South Carolina lowlands, there were no stars. The damp air was too thick and glowed a sickly yellow from the lights on the runway and the sodium lights on the highway. I could see the moon, but barely.

There's probably a manual on how to come out, but I've already covered the issues with this being 1998 in Internet history. I hadn't even chosen an AIM handle. It had, for a time, been easier to just date guys.

Guys were easy. Didn't require words half the time. All I had to do was show up to a dorm party, look in a guy's general direction or stand near him long enough to drain the jungle juice from my Solo cup, and he'd assume I wanted him.

"Wanted" was a stretch. If you ever want to feel like a piece of meat, fuck a lesbian who's trying to figure shit out. The last time I'd gone back to a guy's room, he came so fast I'm not even sure it counted as sex. So I'd gone back to the party, the cluster of airmen drinking at the picnic tables between dorm buildings, and got another one. Back to his dorm, kicked out his roommate who'd been happily playing video games, got half undressed, and he threw up. He still wanted to fuck. But even I had standards. So I went back to the party. The last one fell asleep in my bed. I sat in the stairwell, chain-smoking and wondering what the fuck was wrong with me, after I finished myself off.

It wasn't their fault. Some of them, god bless them, actually tried. Some of them, I'd fake an orgasm to spare their feelings. But I couldn't come. I know this isn't a rare problem and likely had a lot to do with their fucking like they were worried if they didn't hurry it up, I'd leave. Might've been because if they didn't hurry it up, I'd leave. I was always worried if I opened my eyes, I'd laugh or throw up.

These are not the reactions you're supposed to have to sex. I was pretty sure about that. Everyone from Oprah to *Loveline* to the books I blindly grabbed as I walked past the gay-and-lesbian shelf at Barnes & Noble to quickly skim in another, safer part of the store, they all agreed sexuality wasn't a choice. But they also agreed women existed somewhere along a spectrum. That a spectrum has two ends is probably something I'd have learned in school. But I didn't. I'd been busy learning how people like me, women who were attracted to women, were abominations. I could mostly ignore all that shit. Mostly.

I figured if I kept trying, if I got used to it, like any other unpleasant task—running or cleaning toilets—I could learn to enjoy it, or at least tolerate it. And if I could, there was no need to ruin my life by being a lesbian. I could get married. I could have kids. I could be normal. I just fucking wanted to be normal.

It was weird, according to the others in basic training, that I'd been a virgin when I joined the Air Force. Although whether or not I technically was a virgin according to the manual, who fucking knows.

Dry-humping doesn't count. Thank fuck. I had this on good authority from experts on exactly where to draw the virgin-slut line: the basketball team from Amarillo Christian School. (I was homeschooled. My stepdad, Gabe, had cut a deal with the principal to allow us to play basketball. Forced socialization for two homeschoolers who'd still forget not to hug strangers. Whatever he paid, it was too much. There were only seven girls on my team. Even though I sucked, I was a body on the court, a tall body.)

Amarillo Christian School was run by the Church of Christ. If you've ever wondered what's wrong with Texas, they're as good an answer as any other, especially in the panhandle. The church doesn't allow dancing, drinking, or even instrumental music. Go to a Church of Christ wedding and they'll sing "Here comes the bride," after which they'll stand around a room drinking off-brand soda. Lubbock, two hours south of Amarillo, was a dry county until 2009, largely because of the Church of Christ. Just past Lubbock, you'll find Anson, Texas, the inspiration for *Footloose*, because until 1987, dancing was illegal.

They're fundamentalist nutjobs, but their school was cheap. And so the student body at Amarillo Christian was a pretty even mix of good Christian kids and slightly more worldly though also Christian kids who'd been expelled from local high schools. Who could claim virginity was a constant debate.

The Church of Christ kids were sure anything beyond oral was real sex. The worldly kids were pretty sure anal was allowed. Everyone was iffy on consent.

I knew better than to ask for a specific ruling on the state of my virginity from the Christian school kids. But I remember a moment, on a basketball trip to Abilene, Coach Rhodes decided to give us an impromptu sex talk, in case the sights of Abilene-fucking-Texas sent us into hormonal manic episodes. She stood there clinging to the seat backs in one of those warm-up suits coaches buy at a coach supply store and asked us all if we thought it was okay to let a guy feel us up. She knew some of us didn't come from solid Church of Christ homes. Some of our parents drank beer. Some of our parents were divorced. Some didn't attend church at all. You can't expect people like that to vigilantly guard their daughters' sexual purity. She told us if we let a guy feel us up, we might as well give it up right there.

The freshmen boys, separated from us girls by a single row of bus seats, not cool enough to join the senior boys in the back of the bus, giggled. The lesson for them was clear: try to get away with what you can. A girl doesn't stop you, that's on her. I wasn't sure whether "feel up" meant up a shirt or up a skirt. Either way, I let someone else answer. It was still novel for me to hear an adult tell me not to have sex.

———

The only reason anyone's heard of the Family, the Children of God, is the same reason I wouldn't tell anyone I grew up in the cult: it was known as a sex cult. For a long time, until NXIVM, it was *the* sex cult. (Their marketing was better. Didn't occur to us to brand anyone, damnit.)

In the Family, kids were encouraged to express themselves sexually. When a four-year-old boy tried to mount a four-year-old girl, the adults would say, "Oh, how cute." When twelve-year-olds were caught in bed naked, the adults might tell them to be careful—the Systemites wouldn't understand. When an adult groped a preteen girl, she might freeze; she might be called unloving and told to be more receptive. She'd learn, eventually, to only freeze on the inside.

An edict was sent out around the time I was born, one of our prophet David Berg's rambling diatribes, this one called "Child Brides." In it, we got to hear Berg detail one of his dearest memories—a nanny who'd suck him off when he was maybe three. One of his less fond memories was when his mom caught him masturbating and made him wait until his father got home, and finish in front of his dad.

I don't know what made Berg who he was. I don't fucking care. I care that about thirty thousand kids were raised in his sex cult where the manual for raising children, the Davidito Book, showed adult women groping a toddler, Davidito, Berg's heir. It showed naked three-year-olds miming sex with one another. I care that the entire body of literature we were raised with was about sex. I care that in *Heaven's Girl*, a book written just for us preteens, the pivotal scene is a fourteen-year-old girl being gang-raped by Antichrist soldiers, and loving it. I care that girls as young as fourteen were sent out to "Flirty Fish." I care that for a time, kids were passed around between adults for their regularly scheduled "sharing nights." (While we're here, "thanks for sharing" will always mean something different to me.) I care that I spent a good deal of my childhood taking care of the inevitable babies, pacing the halls with them at night while they screamed for their mothers. I care that they only ended Flirty Fishing because of the AIDS crisis. I care that when they did ban sex between kids and adults, only because of legal problems, they never bothered telling the kids. Really depended on whether an adult gave a shit about the new rule. Who were we going to tell? I care that we were taught girls who didn't eagerly participate were selfish. That satisfying men was a girl's duty. And of course, if satisfying men is your duty, sort of rules out being a lesbian.

I'd never sucked a dick (women's anatomy remained unimaginable), though there was that shepherd in Japan with the permanently filmy glasses, who smelled like cough syrup, who'd lick me when I was trying to sleep. I decided what he did couldn't possibly count against me. I hadn't even been awake most of the time.

Dry-humping, though, that wasn't a "one guy" sort of history. I'd participated in dry-humping with exactly as much enthusiasm as I'd participated in prayer meetings. Which is to say I was generally awake for it, daydreaming about anything else, and hoping it would be over soon. Neither activity was exactly avoidable; both occurred constantly. I did push a boy too hard once and he fell off my bunk bed. We both panicked. He was fine. And I had to let him go at it on my leg for weeks so he wouldn't tell on me.

After Coach Rhodes finished her talk with a resounding "If you let a guy feel you up, sex you up, you don't come back from that," and the boys in the back broke into the chorus of that fucking Color Me Badd song, the girls discussed the coach's disjointed lecture on which body parts we could let a guy touch—everyone agreed that being felt up was fine. There was no consensus on oral, but no one wanted to press too hard and seem like a slut. Then Lisa Collins, who was a very good Christian, whose dad was a Church of Christ elder, said dry-humping didn't count because it wasn't even fun. I never asked anyone else. I had the answer I wanted. I was a virgin. I held to that fact like I'd beaten the Family at the game they played best. I was somehow still a fucking virgin. I won.

That I'd left a fucking sex cult a virgin might've been why I was so reluctant to give it up to my first boyfriend. I met him at the off-brand Taco Bell where Lisa's older brother got me a job. My main attraction to John was he was taller than me and we didn't look stupid standing next to one another, and his family had horses. He worked in the kitchen and drove a truck and wore a cowboy hat and walked funny because he'd already broken several bones riding bulls in amateur rodeos. The bulls were smaller but still bulls. The bull riders were already the sort of stupid that makes someone think riding a bull is a good idea. He wanted to drop out of high school.

Auto techs made good money, he said. He didn't need a diploma. John was stupid or sweet or horny enough that he didn't mind my cupping his boobs while we dry-humped in the back of his truck. I didn't mind the dry-humping because that's the price you pay for not getting told on, or for riding horses. I liked horses. I should've let him fuck me, but getting pregnant meant staying in Amarillo to get pregnant again, and again. Maybe go to dental hygienist school once the kids were self-sufficient. But John found someone else who would go all the way and took her to prom. I pretended to care. My mom took me to Olive Garden. She ordered a bottle of wine with two glasses, and when the waiter asked for my ID, she said, "She's my daughter." Enough for Texas law. But of course she added, "Are you dating anyone?" Like there might still be time for him to take me to prom after his shift. He wasn't single, or claimed not to be. So once I was good and drunk, Mom and I saw *French Kiss* over a large popcorn with butter because Mom doesn't believe diets exist in movie theaters.

Then I joined the Air Force. They sent me to the Defense Language Institute (DLI) in Monterey to learn Vietnamese. Why the Air Force needed Vietnamese interpreters in 1996 is beyond me. I never got far enough to find out. The point here is Monterey is a short drive from the storied gay mecca of San Francisco. And I knew I was a lesbian by then.

Airman Eudy, who was from San Francisco and therefore an expert on all things gay, had told me so in basic training. I respected Eudy because when they marched us to church that first Sunday, Eudy said she wasn't going in. She was an atheist. I'd never heard someone say those words, "I'm an atheist." I wasn't expecting her to burst into flames, but I wouldn't have been surprised. They said she could fucking sit outside if it was that fucking important to her. (I don't think our training instructors gave a shit about our souls. That Sunday was the first time they'd get a few hours away from us, and they probably had laundry to do.) There'd been an ice storm the night before. But Eudy happily sat outside, freezing her ass to a stone bench. I was in awe. But I wasn't an idiot. I went to the three-hour-long Mormon service with Airman Mock. Three hours in a warm room with no one screaming at me sounded like heaven. Sure, I had to listen to Mormons. But I was having a hard enough time expelling the Family's crap from my brain. The Mormons didn't have a chance. Then I kept going to Mormon church because I'd developed a crush on Mock.

The night Eudy broke the news, we were a couple days away from graduation, final inspections done. Most of the airmen were huddled in groups, discussing their tech school assignments and the first thing they'd eat once we were free. I was sitting on my bed in my PT shorts and T-shirt, writing a letter to my grandma. Airman Mock was reading a letter from her boyfriend. She was lying on her back with her head resting on my leg. Just normal straight-girl stuff that straight girls do. Except one of us was straight and probably well aware the other was not. And I was way too fucking aware of the heat of her head on my thigh and trying to resist the urge to stroke her hair. It wasn't gay at all. It wasn't gay that we bought rings outside the PX with each other's names on them. It wasn't gay that I polished her boots for her. I was just better at polishing boots. Then Airman Eudy had to fucking ruin it. She walked past my rack in her towel and laughed and said, "You fucking lesbians." Like that was a normal, friendly thing to say. Airman Mock laughed and sat up. I probably made a laughing sound. Odds are, no one heard it and no one cared. But I was humiliated. And I was pissed because Airman Mock would probably never lay her head on my thigh again. But I believed Eudy. Like I said, Eudy was from San Francisco. And it scared the shit out of me.

I think I was twelve the first time Gabe decided to name the problem: I had a homosexual spirit. I wasn't yet possessed by a demon, thank God. But possession could happen anytime if I wasn't careful.

It wasn't anything I'd done. It's not like I had a secret stash of Indigo Girls tapes or got caught watching *Desert Hearts*. I was in the Family. I watched the same shitty movie everyone else watched on movie night and listened to the same Family tapes we all listened to. I simply wasn't sufficiently feminine. My preferred look was homeschooled boy, which is to say polo shirts buttoned to the top and tucked neatly into my shorts or pants. The only thing I ever did with my hair was scrape it into a ponytail. And for a while, I got away with it.

Then we moved to this massive commune up in the mountains north of Osaka. I was grouped with the preteens, the Junior End Time Teens—JETTS, because the Family loved acronyms—and surrounded by appro-

priately feminine girls with appropriate interests, man-
nerisms, and style. I stood out as "that tall girl—you
know, the tomboy." And I tried. I really fucking did.

The girls tried to help. Come dance night, and there
was always a fucking dance night, they'd lend me shawls
and tie ribbons into my hair and choose my skirt. All so I
could look like a godly woman. But then we'd sit in chairs
around the dining room, tables shoved against one wall,
scarves draped on lamps to create mood lighting, the live
band (a few teen boys with their hair slicked back) playing Family songs, and the girls sitting with posture like
trained dancers, their ankles perfectly crossed, knees
together, and me slouched back and legs spread like that
asshole taking two seats during rush hour.

The girls would practice walking with the encyclopedias we weren't allowed to read balanced on their heads.
I'd sit in a corner reading the encyclopedias we weren't
allowed to read, grateful they'd convinced someone to
let us use the books. Gabe called me "moose" because
of my awkward, loping, legs-grew-too-fast-for-my-brain
gait. I couldn't walk right. I couldn't even run right. I
liked winning races too much to worry about whether
my arms looked dainty.

What I'm saying is whether or not I actively did anything wrong that time or any other time doesn't fucking matter. Once the shepherds and Gabe agreed I was a
problem, I was a problem. They skirted around the issue
at first. Reading assignments on how a godly woman
should look and act, increasingly harsh warnings to stop
acting like a bull in a china shop, a moose, a tomboy, a
man. Be ladylike. This masculine spirit, this homosexual

spirit, this evil, you have to fight it. We'll help you, of course, with public shaming, isolation, and occasionally by beating the shit out of you.

Gabe was especially invested in my spiritual health because he had aspirations. His lesbian daughter reflected poorly on his leadership skills, not to mention his entire manhood. I mean, if you can't control one little girl . . . The only part I understood at the time was he was ashamed of me. So I got better. Wore skirts. Let my friends do my hair. Sometimes sat with my knees together, if I remembered. Then we moved to Switzerland.

Part of the problem was an item written in bold print on the list of why any of this act-like-a-lady shit mattered: I was supposed to make myself attractive to boys. This was what you might call a cornerstone of Family doctrine, and entire volumes of our literature were dedicated to pounding that fact home.

They weren't wrong to be worried about me. Ignore the apocalyptic shit, and some of the sex shit, and the cult wasn't all that radical in its doctrine, especially on the role of women. Those who write the rules will always give themselves an advantage over those who are "other." Difference was, our patriarch said the quiet parts out loud—that women were created to serve men, that a woman's value was determined by men, that women should submit to men, that a woman's ultimate purpose was to grow babies, that rape wouldn't exist if women weren't selfish. You can't have a lesbian, even if she is just a girl, running around acting like she doesn't give a rat's ass what men think of her. That'd be fucking chaos.

They'd ask me why I wanted to be a man and I'd tell them I didn't. Because I didn't. Just, the boys had all the power. The boys got to build things with wood while the girls had to sew curtains and bedsheets. They'd ask me why I was acting like a man and I'd tell them I wasn't. Because I wasn't. I just didn't think they should get to decide how a girl should act. I just wanted some fucking control. They'd tell me to read *The Look of Love*, about how God wanted me to flirt with men, and I'd have to write an essay on what I learned about flirting. I wouldn't flirt because all those coy glances and half smiles the other girls performed naturally felt ridiculous on my face. And they'd warn me no man would want me.

Part of the problem was the possibility no man would want me was fucking fine with me. There was a time in Japan, may have been the conclusive symptom in my homosexual spirit syndrome diagnosis, when I stopped showering altogether to make myself less attractive to boys, or specifically men. We only showered once or twice a week anyway and were only allowed three minutes with a bucket, a stool, and a cup. It took a while for anyone to notice. I mean it took a couple months. I'd sit in class half listening to our shepherd explain why God made it possible for girls to have babies at twelve, and I'd scrape the film off my forearm to reveal the angry pink skin underneath. I wondered if I'd eventually molt like a snake, but I never found out. Someone would make me shower. I'd have to start all over with my project of being the dirtiest girl in the room, the girl the men didn't want to rub against in the dish line, the girl our shepherd didn't want to fondle at night.

People hear "sex cult" and think it sounds fun. They don't consider that cult members are who they'll be fucking. They don't consider that there's a schedule right on the dining room wall—laundry, dishes, toddlers, all those babies, bathrooms, the herpes bathroom, and "sharing night." It's okay. Gabe didn't think it through either. For a few months when I was pissed at him, I used to switch the schedule around when no one was looking. Assign him to women he loathed. Hope you enjoyed your free love, asshole.

Part of the problem was my stepdad and the shepherds were full of shit. Probably why I backslid into my old ways in Switzerland—the boys liked me just fine. The girls could go either way. I wasn't interested in being pretty or talking about which boys were cute. The boys were my friends, except for Samuel, who didn't brush his teeth and was always trying to kiss me or crawl into my bunk and hump my leg. (He's not the boy I managed to shove off the bunk. I considered it. But he might've told, and I'd have been in for a world of hurt.) But that first home in Switzerland, we were barely supervised. I was free to punch Samuel in the stomach when he got too pushy. But I took the continued leg-humping from boys and the constant casual groping from men as proof that Gabe and the Family were wrong about me.

Besides, I wasn't a lesbian. If I were, wouldn't I be compelled to hump girls' legs? I tried to picture it sometimes. The prettiest girl in the house was my sister's friend Theresa. I had a massive crush on her, but I didn't recognize it as a crush. I recognized it as wanting her to like me. She taught me how to play bar chords on the guitar. I tried to make her laugh.

My sister Valerie shared a room on the top floor of that Swiss commune, up in the mountains near the French border. As older teens, they had a little more privacy.

They even had a razor. I found out about the razor while hanging out in their room one Sunday. I was telling a story, waving my arms around, and Valerie said, "Wait. Put your hand up?" I didn't know what she was looking for, but I heard that tone, like she was about to tease me for something. I did not want her to tease me in front of Theresa. But I was little scared of Valerie. (I still am.) So I raised my arm and my shirt sleeve slid down to reveal just enough, I guess. Because the next thing I knew, Valerie had grabbed my hand and was dragging me to the bathroom. "Take off your shirt."

"No. Why?"

"Lauren."

Listen. She used to pinch us if we didn't obey when we were little. I took my shirt off. And I swear to Christ, I can still see the look she gave me, covering her mouth like my armpit was covered with ants. "When did you get hair? Why didn't you tell me? Lauren. Oh my god, you're *hairy*. Stay here. Lock the door." And then she was gone.

She came back with a little pink razor and told me to get in the shower.

I said, "I can't. I'll get in trouble." Which was likely true. Shaving wasn't strictly outlawed but didn't fit with Berg's image of a godly woman, a position happily accepted by the hippies who were now our elders. Either way, it's not like we could run to town to buy a razor. Unlike my sister, I was still sleeping and changing and showering with twenty other kids, any of whom might've reported me. And my shepherds were assholes.

Valerie said if she hadn't noticed my hair, no one would notice I'd shaved it. It's not like anyone looks at anyone else while they're changing (a fact that took another twenty years to sink in).

So I undressed and Valerie stood there and told me to soap up. I don't know how long she and Theresa had been sharing that razor, but it was a fucking butter knife. The single blade kept getting jammed up and I sliced my thumb trying to pull hair from it. Do another stroke. Bleed a little more. My sister, her hair growing frizzier by the moment, making her look even scarier, critiquing my technique. "Just short strokes. Stop being foolish. You have to go fast. No. Fast. Push down harder."

"It's pulling my hair out."

"Don't be a baby."

Next armpit. She told me not to shave my legs yet. That would've been too obvious. Or my arms. I don't know why she thought arms should be shaved, but she did. It's not like we had access to *Seventeen* magazine or normal adults to teach us these things. I still shave my arms for no other reason than my sister told me to. I liked that we had a secret between us. Like she'd let me into her cool secret life.

Once we were done and I was dressed, most of the bleeding stanched, the razor burn just beginning to flare, we returned to her room. "Show Theresa," she said, proud of her work. I kept my arms pinned to my sides. "Show her." So I did. Theresa winced and I dropped my arms.

"You should give me that shirt," Theresa said. "I can get the blood out." And she offered me one of her own, a pink strappy thing.

I shook my head and said, "It's okay." Getting blood out of things was an earlier sister lesson. Valerie was hav-

ing fun by then, the grade-A high of bossing your siblings around. She said, "Oh, Lauren would never wear
that, my little lesbian *seester*," in that silly baby voice she
used to make fun of me. I told her to shut up and I know
she heard it in my voice, that I was about to cry. So she
stopped. The line we've never crossed, that unspoken
oath of sisters: you don't make each other cry in front of
others. Still, I was worried Theresa would think I was
some sort of pervert.

Theresa, saint that she was, just smiled at me and
picked up her guitar. And I thought, *No way I'm a lesbian.*
I was watching Theresa strum away and I tried to picture
fucking her. I couldn't even figure out what to picture.
I imagined grinding on her like the boys were always
doing to me, and I nearly burst out laughing. I might
have if I weren't so sure Valerie would've demanded to
know why. So there it was—I was not a lesbian. Sure,
Valerie kept calling me a lesbian. But I called her fat.
Sisters say stupid shit.

Gabe never did stop warning me about what could
make me a lesbian. Even long after we left the Family.
Watching *Roseanne* could do it, tip me over the edge.
90210 was safe as long as I made it clear I wanted to
kiss Brandon, not be Brandon. Music was dangerous.
Alanis Morissette was definitely a lesbian. So was Dolo-
res O'Riordan, with her manly shaved head. He said his
cousin had seen Melissa Etheridge in Los Angeles, with
a woman who looked like a man. He didn't mind if I listened to country, but not that Mary Chapin lady. Something wasn't right with her. No Reba either. He knew
Dolly Parton wasn't a lesbian. Obviously she was too
pretty. But it was suspect how much I loved her. Really

all celebrities were suspect. They were either queers
or feminazis. (Gabe had found a new prophet in Rush
Limbaugh. All the misogyny and none of the work.)
Books were a constant danger, but he couldn't be bothered to read them for content. He'd just helpfully point
out that I'd been reading a lot of that Agatha Christie.
He was a slightly better judge of movies. *Silence of the
Lambs* was banned, and *Thelma & Louise*, but so were
9 to 5 and anything by John Hughes. Anything I liked
too much. It sounded like a recipe warning. Whip the
cream a little too much and it'll break and there you have
it—homosexuality.

Knowing I didn't consider him my real dad, Gabe
used my father as a weapon: "If he saw you do that"—
whatever it was that time—"what would he think? He'd
be disgusted. And it won't be on me. God knows I tried."
My dad came to visit once, when I was seventeen. He
was living in Poland, I think. Who cares. He brought his
stepson and wife. And after he left, Gabe was relentless.
"You know he already has a new son. He doesn't need
either of you." (Mikey didn't fare much better under
Gabe's homo-inquisitions. He was "a wimp," a "little
limp-wristed," "a fag.")

Gabe was an idiot. Mikey's straight. And I didn't want
to fuck Dolly Parton. (It feels disrespectful to even write
that sentence.) I did have a lot of feelings about Linda
Evangelista in the "Freedom! '90" video. But I didn't
know not being able to breathe was a symptom to look
out for. No book I found in the Amarillo public library
made me want to hump girls. And I certainly wasn't
checking out my teammates in the locker room. More
than that, I usually changed in a bathroom stall. If some-

one talked to me in the locker room and I wasn't sure she was fully dressed, I'd stare at her shoes, the ceiling, the locker behind her, anything. Up until Eudy's lesbian accusation, I'd made it through most of basic training without showing signs of catching something lesbian. And in basic training, we had to shower together.

The first few weeks, I didn't have time to notice. There were fifty of us, eight showerheads, and we had five minutes. We didn't have time to get wet. But later on, they relaxed a little. There was even time to shave your legs. This is what the entire country was shitting itself over—the clear and present danger of homosexuals in showers. But anytime I was in the shower, I stared at the ceiling tiles in absolute terror I'd accidentally see the naked body of another airman. (I didn't know at the time that counting ceiling tiles is the customary practice of homosexuals in communal showers.)

Once out of basic training, I could watch any Jodie Foster movie I wanted. I could read any book I chose without someone keeping score of how many women I'd read that week. I was free to buy Indigo Girls CDs. It wasn't because they were gay. I didn't even like Melissa Etheridge. If I played that Sarah McLachlan CD every single night, maybe it was just to drown out my room-mate's Bone Thugs CD. None of it made me gay. I never even went to San Francisco, though the rumor was gay bars didn't ask for ID. I was perfectly happy drinking on the beach with the rest of the underage airmen. Sure, I had the occasional crush on a girl. But as long as I avoided her completely, I could tell myself I was normal.

The first time I spent the night with a lesbian, it wasn't sexual. The first time was the exact opposite of sexual.

She was a salty old Marine staff sergeant who looked like Sam Shepard, but butch. She was a class ahead of me in my Vietnamese school at DLI. We'd talked a few times in the bathroom—in the bathroom because I didn't want anyone seeing me talking to an obvious lesbian.

I'm sure she knew I was gay. I'm sure she knew it would do no good to tell me. She did tell me I was pregnant. She asked if I knew. We were in the bathroom in one of the old WWII-era buildings they still used for the school. I'd left class to throw up, and when I came out of the stall, she was leaning against the sink with her arms crossed. I thought she was going to chew me out for drinking. Then I remembered I wasn't hungover.

She handed me a paper towel and stepped aside so I could use the sink. She asked how late I was. I spat into the sink and told her I wasn't pregnant. That was ridiculous. Jesus. That's how rumors start. I fixed my uniform like I was ready to leave. But now she was standing in front of the door, chewing her cheek and shaking her head like it'd be a shame if she had to fight me. I wasn't stupid enough to barge past a staff sergeant. So I just stood there, admiring the shine on my boots. She said, "You need help, you'll let me know." It wasn't a question. I nodded because I wasn't going to cry. I said, "I'm not pregnant."

But I wasn't sure.

He didn't use a condom. That's what pissed me off more than anything. We were leaving the beach, a little campfire, a bunch of idiots passing around a bottle of vodka, telling jokes, daring one another to run into the icy surf, smoking clove cigarettes, "Don't Speak" blasting on someone's boom box and the sailor from Long

Beach swearing he used to smoke weed with Gwen Stefani's brother. I was having fun. I thought, because I'm the type of person who catalogues these sorts of things, that this was the sort of night I'd remember. Nineteen years old, sitting on a beach with my friends. Then I was too drunk. I didn't want to pass out or puke, didn't want to seem weak. I wanted to go to sleep.

He said he was leaving too. And someone said, "Hey, you guys want a condom?" It was a big joke. Someone saw Markowitz buying condoms, like that dipshit would ever get laid. But this guy wasn't a dork like Markowitz. He laughed and kept walking. He said, "God, they're such children." And it felt nice, like I wasn't one of those dumb children.

He raped me in the woods just outside the gates. But it wasn't a real gate and there were no guards to hear me, if I made any noise at all. I didn't realize what was happening at first anyway. There was a moment when it seemed like he'd stop because I told him to stop. He didn't stop and I thought, *Oh, I'm being raped*. Just like that.

Six weeks or so later, I was running out of Vietnamese class to puke. After the staff sergeant clued me in to what I didn't want to believe, I stole a pregnancy test from Safeway. She drove me to the appointment on a Saturday and waited for me. I thought it was strange there was only one protester outside. And he was phoning it in, really. Just sitting in a lawn chair.

I was lucky I was stationed in California then. You get pregnant in a backwards state or country where people think a woman should raise her rapist's kid, getting an abortion can be a hassle, if not impossible. I didn't have to wait. I didn't have to take extra leave and get permission to miss school or watch an ultrasound to make sure my nightmares had appropriate visuals. I just walked in at my correct appointment time and walked out a couple hours later knowing at least I wouldn't have to suffer a life sentence because the asshole didn't go back for a condom.

The staff sergeant picked up McDonald's on the way back to post. She let me hide in her room to recover so I wouldn't have to deal with my roommate or anyone else who dropped by. Because she was a staff sergeant, she had a room up the hill in an NCO building with private bathrooms and no roommates.

I fell asleep watching *Seven*—maybe not the best movie choice for the occasion, but I doubt she knew the plot beforehand.

When I woke up, she was asleep beside me. And I finally cried. And I mean I was bawling. I wasn't crying about the abortion. The only thing I felt about that was relief. I was crying because somewhere along the way, sometime after leaving the Family, I somehow started thinking, *Okay. I'll be safe now.* I truly believed it. I thought once I was free of those fucking perverted old men copping a feel any chance they got, once I wasn't destined to marry someone at twelve, fourteen, or whatever arbitrary age David Berg decided girls were ready that year, once I'd never see my name on a sharing schedule, to share free love with whomever the home shepherds designated my partner that week, I'd have some fucking control over who I fucked and when. I would get the one thing no cult baby is allowed: a fucking choice.

But like I said, the Family, once you get down to the

nut of it, wasn't all that radical. If it hadn't been that guy, it would've been some asshole somewhere else.

The staff sergeant woke up and held me until I stopped crying. She fell asleep holding me, and I cried again, but quieter this time. Because she was comfortable and I felt safe, if only that night.

You tell that story to a guy and all he'll want to ask is, "So did you fuck or not?" But I wasn't much interested in making friends with guys anymore, let alone telling them why.

For a long time after, I didn't cry again. I didn't feel much at all. I'd always heard people describe depression as deep sorrow, rock bottom, the blues. But there's no bottom. There's no sorrow. There's just falling. Maybe that's why I didn't recognize it when it hit. I felt nothing at all and cared less.

I failed out of Vietnamese school and didn't care. I stayed up all night polishing my boots and ironing another bottle of starch into my uniform until it stood on its own. I'd switched into the same survival mode I'd learned as a kid. Be good. Be perfect. But studying didn't occur to me. Being a good airman became a compulsion. Volunteer for everything. Anything. Give up weekends to work guard duty. Be good. Be perfect and they won't hurt you.

It kind of worked. They stuck me in Russian to give me another chance at a language. I couldn't read in English at that point. I only lasted a few months. I still wasn't studying. I'd borrow someone's car—any airman will rent you theirs for a twenty—and drive the cliffs and bridges of the Central Coast trying to find the courage to gun it into the ocean. But I couldn't do it. I was afraid I'd survive and I couldn't live with that.

The System had finally done what the Family never could. They made me compliant. Anyone who wanted to fuck, I was game. Sure. Why not. At least it was my choice. The Marine barracks were right next door to ours. Identical buildings, though our doors were painted blue and theirs crimson red. But mostly we fucked on the beach or in cars.

Somewhere in a place I didn't think about when driving near cliffs, I thought maybe the God I was trying so hard to not believe in had found a way to fuck me.

Then I was transferred to Shaw, but nothing really changed. Some people cut themselves or hit walls or fought. I fucked random guys. There wasn't a single moment wherein I thought, *This is fucking ridiculous. You're gay. Christ.* There was a phone call from my sister in Massachusetts who said, "Come visit." So I did.

She'd left the Family with her husband and their two kids. We spent the weekend peeling smoke-stained wallpaper off her kitchen walls while her son and daughter played in the living room. And I told her I was gay. I didn't say "I'm gay." We were standing in a pile of shredded wallpaper, drinking cheap wine from paper cups. I said something like, "Hey, what if I'm a lesbian?"

She dropped her scraper in the sink and said, "I knew it! Lauren! I knew it!" She was shouting and ran into the living room like she was looking for someone to tell she'd been right about me, someone to confirm.

Upside of sisters. It doesn't really matter what you just confessed as long as they were right. She came back in after deciding not to explain lesbians to the three- and one-year-olds and said, "Remember when I told you and you started crying?" I just stared. She called me a Pisces. I started crying, to prove her point. Goddamnit.

I didn't tell her everything. I couldn't then. But once I said it, once I knew at least I wouldn't lose my sister, once I said it out loud and nothing changed between us, I figured maybe I'd be all right.

Though I'd achieved a degree of self-acceptance, I was still paranoid. I already had one secret, the Family, and now another. Or maybe I'd always had that secret. Either way, I wasn't risking any more than I had to. So I waited until I was twenty-one, until I found that gay bar in Florence, far enough from base, to go home with the first of many women who'd play that Sarah McLachlan CD while we fucked. Sometimes I'd go home with them more than once, which is practically marriage if you're a lesbian.

But that night, I didn't hit on her. She came over to where I was standing at the end of the bar, nursing a Bud Light, the label crumpled somewhere on the floor. She said her name was Dana. She was cute, but I don't think it mattered by that point. I was clinically horny and would've convinced myself I was attracted to any-one. I couldn't hear a word she was saying over the music and just nodded dumbly while she talked. Then she kissed me and I'd like to say the world disappeared, but the world remained. I kept thinking, *This is what it's supposed to feel like.* We made out against the bar, then on the patio, then against her Ford Escort with the missing bumper. She said I should follow her home. It was all I could do to not shout, "Oh, fuck yes. Finally."

The moment we stepped into her shabby living room with the cat-stained beanbag chair and the trucker-blanket-covered couch and the cigarette holes in the carpet, she said "Hold up," and dropped that fucking CD into the player. You know the one—"I would be the one to hold you down . . ."

I was thrilled because I'd always wanted to fuck to that song and didn't know I'd be fucking to that song for years to come. I don't know if we talked. I couldn't understand her well anyway. The Jack and Cokes she'd been downing at the bar dampened her accent into an unintelligible slurry of sounds. It didn't matter. I wasn't in a position to make decisions. By which I mean, I'd accidentally gone home with the rarest of all lesbians, the femme power top.

I didn't know about tops and bottoms yet. I didn't have gay friends yet. I didn't know that, as Jay would eventually tell me, "Girl, you just ask if you can't tell. But trust me, you can always tell." I asked him if he was a top or a bottom, and he giggled, ruining his entire butch persona that he nearly managed to pull off anytime we were around other military. We were eating dinner in the chow hall at the time, so I gave him a minute to get his bearing back. He told me I was an idiot. But that was long after I met Dana. Or he might've warned me and ruined everything. For a kid from nowhere, he somehow knew an awful lot about being gay.

Again, even if I'd owned a computer, what were the options for research then, Ask Jeeves? You had to go into a physical store to rent porn. And lesbian porn isn't made for lesbians. There were lesbian movies, sure. But the common theme of lesbian movies in the '90s was: There's this lesbian who's in love with Mary-Louise Parker, who's nice to the lesbian. Then Mary-Louise Parker dies. That was the dream back then: one day you might have a straight friend who isn't shitty to you. The other lesbian movie, released just that year, was *Chasing Amy*, in which Ben Affleck, who draws cartoons and has questions about fisting, proves the thesis of the film, of my entire sexual education: lesbians just need a good deep-dicking. Wasn't the most helpful storyline to hand a generation of men.

I've rarely found it in me to respond with, "I have tried dick, Greg. I have tried so many fucking dicks. So many." I'll grant you that younger guys just don't know how to fuck. But you'd think I'd have managed a single orgasm, even accidentally, after fucking . . . (I really don't know how many. I tried to make a list one time, but it's hard to come up with a definite answer when number thirty-eight is "dude in red shirt with chipped tooth." Let's go with fifty.)

I had six that night with Dana. Could've been more, but I had to take a break to pee and give myself a pep talk in the mirror—something like "You will do this. You will go down on her and you will like it." I did. She was the easiest first time I could've drawn. She told me what to do and made it sound hot instead of what I was used to—the wordless shoving of my head down onto a dick, followed quickly by the desperate removal of my head from a dick in serious pain. I'd gone from staring at the ceiling while some guy grunted on top of me to a woman choking me and calling me a whore while I came. It was like suddenly getting to play in the World Cup when all you've done is play pickup soccer with the local divorced dads.

I rarely spent the night with guys, preferred going to their dorm rooms because it was easier to leave than throw them out. But even though my contacts were shards of glass in my eyes and I was wheezing from my cat allergy, it never occurred to me to leave that night. I wanted the whole experience. I wanted her to fall asleep on my shoulder. And she did.

How to Make an Enemy

The first time I tried to break up with someone, I planned that shit like a museum heist. I chose a bar where I didn't work but knew the bartender—Jay, my roommate, my friend, who'd serve me free drinks once the deed was done. Walking distance to my house so I wouldn't need a ride or have to wait for a cab. I picked Thursday night so she'd have to keep her shit together through work on Friday, wouldn't be able to blow up my phone or show up at my door, and she'd still have the weekend to binge. If you look at it that way, I was downright considerate. I had to be.

This was a big moment for me. I'd never ended it first. I'd been dumped. As an airman, I'd faked a deployment once, okay, maybe twice. Hid behind the base gates. Allowed nature to take its course. But I'd never looked into someone's eyes and said, "It's over."

I wasn't passive. I was fucking play dough. Survival by bending, twisting, and flattening in whatever manner was required to keep someone from getting mad. Avoid conflict by being amenable. I fell into relationships just as casually as I eventually ended them. Easier to fuck someone than deal with what happens when you say no. Easier to stay the night than try to leave. Easier to see them again when they ask.

She wasn't my first girlfriend, though it's hard to say exactly how many girlfriends I'd had. Dana doesn't quite count, nor does whomever I slept with next because, like I said, it was easier than saying no. We'll skip Michelle because, though I gladly would've dated her, married her, divorced her bitterly a few months later, Michelle wasn't interested in dating. And we'll move on to Allie, who I loved. I still do. She may have been my only intentional relationship. But she didn't want to leave South Carolina and I couldn't stay. She's happy now, in South Carolina with her wife and their kids. I still mute her on social media. Because she's happy. So I won't talk about her here other than to say I loved her.

Moving on. I met Rhonda one night at Nation. I was tripping balls on ecstasy and dancing in the heaving crowd when this woman started dancing *on* me. She had Emily Valentine hair, and her face was a blur of lights and smeared eyeliner. I liked touching her sweaty skin. I liked it when she kissed me. She tasted like the color orange. Because again, I was on ecstasy.

She said her name was Rhonda and I started singing that song. I could not have been the first. I said—and again, tripping balls—"That's not so bad. I have a friend named Whisper." She kept dancing. I was sitting on the rail at the edge of the floor. And she was writhing between my knees. I was coming down, and the thought of people with shitty names was depressing me. That she was still dancing after I'd started to come down was getting on my nerves. I wondered if she had any coke. I thought at least my mom didn't do that to us, fuck up every future introduction with a name that required its own conversation. I said, "You should get one free name change when you turn eighteen." (Maybe another when you turn twenty-five, in case you thought "Thor" would be cool.) She stopped dancing and I thought, well, that was fun making out. At least she'll go away now. She said, "I love my name." And I realized then she was completely sober.

I must've told her where I worked because she showed up at Badlands on Tuesday, grinning wide to show off her gummy, baby-toothed smile whenever I walked past her, raising her shirt to show off her abs while she danced. I made a point to never be without a tower of empty glasses to leave at the end of a bar, a mop to leave in a bathroom, or the arm of an underage kid to leave outside the door. When I was a kid, it was a broom. If you're carrying a broom, you must be on your way to sweep something. Too little had changed. She came the next night. And the next. Staying until close every time. I wondered if she had a job.

Because it was unthinkable to say, "I'm not interested," I told her I didn't get off until four a.m., an hour after the club closed. No, she couldn't wait in the club. I'd been working at the club a while. "I don't get off until four" worked so well to get rid of people, it had been a problem. So it should've been enough, I thought, to convince her I wasn't worth it. And I had to convince her, or I'd have to fuck her and then, inevitably, date her. I did not want to date her. I didn't want to date anyone. But it would have been nice if I were attracted to them while sober.

Rhonda was waiting at Soho, the shitty twenty-four-hour coffee shop where they hung shitty artwork and sold Costco pastries at a 300 percent markup. I only wanted a coffee and a ride over to Nation. It would be open until six a.m., at least. She wanted to take me home, so I got in her car. I wonder sometimes, if I've ever been kidnapped, would I have even noticed.

She played Ani DiFranco the entire way. There are two Ani songs I like, and they're not the songs anyone else likes—her tempo makes me bite my teeth. But I thought we'd all moved on from Ani by then. I'd taken a pill because I thought I was going to Nation, not home with someone who kept talking about her car and how hard it was to find that model Jetta with a black interior. She talked like she was from the prairie—lots of "anyhow" and "gal." I tried to tune her out. The streetlights were dancing. She backed into the parking spot, pulled out, tried again. Three fucking times. When we got to her bedroom, she fiddled with her computer until Sarah McLachlan came on.

If you've never tried to fuck someone while on ecstasy, it's only fun if there's chemistry or they're on ecstasy too. Otherwise it's like trying to put makeup on a cat. Everything's hilarious—your terrible technique, the ridiculous sounds, the fact the cat might kill you.

When the sun came up, I slipped out of bed and stepped outside to smoke a cigarette. Everything was too bright. Every sound sharp. A family of Koreans were loading the kids into a minivan, dressed for church. A salon-tanned woman in leggings walked by with a pure-bred beagle. A fat guy in a Colts jersey was washing his car, beer in hand. I was standing mid-row in a patch of identical town houses, behind identical cubed hedges, behind identical green mini-lawns, behind power-washed sidewalks. I was in the fucking suburbs—Virginia, if I could believe the license plates. My nerves were still bare from the ecstasy. I felt my jaw clench like my body was readying for a fight. Down the road, someone cranked up a leaf blower and I reacted like a bomb had gone off.

I leaned against the inside of the door until only my hands were shaking. I had to find something with an address, a roommate with directions to the metro, any-thing. The suburbs weren't safe. The city was safe. I might get mugged, sure. But the mugger wouldn't give a shit that I was a dyke. I had to calm down. Breathe.

I saw a bookshelf and thought, okay, I can read something. Just read something and focus on that and wait it out. Maybe make some coffee. Have a relaxing Sunday morning, in a complete stranger's house. But every goddamn book on the shelf was a manual for something—VW repair, Linux, Unix, sex, marathon training, hikers' guides. And *The Secret*.

When she dropped me off at home, I told Jay I'd fucked a Republican. All he said was, "Honey, next time, you better get the money first."

I told myself there wouldn't be a next time. She told me she'd buy me dinner. It was her birthday. She'd got-ten a hotel in the city. And I thought, well, at least in the city, I can get to the metro, easier to escape.

After dinner, we ended up at a club where someone in the bathroom offered me a bump of coke, and thinking I was among gays, I accepted. Rhonda said something about a security clearance and declined free drugs. I wasn't going to hold a security clearance against her. Then she told me I only needed drugs because my mind was weak. And asked me to score ecstasy for her friends.

Back at the hotel, she told me I wouldn't be in this mess if I didn't waste money on drugs. I'd never paid for drugs. She told me I wasn't even trying to dig out of this hole. I should go to school. I should apply for better jobs.

I stole a twenty out of her wallet once she was asleep and took a cab home. I'd like to say I needed the money, and I did. But what I needed more was to make sure she wouldn't call me again.

She called. I didn't answer the phone, so she showed up at the club. Every night. So I went to dinner again.

She kept buying dinner. Always in the suburbs, Alexandria or Tysons. She'd been stationed there in the Army and liked chain restaurants. I kept my guard up like a mob of evangelical suburbanites with pitchforks might be waiting in the bathroom. But chains serve massive portions and I'd bring leftovers home to Jay. Every goddamn time, I'd tell him, "This is the last fucking time, though. I'm serious. She went off last night about flag burning. How you should be shot."

Jay called me a communist and said, "It is weird. Like, the first time I saw her, she looked like a power lesbian. But girl, she's butcher than you are." It was true. She wanted to take me to a salon to get my hair cut. I said I cut my own. She insisted. I hated feeling like I owed her. So I said, I just go to barbers. So she came with me. And came out looking exactly like me. High fade, leave the front longer. I swore I wouldn't see her again.

I was living off three-dollar gyro platters from the shop near Badlands. The air was getting colder and I needed new shoes. The drag queen who ran the coat check found a good peacoat for me, but no one was checking shoes my size.

Rhonda bought me shoes. I didn't ask. She just showed up one day with a pair of Doc Martens that matched the pair she was now wearing and said we should go eat. She was wearing a flannel shirt with the sleeves cut off like a lesbian punch line in a sitcom. A few weeks before, she'd been wearing makeup.

In the car, Ani DiFranco again. I forgot how to breathe on the 14th Street bridge into Virginia. In daylight, the border into enemy territory seemed as forbidding as the Berlin Wall. I shut Ani off like the radio was leaking gas. The staccato guitar and screaming were making me want to stick my head out the window and hope for a truck. Rhonda turned the radio back on, said, "My car, my rules." I tried to light a cigarette, but my hand was shaking and I couldn't let her see. We'd had this fight already. Look at us. Our first couple fight. I didn't want to leave the city. She said I was being unreasonable. Just because they vote Republican doesn't mean they hate gay people, she said.

The farther we got down 95, the worse the panic got until finally, she pulled off the highway and pulled into a motherfucking Cracker Barrel. I just started laughing like it was a great joke, because it was. When I finally caught my breath, I asked her if she'd lost her fucking mind. She was working on backing into the spot and

I said, "Don't bother. I'm not eating here." Maybe I would've argued with a kidnapper after all.

She looked at me like I was the crazy one and pulled the hand brake and said they have great brunch. I looked at the crowd outside the restaurant who used the word "brunch" twice a year—Mother's Day and Easter. White-haired men in Sunday suits sitting on the rocking chairs. Little kids in patent leather shoes jumping off the patio while their parents milled around in varying pantomimes of impatience. They looked like people who drink milk with dinner.

I said, "We're in the fucking suburbs, in Virginia, and you want to walk into a fucking Cracker Barrel on a Sunday." A mom in a church dress walking past the car yanked her kid closer to her. I may have been shouting. Who knows. I felt like a guitar string wound too tight by a queer folk singer.

Rhonda stared at me like she was actually confused. And I remembered the magnets on her fridge—rainbows and "Queer as FUCK" and "Sorry I missed church. I was busy practicing witchcraft and becoming a lesbian." The shit tourists buy in a gay bookstore the first time they walk into a gay bookstore. It's only sort of funny the first time because it's so aggressively gay and you've been in the closet. I looked at her in that haircut, my haircut. The cutoff flannel shirt. The Doc Martens. She was wearing boxers nowadays instead of panties. And it finally hit me. I asked her how long she'd been out. I'm sure I worded this sympathetically, something like, "Jesus fucking Christ, did you come out yesterday? What the fuck."

I knew the answer by the time I formed the question

and I still wasn't prepared. She'd only been separated from her husband a few months. She was thirty-six, and she'd waited until she was thirty-six to come out. I said, "Do you not understand it's not safe to be here?"

She said, "That's crazy." And opened the door like we'd be getting out of the car. I held onto my door like it might open on its own.

There's safety in the closet. It's why people stay. As long as you act like them, look like them, dress like them, and live like them, husband and all, you can walk among them. They won't suspect you because to them, assuming someone is gay is rude, because to them, being gay is wrong.

I had no plans of getting out of the car. I figured, in that Cracker Barrel parking lot, I was the subject matter expert on where it was and was not safe to be gay. I thought she was an idiot to not believe me. But then, she hadn't been visibly gay long enough to know. I had to calm down and get her on my side if I had any chance of convincing her to leave. The survival strategy I'd mastered in my youth: make them like you, pity you, anything to make peace. I said, "Listen, best case, we get a few weird looks. A few people will stare, and they'll want us to see they're staring. I won't feel safe. That's the best case. It only gets worse from there."

She said, "That's crazy. No one cares."

I said, "Have you seriously not seen the looks we get? Do you understand Cracker Barrel fires gays, as a policy?" She told me I had a victim mentality. I wondered what it would take for her to even notice they hated her. But then, she thought she was one of them. Why shouldn't she? High-paying job with a government contractor, a husband to confirm she belonged. She even talked like them—the bumper sticker patriotism of post–9/11 America—and up until she decided to become me, she had looked like one of them. Ambiguous enough for corporate America to tolerate as, sure, she could be a lesbian, but she's not one of *those* gays. She's not shoving it in anyone's face. She'd lost that privilege with a haircut. She just didn't know it yet.

She said I was imagining things. She said this to me. She knew I had a car that had been torched, that I'd been kicked out of the Air Force. That I'd received death threats. For being gay. I was fucking shaking. I wanted to leave so fucking bad. I wanted her to turn the car around and take me back to the city, back to safety. I tried to keep my voice flat, but it just made me sound angrier. I said, "It gets worse. They won't serve you, they'll call you a dyke, they'll tell you you're going to hell, they'll spit on you, they'll ask you to leave, and you do have to leave. That's if you don't use a bathroom. God fucking forbid one of us has to pee. They will call the manager. They will call the cops. That's what they feel safe doing with witnesses."

A guy in a Redskins jersey approached and I tensed again. But he hit the button on his key chain and unlocked the car beside us.

She said, "You're being paranoid. This is Virginia." I shook my head. I was gearing up for a hell of a monologue. I'd start with the Air Force. Alabama. I'd tell her about the time I got jumped walking out of a gay bar in Columbia. I'd tell her about the death threats. I'd tell her about the threats Jay received. I'd tell her about Matthew Shepard. Arthur Warren. Barry Winchell.

Brandon Teena. The Backstreet Café. The Otherside
Lounge. Julianne Williams and Lollie Winans. I'd tell
her every goddamn story I'd ever heard or read. I was
going to make her understand she wasn't safe. I hated her
for feeling safe. I was going to take that from her if it was
the last fucking thing I did. But I didn't have to.

The Redskins fan got into his car next to hers, looked
at us, and hocked a fat, bloody loogie onto her window.

When I got home, I told Jay I was going to end it
before she got me killed, or got tattoos matching mine
and started using my name. So we came up with the
plan. I waited another couple weeks because, as we've
established, I'm a coward. But finally I sent her an email
and told her to meet me at Remingtons.

Remingtons was a gay country-western bar. (I know.
Blew my mind too. And yes, there's line dancing, with
an extra shimmy.) Jay'd been bartending there for a couple months. His accent alone qualified him. The bar was
a perfect choice for a breakup. Music just loud enough to
allow a little privacy and just enough customers to prevent a scene.

Rhonda was telling some story about her husband
that I'm sure would've been funny had I been there, had
I not been bothered by the idea she was still married.
Now that she was out about having been a closet case
for most of her adult life, she felt free to discuss her husband, in painfully intimate detail. I mean that I knew
that his penis curved, and in which direction. I'd have
been more irritated if I hadn't needed the excuse to end
things. And that was my plan.

I'd tell her she needed time to figure out her life. Why jump right into something serious. I needed to get my shit together. We could be friends.

She ordered another drink and Jay gave me an audible look: *Honey, just do it already.* The phone behind his bar kept ringing, making me more anxious. So I downed my Jack Daniel's and lit a cigarette and took a breath— actions I'd regret for years. Finally I said, "We do need to talk about something." But Jay said, "Hold up. Honey, it's for you." And he handed Rhonda the phone.

Turns out when your dad dies and they can't find you, they'll send state troopers to your house. The troopers won't leave until your roommate gets ahold of you. And since she wasn't answering her cell, her roommate thought to call the bar.

I may have been a coward, but I'm not a complete asshole. I couldn't break up with her that night. I couldn't break up with her before the funeral, or a week before Thanksgiving. It seemed shitty to end it right before Christmas, or during Christmas.

There's no easy way to say this: I dated her another two years. Two years that felt like getting a tattoo. Tiny needles piercing your skin while you listen to shitty music someone else chose, for two years. Not exactly painful, just profoundly irritating. And I'd be stuck having to explain it forever.

We established our roles early. She'd pay for things— my share of the rent, food, cell phone—and in turn, she could say mean things to me, fuck anyone she wanted, control me, and I'd forgive her. I could do that. She could get drunk and hit me. She could try to fuck my friends. She could tell me I shouldn't see them anymore;

they were tearing us apart. I'd agree. And I'd forgive her. I was miserable. But I thought my misery was proof I was doing something right.

I quit my job at the bar because she didn't like that it took me away from her. I applied for the jobs she thought she could get me into and took the jobs she said were beneath me—construction worker, barista, town car driver, call center tech. She said I should plan for my future, our future, and I tried not to laugh.

I wasn't imagining a future together, or alone. I couldn't imagine a future at all. Which is, I think, the very definition of depression. I know that now. I also know some part of me was planning for a future, if only in the small sense that I knew I would leave her. I just had to wait until I could pay my own rent, which was shitty but necessary. That this was, after all, what I'd been trained to do, to live off what others donated, didn't make it feel less shitty. It did make me refuse to consider how manipulative it all was.

There's something beautiful and terrifying about the human mind, that it learns what we need to survive and allows us to hide away in the recesses while it handles what it does best. In my case, I'd learned to survive by becoming what they wanted me to be, as best I could. And when I couldn't, I hid, erasing those parts of me that offended.

I wasn't always so good at survival, but I'd had something like thirteen years of training, if you go back to the beginning. And because I remember a time before, a time when I could just be me without fear, the beginning was the guy we've been calling Gabe.

Gabe was the bartender at the chain steakhouse

where my mom waited tables in Amarillo. He was cool and funny, and always made us a Cherry Coke while we waited for Mom to get off work. Plus he liked dogs. Not the worst guy for your mom to start dating. Then he became my stepdad, and as everyone knows, when the cool guy becomes "Stepdad," he turns into an asshole. It starts when your mom asks you to call him "Dad" because his own name hurts his feelings. But my dad had left, and I missed my real dad. I wanted the new dad to like me because I was a fucking seven-year-old who missed her dad. He didn't like me.

He didn't like that I wore trucker hats my grandma gave me. He didn't like that I wore the same pair of shorts all summer. Listen, they had a cool clip where I could attach things like keys I found, or a knife—before he took that away too. He didn't like the Ramona books I read about a girl whose dad didn't leave. He didn't like the scabs on my knees, my gnawed fingernails, my unbrushed hair, my loud laugh, or the way I chewed, walked, and most of all talked.

He wanted a little princess to slavishly worship him. And when he didn't get what he wanted, he did what that kind of asshole does—humiliated or hit me. Sometimes both, but he liked to mix it up. But I learned, slowly, for the most part. It's not easy changing your entire personality. It's sort of ingrained. You end up always scrambling, always worried about what you forgot.

I went from a reasonably happy kid to an anxious, angry, twitchy little bastard, never sure about what would set Gabe off. The thing that was funny yesterday, the burp, the fart joke—if you've never met a kid, they generally adhere to the repeat-until-it's-funny-again school of comedy—any joke was as likely to get a laugh or a "stop beating a dead horse" or a slap in the face. (For the record, and this is coming from someone familiar with a variety of belts and paddles, makeshift or otherwise, slapping is worse. A slap's a surprise even when you see it coming. But more than that, it's humiliating.)

I'd rush in when he was yelling at my mom, armed with a Nerf bat, and tell him to leave her alone. He'd slap me, and I'd wish he would've punched me. One minute I'd be enjoying the weird sound mac and cheese makes in your mouth, because I was seven; the next, I'd get rapped on the head with his marble knuckles. Makes your eyes water. Makes you taste pennies. I'd jump off the top bunk, wearing a towel for a cape, like I always had, and end up bent over his waterbed for swats. Staying out of trouble was like trying to win at fucking Calvinball. New rules were enforced before they were even introduced.

In fairness, Gabe was twenty-three when he met and married my mom. Suddenly he had two kids and had to give up things like dirt bikes and coke. But he didn't have to be an asshole about it.

I was a nervous wreck long before we rejoined the Family. The Family meant another list of ever-changing rules I had to keep track of or suffer the consequences. The Family meant it was even more important my stepdad cared what happened to me. And I still wanted him to like me.

Gabe was as charming and funny as any successful asshole, and he loved an audience. I used to watch the way he'd hold the attention of a room. Everyone laughing tears listening to one of his stories. But his stories required an idiot. Someone who never looked where they were going. Someone to trip. Someone to fall into the sewer. You didn't want a starring role in one of Gabe's stories.

He dangled love and affection like a prize to be won. Worked great for him because the onus was always on us. When a record-breaking day selling Family music tapes door-to-door turned to shit because I left his boom box on the train, I knew it was my fault that he changed the plan from celebratory ramen to watching him eat McDonald's. When a fun day selling posters at a Japanese castle ended with his slapping me around in a parking garage, I had it coming. I'd tried to sell a poster to a cop. Granted the cop was dressed like everyone else, but the Family'd handed Gabe a new reason for my fuckups: I wasn't listening to the Spirit, who's supposed to tell you when you ask if that guy's a cop. (It doesn't work. I tried.)

But if I was good, if I was perfect, Gabe could be so damn cool. Running into our Osaka apartment one time and rescuing me from a prayer meeting because he'd met an Akita in the park he wanted to show me, hiking mountains with us in Switzerland and buying us hot chocolate at the top. Sometimes on our Sundays off, if we made enough money selling the posters he'd steal from the home stash, we'd go to a swimming pool or sledding up in the mountains. Unless he critiqued the way I rode a sled, and I rolled my eyes. Then the asshole would drive us back early. And we all knew whose fault it was.

Back at the home, the commune, whichever home that was at the time, I'd have to worry about following their rules, which weren't all that different from Gabe's, and earning God's love, which was just as erratic. Yeah, I know the verse, "God is love," but he feeds children to bears for mocking bald men, drowns people and animals, and turns women to salt for missing home. At least around Gabe, you could usually laugh at something funny, but the Family called it foolishness, so I learned not to laugh. Except then Gabe thought I was being rebellious if I didn't laugh at his jokes. The Family didn't allow unclean meats, but Gabe thought turning down pork was my being ungrateful. They all agreed I wasn't feminine enough, but Gabe thought I should help the boys masturbate . . . Actually they agreed on that. But I did what I needed to do because I'd learned not to make an enemy. Sometimes that meant not showering. Sometimes it meant befriending the boys the way you're supposed to talk to a potential murderer, make them see you as human.

I learned to watch adults for any hint of a mood change. I learned to keep stray words away from their hot plate tempers. I learned to anticipate their whims. I learned not to cry because crying was manipulation, crying was the demon defending itself, and demons only respond to violence. I learned to befriend those who despised me because you can't afford to have nemeses. Most of all, because I couldn't change who I was, I learned to subdue myself, to shut off, to hide somewhere in the dark of my mind so I didn't anger the people who could hurt me, so it didn't hurt so much when they did.

I didn't accept abuse. I expected it, welcomed it. It's the lesson not only of asshole stepdads or cults, but of evangelical Christianity. You're nothing without "a relationship with Jesus." You'll take anything, from a healed flu virus to a pretty flower, as evidence your love is reciprocated. Shit luck is the devil testing you, or punishment for sin, because a loving God hits you sometimes. He hurts you because he loves you, to teach you, to make you better. (Or he had a bet with the devil. See: the entire book of Job.) You reject doubt the same way you reject your friends telling you your girlfriend's a fucking asshole. When she tells you your friends are jealous of your relationship, it rings true, because you were taught doubts are evidence the devil is fighting for your soul. When your stepdad tells you that he only hits you because he loves you and wants you to be better, well, that tracks. (See: the entire Bible.) The pain you suffer is accepted as proof of your faith, your love. You're supposed to welcome it.

I grew into a person you see as empathetic. But it's not empathy. It's survival. That watchfulness can be pretty damn useful in dating, though. I don't just memorize how to make your coffee. I memorize everything. I know how you like to be woken up in the morning. I know you're having a bad day before you do, and I've got a list of ways to fix it. I'll burn you a CD of your favorite songs and songs you'll like, and it won't occur to you I'd rather listen to anything else. I'll make sure we have tickets for the concert. We'll listen to your music on the road trip. I know mine drives you crazy.

After Rhonda, I dated Autumn, the Korn fan. Try putting that mixtape together. I fell for her because she had kind eyes and she liked to steal. I mean that she was fun. Where I couldn't drive to CVS without fighting with Rhonda, Autumn and I never fought, not in the beginning or even the middle. Road trips were the sort of adventure you imagine before you've had to drive twenty-two hours in aggressive silence back from New Orleans because she wanted to do a threesome and you accidentally enjoyed it. Autumn and I went to Provincetown once, midwinter because that was our budget. And we got thrown out of the one open head shop because she didn't know you're not allowed to say "bong" in a head shop. (This was in the beforetimes, for you assholes who live in legal states.) Anyway, the whole way out of the store, Autumn was knocking shit off the shelves, throwing handfuls of hemp bracelets and puka-shell necklaces into the air, just fucking making it rain with those tourist-stop gay postcards. It was sexy as hell. I mean that we actually liked hanging out together.

I remember my brother came to visit once, on his way up to New England after college, and I was so proud for him to meet her. *This is my girlfriend. Isn't she fucking cool? Dude. This extremely cool person loves me.* I mean, goddamn, she was cool. And really fucking good at shoplifting, which she did constantly, and not because she couldn't buy something. She just refused to believe a razor blade was worth five dollars or that a restaurant would miss their ramekins.

But in no time, I slipped away again. A dish in the sink could send her into an anxiety tantrum, and then came the list of all the messes I'd made. I kept lists too. Of things to clean before she got home from work—coffee

table, bathroom, bedroom. Of the morning routine—
make bed, fan off, curtains open, sink dry. Of foods she
didn't eat—tomatoes, onions, mushrooms, celery, water
chestnuts, apples, cucumbers, any vegetable that hadn't
been canned, whole wheat bread, any dressing but bleu
cheese, any booze that wasn't Smirnoff Ice. Any variation
could send her into a panic attack that felt like rage. But
always, I'd forgive her. Because I understood.

I became the person she needed. I could love her
enough for both of us, until someday, she could love me.

I made her lunch and drove her to work at four a.m.
on my days off so she wouldn't have to park. And slept on
the couch those same days because I breathed too loud.
I don't like horror movies, but I've seen every *Saw* and
Hostel in the theater, more than once. I don't like roller
coasters because I can get just as sick on a hammock and
throw up in private, but I've ridden every coaster within
a hundred miles of D.C. And if you asked her, she'd
tell you I loved that shit. Because I made her believe it.
Because I loved her. And I wanted her to love me.

When it was over, I can't say there was much left of
me to love. I became the person who answered the phone
when she needed me. I didn't matter. I needed nothing. I
could take a pill or drink enough that nothing mattered.
I could fuck her when she was lonely. I could hold my
dog when I was alone.

I wasn't done seeking love. I thought if I could find
that, have that one answer—*This is who I love, and this is
who loves me*—if that were no longer a question, I could
deal with the rest. I wouldn't mind so much the mess I'd
made of my life. I wouldn't mind knowing it was too late

to change it. And I believed by then that it was too late. So I fucked anyone who needed to feel something.

I was working as a cable tech at the time. I used to tease the guys who claimed they'd fucked customers, though I knew it happened on occasion. Then one day it was me, though I'd never tell the other guys.

One of those apartments for the newly divorced or extremely busy, already furnished, four plates, four bowls, four glasses. Coffee maker. The moving boxes stacked against the wall. She'd been workshopping innuendo about laying cable. She gave up and asked if I'd ever fucked some lonely housewife. I was waiting for the cable box to load, staring at the lights on the front of the box. I said I hadn't.

She asked, "Lack of opportunity or lack of interest?"

I couldn't figure out if she was hitting on me or teasing me. Not something you want to misjudge and have to wait around in awkward silence while a cable box decides if it'll work. I shrugged and turned around. She took off her jacket, and I saw the gun under her arm. She said, "FBI," then added, "really."

I said, "In this neighborhood, most people will believe you the first time." Then she took the harness off.

I'd watched *Silence of the Lambs* too many times to even think of turning her down. I was lucky our cable boxes were being upgraded and I could excuse a missed hour with, "I had to try three of those fucking things. Sorry. Yeah. There's just no phone signal in Falls Church."

There may have been a couple housewives after that. But mostly it was women I met at bars or met on the Internet. I stayed when they wanted and left when they wanted. I listened to their breakup stories and bad-marriage stories and childhood traumas. I could be the person who did that for others.

I used to think I'd somehow escaped a sex cult without sexual hang-ups. I didn't have an education, or a healthy mind, or healthy relationships. But I could have sex with women, and even when it wasn't great, it was still usually fun. I thought it helped that I'm gay and didn't have to sleep with men. I told myself I had no fear of women. But then, I never did say no. Still, my paying attention to every breath made me really fucking good in bed, whatever that means to you. You want to go slow and eventually, carefully, try oral, I can do that. It's my favorite thing. You want someone to make you come with a strap-on, want to call it my cock, I'm all about it. And you'll believe it. You want to be held down and choked, fisted, spanked, called names, I can do that too. Love it. You want to wear a dick to the club, I'll suck it on the way home, then fuck you over the couch when we get there. You'll think it was my idea. It's that thing you call empathy. Maybe it is. Sometimes it's enough just to make you feel. Sometimes, I'm still surprised by someone, and the sex is amazing, if only the sex. I still want more.

I dated a woman because she was sad and followed me home. I thought I could make one of us happy. But making her happy required I fill the role of a mother who enjoyed watching someone play video games after I'd cooked dinner. I dated a woman who said I was brilliant—she just couldn't introduce me to her friends because I was blue-collar, just a cable guy.

People describe falling in love as meeting someone who they feel like they've known all their lives. Someone who understands them immediately. To me, that seems more like a nightmare than a fantasy. I always thought love meant the process of discovery, the work to understand someone. I want to know what it feels like when someone tries to figure me out, and keeps trying. I want someone to ask the questions and listen to the answers. I want to be studied the way I study others and learned the way I learn them.

The closest I found was someone who played the perfect role, nearly. When she didn't know the answer, she filled in the blank with an errant assumption, what she wanted me to be. She shared every interest of mine. Music. Movies. Books. Dolly Parton. Dogs. Cooking. Red Bull in the light blue can. American Spirits in the yellow box. Those little Nutella snacks with the dipping sticks. You'd think I'd have noticed she was playing my game—how to survive a world that cannot love you. In the end, she couldn't keep up the act. But neither could I.

The funniest thing, to me, or maybe it's sad—fine line, really—is that a lot of my story doesn't even require much work. But no one, not one person in the history of my dating life, has ever googled it. The big story I don't always want to explain, a whole lot of it's on the Internet, websites, books, documentaries. No one has ever bothered to look it up.

Maybe if they knew the story they could forgive me

too. Maybe then I wouldn't be invisible. But then, all those times, trying to be enough for someone to love, I'd forgotten something I'd already learned.

We'd broken up once before, Rhonda and me. I don't remember who broke up with whom that time. She was fucking someone else, but I couldn't tell you if that started before or after. I'd been living with her in a basement apartment in Logan Circle. But if we weren't together, I had to find a new place to live. I spent a lot of nights on the upstairs neighbors' couch. They'd smoke me up and tell me to leave her. And finally I did.

I was back where I began in D.C., looking at shared town houses where I couldn't afford to rent a closet, much less a room. So when she wanted to get back together . . . I thought it was a good thing that I knew how to forgive. And by "forgive," I mean shove all that shit, my hurt and anger, down, way down, and pretend everything was fine.

Forgiveness is, after all, the ultimate virtue; the only other option is becoming one of *those* people. You know the type. The bitter, angry, crazy shell of a human played by Kathy Bates on a quest for an Oscar.

Whether someone forgave or is still angry is the question we ask before we allow them empathy. We shame those who don't forgive and treat their instincts of distrust, anger, and hurt as something shameful. Maybe it comes from Christianity. Never mind that Jesus is shit at forgiving. I mean, yeah, he died for our sins. But he passive-aggressively reminds you of them and punishes you anytime you disagree. Forgiveness is a sign of good moral character, maturity, good health and fortune, white teeth and a clear complexion. All this can be yours for the small price of existential pain. The person who forgives takes the higher ground; they're the bigger person. And goddamn, if I didn't want to be the bigger person. But what if I didn't? What if forgiveness was a trick I played on myself so that I wouldn't have an enemy or wouldn't be alone?

It took a few tries with Rhonda. But when I did finally leave, when I stopped letting her hurt me and stopped calling it forgiveness, when I accepted she was an asshole who'd never not be an asshole, that's when I was safe. I was safe because I recognized she was my enemy. It helped that she sent me a bill.

I was sitting there in the living room with my new roommate, Nathan, and a friend of mine we'll call Brian. Brian had been a sex worker. What else are you going to do when your parents throw you out at sixteen. I remember they were watching *Veronica Mars*, and I borrowed Nathan's computer to check my email. I opened an email from Rhonda to find a fucking itemized bill for every meal, every coffee, every vacation, and every gift she'd ever bought me. I jumped back from the computer like it'd slapped me. When the guys asked what was wrong, all I could do was point at the screen.

Nathan didn't waste any time. He nudged me out of the way, opened a spreadsheet, and asked Brian, "Hey, how much is oral anyway?"

"Giving or receiving?"

"Both. Lauren, what else was there? What did you two do?"

And so we sent her another bill in return, for every sex

act I'd ever performed. Turned out she owed me. Never heard from her again.

Fact is, there are more than two doors, forgiveness or Kathy Bates. The third door is, you don't have to forgive at all. You can just go right on living your life with one less asshole to deal with.

The last time I talked to Gabe was right after my mom left him. She called me from her new apartment. She'd been complaining of the quiet, the shock of living alone for the first time, and I'd sent her a CD player and a bunch of CDs I burned off Napster—Neil Young and Emmylou Harris and Townes Van Zandt and Bruce— the essentials. She was calling to thank me. She said she was sitting out on her porch with a glass of wine, listening to Emmylou. And it was just "so wonderful, Lauren. Gabe never liked Emmylou. Never. I should've known then."

I told her I'd never dated anyone who liked Emmylou either. She said we should make a pact to never make that mistake again. (I broke it immediately. But in fairness, I was twenty-one, still in the Air Force, hadn't even met Rhonda yet, let alone the rest.) I said, "Well, he never liked me much either."

I heard her muffled sob while she tried to find words. Eventually, she said, "I hope you forgive me someday." I told her I already had. I told her it wasn't her fault. She was like me, or I was like her. We learned how to survive. She said, "I was so lonely. And now I have Emmylou."

There's a difference there too, between loneliness and

solitude. One wretched. One peaceful. Solitude's easier
to get to when you don't have to listen to some asshole's
shitty music. I wrote Gabe a letter that night. Only
needed three sentences. "I'm glad my mother's free of
you. I'm a lesbian. Go fuck yourself."

Cell Block

On the third day, the woman in the next cell stopped screaming. On the third day I punched the wall. Maybe it was the second day. Hard to tell. We liken things to a cell, to jail, to prison. But there's no metaphor for actually being locked in a cell. You just are. The door doesn't open and the air doesn't change. There's no day and no night, no sunrise or sunset. In a cell it's always bright light and piss yellow, hard edges and corners and walls, steel and concrete, concrete and steel. Nothing gives. Nothing bends. Nothing breaks. But something has to break. It's the purpose of the cell.

So I hit the wall that won't break. The first hit is weak. Some part of my mind, the part that keeps you from sticking your hand in a fire or hitting walls, slows my arm. I mime the action a few times. Manual override. And I hit the wall again. I taste copper. The pain like that first hit of weed that clouds your head and wraps the panic in cotton. I hit it again and felt my skin burst. Again and a warm trickle of blood. Again. More skin. The next hit leaves an imprint of blood on the wall. The next smears the bloody imprint on the yellow cinder block. Again. And for the first time in three days, I can breathe. Maybe it was just two days.

I shouldn't have been in that cell. That's what everyone in a cell says. The screaming woman in the next cell says she isn't supposed to be in a cell. She's supposed to be at work. She'd felt a pain in her back, couldn't take off work. No one in jail has a job that hands out sick days. *Had* a job. No one in jail has a job anymore.

A friend gave her a few Percocets. One Percocet's a felony, felony possession of narcotics. A cop pulled her over for swerving when the pain pierced through. She was a good driver. Not even a traffic ticket. Now she's locked in the cell next to mine. Now she's passing a kidney stone. That pain in her back.

This isn't gen pop. This is the SHU. They don't hand out aspirin in the SHU. A magistrate set her bail at a thousand dollars—a hundred to a bondsman. Her husband didn't have a hundred dollars. The maid service where she worked, used to work, wouldn't hand her paycheck to her husband. Her husband is a tile setter. He'd scraped enough together for rent. Maybe next month, he can pick up some side work.

She's not supposed to be in a cell. When she isn't screaming, I hear another woman, farther down the block, the woman groaning or vomiting or dry-heaving into the stainless steel seatless toilet.

"What did you do?" I asked her when she wasn't screaming.

It's better when we talk. I thought so then. Then I wasn't sure anymore. They don't let us talk much anyway. We can't talk if deputies are in the hall. We don't talk at night, mostly. But after the third meal, we talk. I thought that this is what people talk about in jail.

The groaning woman said that's not how to ask. Then, to no one, to everyone, "White lady over here asking what I did. Shit."

Another voice, a helpful voice, says to ask what someone's in for, not what they did. Even if the deputies don't hear, snitches are everywhere. Maybe I'm the snitch. I'm not the snitch. That's what a snitch would say. I say if you ask a snitch if they're a snitch, they have to tell you if they're a snitch. It's the law. The voices laugh. I kill in this club.

I ask right the next time, "What are you in for?" I add, "Sorry, I'm new at this." First thing I learned. Acknowledge you don't know shit. This is easy. I'm good at jail.

The voice gave the police a blow job. He arrested her anyway. Police are liars. Everyone knows that. Even I know that. Another voice says police always do that shit. Except sometimes they let you go. The voices agree. The police are not to be trusted with bargains.

"Jesus. That's rape," I say.

"I'll be sure to pass that information to my attorney," says the voice in mock white lady. The inmates laugh. I laugh. I'm an inmate. The voice says she's a prostitute. She prefers call girl. No one cares. She's an alcoholic. No one cares. Withdrawals can kill you. No one cares.

The voice with the kidney stone asks for a song. The voice who sings sings Aaliyah. She sounds better than anyone on the radio. I like it when she sings. I can close my eyes. Her voice feels like a warm hand on my chest.

"Shut the fuck up." Man's voice. Deputy Day-Day is what everyone calls him. If you're naming sheriff's deputies after *Friday* characters, he's more of a Deebo. But he'd probably like being named after a bully, so we don't call him that. The other voices hate him. The inmates hate him. I'm an inmate. I hate him.

A voice asks, "What you gonna do, Day-Day?" Then, "You go on. He's just mad no one sucked his dick."

The voices agree he can't find his own dick. The song changes. Something mournful. I don't know this one. I don't care. I hope the voice never stops singing.

The voice who sings Aaliyah is the only other inmate I've seen. That was the first day. I was being led from the nurse's office, the skin on my forearm freshly lumped with a TB test. Me, still thinking the worst humiliation was a squat and cough when they took my clothes. When they handed me these green coveralls that smelled like ammonia. The woman who would sing Aaliyah stood in the hallway between two deputies. Her arms and face and legs more scabs than skin. Her hair wild and greasy and flecked with dust. Her eyes swollen. I nodded. She looked at nothing in front of her with nothing eyes that see nothing. She wore a blanket like the inmates sleep under, like the kind they hang in an elevator when someone's moving. But hers is sewn into a tunic that closes with Velcro. She tried to kill herself. She failed.

I remember the tunic, and I wipe my blood off the wall

with a wad of toilet paper and flush the wad. I look at my hand, at my mincemeat knuckles, and I'm afraid. The worst thing I can think of, a loss of freedom worse than this—no way to take my own life. I can't let them see I'm losing my mind. Or I've lost it. I can't tell anymore. They closed the asylums, too inhumane. Now they just watch and wait for the lunatics to commit a crime. This country's a hell of a place to lose your mind.

There's no moment when you know you've lost your mind. That's the upside. You slide into madness and the madness tells you you're fine. The madness tells you to hit the wall. Pick a hole in your arm. Nothing better to do. The voices ask if you're okay and you know you screamed, but you didn't hear your own voice. The voices ask you to sing the "Angel" song again. The voices are getting on your goddamn nerves. But you sing the "Angel" song that John Prine wrote that Bonnie sang. The voices like the song. You understand the voices are trying to help. They feel bad for telling you to hit the wall. They feel bad for telling you to try again with your head. You sing the song about the angel from Montgomery to keep the voices happy.

The voices have no faces. That's the goddamn problem. On the outside, you hear a voice and it's attached to person with a face. Maybe it comes from a radio or a phone, or the neighbors in the toxic relationship. But the voices are attached to a face or a speaker, something made of carbon. In this cell, every voice comes from everywhere and nowhere. Some are farther away. They bounce around the walls and concrete with nothing to slow their journey. The voices closer in are still warm when they arrive. Those voices that travel with accents and stories and questions—they're real. I know that. The voices who want me to do things, it's getting harder to tell. I know they're angry. I know they hate me. So I know they're me. Most of the time.

Day 3, maybe 4. I've been waiting for hours for the nice deputy. The deputy who, when I asked for tampons and she brought me pads and I said I wear boxers, fuck am I supposed to do with these, looked sad. I sat there all day on bloody pads, holding the pad in place when I paced my cell. The nice deputy, whose face is tired and chapped but kind. The nice deputy came back the next night with a pack of granny panties from Walmart and dropped them through the feed slot in my door. She's all right. She'll tell you what time it is when you ask.

I'm obsessed with knowing the time. No windows. No sun. No moon. The lights never go out. I can't sleep. I can handle the noise. Mostly. Baby screams are the only screams you don't get used to. Mostly. No babies here. Mostly. Where I used to get locked in rooms, I'd hear the babies cry. Soundtrack of a sex-cult commune. I thought that was the worst thing. They used to lock me in rooms. To read and pray and think about my sins and write about what I'd learned. I'd hold on as long as I could. Then I'd break. I think now, I was dumb as shit. All I had to do was cry and tell them I was sorry. They'd let me out. I was proud of holding out. Stupid. But I had things to read there. There's nothing here to read. Nothing to write with and nothing to write on. Those rooms, there was a light switch on the wall. But here the light above my mattress, above the cinder block bed, shines in my face.

I know it's still night because they've set two meals in my feed slot since the hard-boiled egg for breakfast. A deputy comes through. Keys jingle. Everyone in power has keys. Everyone in power knows the time. I ask the time. Like I do every time. And this time, like last time, I'm ignored.

Time is what they're taking from us. We're doing time, but most of the inmates haven't been convicted of a crime. And when we're free, it's the time we've lost. Time at work and time at home. The time passes, and someone loses a job, and someone loses a home, and someone's kid has a birthday, takes a first step. Time we have to make up, but it's gone. My brother gets married and I'll miss it because I've lost time at work.

It's Deputy Day-Day. He shouldn't be here if it's night. Maybe I counted wrong. Maybe it's morning. He's talking to the voice three cells down. Tells her to get up. He has to read her charges. She was in gen pop, but she kept food under her mattress. Thirty days, even if she makes bail. She has thirty more days. Her bail's two grand. No one has two hundred for the bondsman. The voice who hid food got a fifty-dollar ticket for turning right on red that she couldn't afford to pay. They suspended her license, but she still had to get to work. So she drove. Suspended license. She doesn't belong in a cell. She's been here three months.

I try to see out the slit in my door. I can't see the deputy.

"Deputy!" It's the voice with the kidney stone.

"Why the fuck are you screaming at me?"

"I need a nurse."

"Take that shit off your light." A rustle. I'd tried that too, covering the light.

"I need a nurse."

"The nurse doesn't work weekends. You know that." It's the weekend. I know that now. Then, "Stop your fucking screaming or I'll put you on loaf."

Keys jingle.

"Deputy." This is me.

"What." A challenge, not a question.

"She's passing a kidney stone. She needs to be in the hospital."

"Mind your fucking business." There's a smear of dried brown mucus on the glass. I don't get too close.

"You know you can get sued," I say. The voices are right about me. I'm this fucking white.

"I said mind your business. She's been screaming since she got here."

"And that proves what exactly? I need to speak to your supervisor." I'm on the phone with the billing department. There's a discrepancy. But I'll speak to the right person and the discrepancy will be fixed with an apology for the inconvenience.

"You want the loaf too?" I can smell his coffee through my slot. He sees me look. I'm not looking at his coffee. I'm trying to see the time on his wristwatch. I came in wearing contacts. I came in with a wristwatch, but they took the watch and left me with my contact lenses. I peeled them off my eyeballs the second day. Nowhere to store them. No saline. They've hardened into crinkled glass. I play a game with the lens chips sometimes. Flick one at the other across the concrete floor. I didn't say it was a fun game. For years after, I won't wear contacts. You never know.

Everything's a blur without my glasses. Including the face of his watch.

"You want me to put in an order for you? Soy, right? No sugar?" Day-Day laughs.

"What time is it?" I ask.

He's already walking away. "You got an appointment or something?" He says this over his shoulder and laughs at his joke. I wonder how to start a prison riot. I wonder how to make a shiv, but I think you need a toothbrush. His keys jangle down the hall.

The voice with the kidney stone says, "Thanks for trying. He's a cunt." (I'm paraphrasing. I'm not bilingual, but I get the gist.)

"What's 'loaf'?"

"Punishment food. Like one of those energy bars you people eat. 'Cept made of shit and mashed cardboard."

I don't want the loaf. I don't even like energy bars.

I hope the nice deputy's working tonight. I try to punch the wall again. But I pull the punch before impact. My hand knows the pain now. I'm a coward.

When I was a kid, Grandma got us a few free lessons at a dojo. The karate instructor broke a cinder block to show us what karate could do for us. I think now the cinder block in the dojo was fake. No part of these cells is destructible, nothing but the contents. The toilet and sink are formed of a single hunk of gray steel. You could flush your entire mattress down the toilet. Nothing clogs. The water rushes like it's propelled from a jet engine. I've been flushing my used pads.

I finger the thin plastic on my oatmeal cream cookie. We get one with our cheese sandwich at lunch. The plastic bread somehow both stale and damp. Like they spread the slices on a counter to harden a few days before spritzing them with dishwater. I want to taste the cookie. Just an edge. Something different. The cellophane wrapper means the cookie won't taste like jail. I wonder how long I have, once I pull the wrapper open, before the cookie absorbs the smell of this place where the air and the food and the water all taste the same, like the inside of a dumpster outside a hospital where you stand to smoke.

I've never eaten one of these little oatmeal cream pies. My mom put carrot sticks in our lunch boxes, not Twinkies, not Ho Hos. Oatmeal cookies on occasion, dotted with raisins or carob. Try trading anything with raisins for a Zebra Cake. I've never tasted anything by Hostess. But I'm scared to even pierce the wrapper for one sniff of something different, scared the damage will decrease the value. The cookie's worth something in here. The cookie's worth a magazine.

The voice who hid food has magazines. One cookie for one magazine. I have two cookies now. But I need the nice deputy. The nice deputy will make the trade. The voices warned me not to trust anyone else. I wonder if I can trust the voices.

The voice who's a call girl asks if the other voice is gonna pass that thing. There's no answer.

Another voice says, "She prob'ly dead." We laugh. Everyone's funny here.

Keys in the hallway. "I hear another fucking word out this block, you're all going on loaf." No one laughs.

It's time for a bath. You watch movies or TV shows

about jail and you'll get some funny ideas. You'll think there'll be things like showers, pillows, an hour in a yard, a TV to fight over, books, pens, paper, photographs to stick on walls, cigarettes, toothbrushes, toothpaste, soap. I have none of these things. I have two socks. I use one for a washcloth. Press the button for water. Soak the dirty sock in the cold metal sink. Wash. Soak again. Wash. Wring. Sop up the water. Wring. I hang the sock on the side of the sink to dry. I use my other dirty sock as something like a toothbrush. Stretch the ankle over my index finger. Wash my teeth. Rinse the sock. I feel no cleaner. I can still smell the acidic, vaguely animal scent under my arms. There's a smell in these halls, in my cell, the smell of caged humans, the smell of fear. Of madness. I'm glad I have my socks.

The voice with the kidney stone's crying now. She's alive. *"Ah, dios mío."* Over and over again. She doesn't belong in a cell.

My first day, after my first night in intake, I spoke to a guy with an expensive haircut and Ralph Lauren frames. He asked what the Wellbutrin and Prozac were for, the meds I listed on the form. He said he was a counselor. I said I was a veteran. I said I have PTSD. He asked me if I was suicidal—trick question no matter who asks. I said no. He said, "You look tired." I said, "Yeah, I can't sleep here." I wonder later if I'd told him I grew up in a cult, if I told him they used to lock me in rooms, if that would've changed anything.

That's when I was still in the fishbowl holding cell where you sit before you're processed. They process humans here. In the fishbowl, everyone does the same thing when the door shuts behind them.

They look around. They don't know if the movies are real, if they'll have to fight. They see the phone on the wall, and someone who's been there longer says to use your inmate number off your intake sheet. You can't call long distance. You can't call a number you don't know. The inmates tell you, for future reference, to always write a number on your arm before you go out. The new inmates make a phone call; then they cry. Every time. Someone tells them it's okay. Every time. For me, the someone who told me how to make a call was a college student, in for a gram of weed. She said, "It'll be okay. It's not as bad as you think." I faced the wall to cry.

The shrink said, "Well, let's put you somewhere you can get some rest."

I was grateful. That's still funny to me. I didn't know that somewhere was the SHU, the punishment cells. When I tell the other inmates how I ended up in the SHU, they laugh. It is pretty funny. I asked for this.

"Honey, you think you're Paris Hilton," a voice says. She says I'm white but not rich. Paris Hilton is rich. Paris Hilton got released early because jail is ugly and we don't like the rich to suffer. The voice says white will keep me from getting pulled over. She says I'm in the system now. I'm just too dumb to know it. Like a baby. The voices laugh. She's killing in this club.

I'm still convinced I've been wronged. I'm not supposed to be here. She accepts this as part of life. I'm a tourist and she's the local giving me directions. She asks what I'm in for. I've already told the story. But this is what people talk about in jail.

I say assault. I add misdemeanor because I think it matters.

She asks if I fought back. She means against a boyfriend or husband. It's a fair question. Women go to jail because of men. Deputy Day-Day comes through and tells us anyone who talks gets the loaf. Story time will wait. We're not going anywhere.

Day 4 or maybe it's 5. The voice who sings Aaliyah doesn't sing anymore. I think the voice is mad at me. The other voices say she's dead. I say she got released. She told me so. She got released and she moved somewhere warm with no walls. The voices tell me to sing a Family song. The one from Psalm 121. Then the voices tell me to shut the fuck up. The voices say if I bite my wrist I can go to a warm place where there are no walls. I tell the voices to shut up. I know they're not real, not all of them. They can't be real. I've heard some of them before. The voices come, but you read to make them quiet. I don't have anything to read. I quote the verses I know. I quote the poems. This is what I know them for. I tell myself the story of the March girls in Concord. But the voices won't quiet. They're older now too.

I cover my head with the blanket and the deputy says show your face. Don't cover your face again, inmate. My name isn't inmate. I tell him my name is Merry. I tell him I'm sorry for talking back so much. I'm praying about it.

A new voice sings and the voices are quiet. The new voice has a deeper voice than the old voice who left. The new voice sings Nina Simone. She sings Billie Holiday. I close my eyes and I'm driving across a desert with the sun in my eyes and the radio blaring and the sand in the wind stings my skin. I'm listening to my iPod.

The new voice brought a bag into a diner for her boyfriend. He said it was safer that way, if she did it for him. She'll be here a while. The new voice says she didn't know what was in the bag. She's not lying exactly. Schrödinger's heroin. Doesn't matter anyway. She didn't have a choice and the voices agree. The voices know about those sorts of choices. The voices understand. You do what your man says.

The voices try to talk to Aaliyah. They don't know if she's still here. She doesn't answer. I say she's gone. She's lost in her mind. Or released. Or dead. The voices say to shut the fuck up.

I wonder how long I have before I pick the first hole in my skin. I look at my mangled hand. I'm already gone.

The voice asks what I'm in for. I was telling a story. I say misdemeanor assault again. The voice only says "Oh." I think she's mad at me now. I don't like it when the voices are mad at me. She says, "Who did you piss off?" The voices discuss. It's a fair question. She's not mad at me. But I am.

Day-Day isn't around, so I tell the story to the voices and hope they understand.

I loved her. Autumn. We were living together, a little town house in Maryland. It was one of those relationships you think are perfect because you don't fight on road trips, or when assembling Ikea furniture. I had a

dog and she had a cat. I painted the walls. We talked
about weddings and children, but neither of us made the
kind of money for all that.

Then, two years in, Autumn texted me and said it was
over. She said she loved me but she wasn't *in love* with
me. She said the problem was I was sad all the time. It
was depressing just being around me anymore. I should
move out and we should date and she'd try to fall in love
with me again. I agreed because I loved her.

I found a room to rent in Virginia, closer to work.
Where I'd been living in Maryland, I had an hour commute each night, which, while standard by D.C. suburbs, was fucking draining. Sitting in a work van in
traffic that never moved. She called when she needed
me. I'd sit in traffic, then make dinner, and she'd let me
stay the night after we fucked. We'd drive down to Kings
Dominion and ride the roller coasters and I'd finger her
in the bathrooms. She'd call and I'd meet her at the security desk of the National Archives, where she worked,
and we'd fuck in the stacks. I pretended I was fine with
it. I pretended I was happy.

I'd been patching myself together so long, hiding
behind whichever version of me I thought would be
least upsetting to everyone else. Meanwhile, the damage
I was ignoring was just festering. That's how life is in
the margins. You can't afford new brakes, so you'll need
new rotors. You can't afford a root canal, so they have
to pull the tooth. You don't have the time, resources, or
money to even begin to diagnose your mind, much less
treat it, so you turn up the radio so you don't hear the
sound of what's breaking. I had kept my anger tucked
away. I liked my anger. I thought it kept me safe.

I went to the VA and told them I was depressed. They gave me meds. Lots of them. They'd assign me someone to talk to as soon as possible. The waiting list was down to three months. I was getting better. I wasn't sad. I was fucking vibrating. I never slept anymore. Who needs to sleep when you're fucking alive. I spent my nights on the Internet.

That's how I saw a picture of them together—Autumn and, let's call her "Karen," because she was one. Some picture on MySpace. Someone new on someone's top eight. Some feed. Here's a funny thing: my ex before had cheated on me with Karen. Small world really.

I had met Karen when I was a bartender. She was camped at my bar one night with her entourage, down-ing kamikaze shots and whooping. One would leave, come back, report on some situation that grew more hilarious each time; they'd laugh and order another shot. I asked what was so funny.

Karen's volunteer spokesperson said, "You know Twofer?" I did not. Karen, exasperated with her spokes-person, said, "Heather. Two for the price of one, get it?" Listen. I didn't like Heather either. Heather was a bouncer who'd called in sick that night. Heather was why I was washing my own glasses—my barback was covering her shift. Whenever Heather did show up, she was rude and never picked up glasses. But Karen and her entourage didn't work at the bar, and I didn't like them talking shit about one of us, the staff.

Karen's spokesperson said, "Heather asked Karen out. So Karen said to meet her next door. She's been waiting there like an hour." This was hilarious to them—the sort of hilarious prank the rich kids pull in a John Hughes movie. I waved down a bouncer and told him to go tell Heather.

All that to say, I thought Karen was an asshole long before she fucked my next two girlfriends.

It happened at the high-heel race, one of those charity events where straight people get to laugh at the queers and somehow money is raised for something. It's held every year around Halloween. I'd never gone because I always had to work. But Autumn invited me, then changed her mind; she was going with Karen and I thought, fuck it. I'm not letting them ruin my night.

I don't know what happened exactly because, while I was completely sober, all I remember is seeing them on the street. Depends on who you ask. I asked Autumn the next day. She said I'd shoved Karen. That it was sloppy. Karen went down hard and broke her wrist on the landing.

Here's a funny thing: I was relieved. After four years as a bouncer and bartender, I can tell you lesbians getting into fights, shoving matches, outright brawls is a running joke, like scissoring but real. I'd never been that lesbian, only because I was the lesbian breaking up the fights that lesbians got into. Didn't have time for my own version. And it was Karen, who was an asshole. I'm not saying it should be legal to assault an asshole. But up until that moment, I can't say it had occurred to me that it might not be legal. I was more worried about the fact I had no memory of the event, and figured at least it was something minor, and Karen was an asshole.

When Autumn said Karen had called the cops, my first reaction was, what kind of asshole calls the cops?

Officer Foreman, the cop who'd taken the report,

laughed when I called her ma'am. She said it was no big deal, just a misdemeanor. She would call when she was finished with the paperwork and I could turn myself in and be out in a couple hours. I made dinner and stayed the night at Autumn's and thought . . . (Jesus, I can hear how stupid this sounds) I thought we were getting back together.

Here's the last thing that's funny: I also thought Officer Foreman was all right. She seemed really nice on the phone.

Then, the Friday before Thanksgiving, someone pounded on the door, and for the life of me, I don't know why I answered. Who answers their door at eleven p.m.? But the way they were pounding made my mind think "emergency" in capital letters.

I opened the door to see Fairfax County cops and thought, *Oh, y'all are definitely at the wrong house.* Then I saw Brett Parsons, everyone's hero. Parsons was the cop who'd march in the Pride parade. The cop who led the unit we could call, who'd understand LGBTQ relationships, who wouldn't call us names, who wouldn't say we brought it on ourselves. Whatever "it" might be.

When I try to explain the Gay and Lesbian Liaison Unit to the inmates in the cells next to mine, they react like I'm telling them cops are heroes and marijuana will kill you. They say, "Honey, gay po-lice is still a po-lice. We don't think a Black po-lice isn't a po-lice because his skin's the same." I say working at a club will give you funny ideas on the kind nature of police.

The voices said, "Yeah. White'll do that too." They

have a point. The voices debate my intelligence level. The consensus comes to "dumb as white." The voices find this hilarious, and I wait for the chant to die down before I continue, knowing the next part will be punctuated by the new slogan.

Brett had said he never pegged me for a troublemaker. I said, "Officer Foreman said I could turn myself in." I explained being arrested was inconvenient. I had to go to work in the morning. I had a dog. Brett let me call Autumn to come get the dog. He said I'd only be in jail a couple hours. No big deal. It's just a misdemeanor. (Dumb as white.)

Here's where it gets confusing: I lived in Virginia. Autumn lived in Maryland. I committed my crime in D.C. In theory, because it was a misdemeanor, I could've decided, instead of turning myself in, to never cross the bridge back into D.C. and might've lived a long life never seeing the inside of a cell. But then Officer Foreman never called me back. So in order for the D.C. police to arrest me in Virginia, a couple things needed to happen—they needed a warrant, and not for a misdemeanor. Or they needed to be a little shady. Since they didn't have a warrant, Brett helpfully drove out to Fairfax and brought the Fairfax cops to my house.

The Fairfax County cop who drove me to the jail said, "Listen, I don't want to say anything about D.C. police, but you're charged with a felony. You better get a lawyer before you talk to those guys again." My brain stuck on the word "felony"—felony will do that to you. I didn't believe him. Told him there must be some mistake. He waited for a light to change and showed me my name on his laptop. "FELONY."

When we got to the jail, Brett Parsons, everyone's hero, said, "Well, yeah. We just bumped it to a felony so we could come get you. It'll get knocked down as soon as the marshals come to transfer you to D.C. Couple hours. You won't even get processed here." (Dumb as white. This is the funniest story the voices have ever heard.)

The deputy at the Fairfax County jail didn't want to take me. He said, "We don't even have a warrant in the system. Yes, I can see the charge. What I don't see is a warrant or order to detain."

Brett said, "Nah. This is standard procedure for a felony arrest."

The Fairfax County cop said, "I don't think this is proper." He was the sort of overgrown Boy Scout who'd make a great cop or a terrible cop, depends on your viewpoint.

Brett said it was no big deal. He would send the extradition order as soon as he was back in the office. The marshals would take over before it mattered anyway. No sweat.

The county cop shrugged. The intake deputy shrugged. They said it was on Brett. Brett smiled, shook everyone's hands—pleasure doing business with you. (Dumb as fucking white.)

Three days in, when they gave me a chance to use a phone, I called the only number I knew by heart. Autumn told me she loved me. She told me she was sorry. She told me she called my boss. My boss said Officer Foreman already called him. Foreman told my boss I'd be in jail thirty days for a violent assault. He said he tried to come see me, but they wouldn't let him in because I'm not an inmate here. I don't get visitors.

Autumn said she'd try to find a lawyer. I told her to call my sister. My sister would pay for it. She said she wouldn't be able to find a lawyer on the weekend. I asked her to drop off my pills. My Wellbutrin. My Prozac. No chance they'd let me have Xanax. I started to hear the electricity in my brain. I asked for Officer Foreman's number. Officer Foreman said the marshals had thirty days to transfer me. She'd let them know in thirty days. I asked to speak to Brett, her supervisor. She laughed and said good luck. The line went dead.

Day 2, day 6. Who gives a shit. The nice deputy doesn't work tonight. I stash my oatmeal creams under my mattress and hope for tomorrow. I'll know it's tomorrow when they push a tray through my feed slot with a hard-boiled egg and a Styrofoam cup of generic cornflakes. Everything tastes the same. The deputies come through every morning to take inmates up to the courthouse. Orders are shouted. Stand up. Turn around. Walk backwards slowly. Are those too tight? (This is a very funny prank. No matter the answer, they tighten the cuffs.)

The voices take the opportunity to shout through the feed slots. "I need to talk to my lawyer. I need to use the phone. I need to see the nurse. My court date was three months ago. What time is it?" No one cares.

I don't yell through my slot today. First days, sure. Every chance I got. "I'm supposed to be transferred to D.C. The marshals are supposed to come get me. I need the phone."

I peel my egg slowly. I try to save the skins. Maybe I

can write on the skins if I figure out something to write with. But the skin sticks to the shell. I think, *Egg skins make good bandages*. I laugh. It's very funny because they don't make good bandages. But that little piece of advice was in a Family book for kids. We'd try to stick egg skins to the mosquito bites we'd scratched bloody. They always got infected anyway, or because we'd introduced salmonella. Who knows. I think I'll stick egg skins to my knuckles. The voices say I'm getting another day if I keep being foolish. I apologize. I tell the voices I don't remember what I did this time. It scares the shit out of me. I'm crazy enough to hurt someone. I'm crazy. I hurt someone. I beg them to keep me here so I don't hurt someone again. I cry. I tell the voices I'll try harder. Let's pray.

The nice deputy comes to my slot, says I have a lawyer. She brings me to a visiting cell and the lawyer tells me he'll get me out.

I tell him he can't let me out. I tell him it's not safe. He says it's his job. I tell him I called Officer Foreman. She told me they have thirty days to transfer me. Foreman said don't worry about work. She'd let them know I wouldn't be back.

My lawyer writes this down like it matters what I say. He says I've been charged with stalking and felony assault and says, don't worry, it's just so they can plead you down. I ask what I'd plead down to if it were a misdemeanor; he says probably disorderly conduct or they'd just drop it. He says I shouldn't be here at all. He says they always think they can get away with this shit. And I want to ask him where he thinks he is. Who is "they"? I want to ask if he hears the voices too. Just my luck. A lawyer as crazy as me.

It's daytime. I've been keeping track of time with cornflakes—one cornflake, one meal. I hear metal squeaking. This sound is new. Anything new is exciting. It takes me a minute to realize I'm hearing wheels. The wheels stop and I see blue hair. I come to the window. And I forget about the mucus smear and caress the little window. An old woman with blue hair has a book cart. Blue-hair lady says I can have two books. She jerks the cart to show me the spines. I want to run my hands across the spines like I used to do in my grandma's house, over her leather-bound *Encyclopedia Britannica*s. Pull one down. Flip to a page. Sit down right there on her pink shag carpet and read. Blue-hair lady says she doesn't have all day.

I can't see the titles. I ask what she's got. "I don't have my glasses."

She says she doesn't have time for this. I'm terrified she'll push the cart away. I panic. "Just the thickest books. You choose. Please choose." Everything I say now sounds like begging. I am begging. "I just need something with a lot of words." Maybe I'll finally read *Infinite Jest* in jail. The deputy escorting blue-hair lady opens my slot. The lady with blue hair hands me Jodi Picoult, *My Sister's Keeper*. And David Baldacci, *The Winner*.

I read the Baldacci back in high school. I don't care. I've forgotten the plot. I know a man saves a woman because it's David and that's what he writes. But I don't care. I've never read Picoult. I hug the books to my chest. I sit on my bed mat and do that, just hold them a while. I open *The Winner* and smell the pages. I lick the pages. I'm weeping. I tell the voices I have books. I'm rich. Maybe I won't go crazy. I already am. This is hysterically funny to me. The voices tell me to shut the fuck up.

I squander the first book in a day. And curse myself. I have to hold the book close to my face to see the words. I devour the words. *The Winner* is the most beautiful book ever written. I curse myself as I near the end. I should have rationed the pages. Sips of clean water on a desert island. Made them last.

Things are turning around. The nice deputy worked today. I now have a *Men's Health* magazine and a *People* magazine. They're both two years old. I read my magazines. I read them again. I lick the perfume ads. They taste like someone else's breath. I read the table of contents. I read the photo captions. I read the copyrights.

Day 3, maybe day 7. I give myself one chapter of Jodi Picoult. I read that chapter three times. I cheat and read the acknowledgments page. I read the chapter again.

My hand's infected. I know the signs. The pus smells worse than me. But it doesn't smell like jail and I'm proud of myself for creating a different smell. They took the voice with the kidney stone this morning. I don't know if she was released or taken to the hospital. She's been quiet the past couple days. The voice who sings Aaliyah is still missing, and the voice who sings Billie Holiday doesn't sing anymore. I don't know if she's still here, or they're still here. The voice who's withdrawing from alcohol, who says she's a call girl, can now hold down food. I asked the nice deputy to give her my last oatmeal cream. The deputy comes back with a sliver of a bar of soap.

I don't know where everyone got these treasures. Maybe if you're in long enough, you earn things like this. A bar of soap after a month. A tube of toothpaste after your first molar rots.

I read another chapter of Picoult. I'll read it again after lunch. The judge this morning said I should be released. I'm not an inmate. I have a sister who'll pay for a lawyer. I have friends who'll find a lawyer.

The sheriff says he can't just release me. He called the judge and asked the judge to assign bail. He smiles and starts to walk away. He thinks I'm an inmate. He thinks I belong here. But here's a thing that's funny: I'm the only person in this jail who's guilty. And I'll be gone before we find another voice to sing Aaliyah. My sister will post bail. Autumn will pick me up and take me to her house in Maryland, where I can sleep with my dog, and the police won't find me. I'm not like the voices. I'll never hear the voices again.

After seven days in jail and two days free, I went to court on the Monday after Thanksgiving. The marshals showed up, finally, to take me to another courthouse, the federal courthouse in Arlington. The judge asked them what the hell I was doing there. She asked me if I could find my way to D.C. to turn myself in. I said I could. She released me, again.

In D.C., Brett, everyone's hero, who swore I'd only be in jail a couple hours, showed up to the police station where I'd asked someone to please arrest me—it was nearly nine a.m., the judge's deadline. Brett said he was very sorry. He'd take my belongings and deliver them to Autumn. He'd take me to jail and make sure I was released the same day.

The judge in D.C. said I wasn't allowed to talk to Autumn, who now had my wallet, keys, and dog. So I was released, without shoelaces or a coat. Autumn had those too. The temperature on the bank said it was below freezing. There was snow on the ground.

I walked to a bar where my friend Jay used to work, where the manager knew me. The bartender fed me and called Jay. I hadn't talked to Jay in a couple years. I had heard he'd moved to Atlanta. Our lives, the way they were, new number each time we moved, new jobs every few months, it was easy to lose someone. Jay changed his number and I changed mine, and someone said, "I think he moved to Atlanta"—I assumed it was for a guy—but he never moved to Atlanta.

Jay showed up in a Chevy and said, "Girl, oh my god. Did you enjoy your bologna sandwich? Get in. Lord. Open a window. You smell like shit. What the hell is going on?"

Strange reunion. Jay drove me to my sister's house. Jay and my sister Ann read the court order that said I was now charged with a felony and stalking.

The problem was, as I've mentioned, Autumn had everything from my wallet to my house keys to my dog. I told them it was obviously a mistake. I just needed to borrow a phone.

Ann was suspicious. "What if she really is claiming that? The cops wouldn't just make it up." Jay burst out laughing. One of those exaggerated guffaws meant to show you how dumb you are. He was treading on thin ice with my sister. I may have had the felony charge, but she's the one who can make you cry.

I shut myself in the bathroom to try to wash some of the jail smell off me while they fought over who would make the call. By the time I came out of the bathroom, they'd finally agreed Ann should call. Autumn had never met Jay. And Jay had no interest in feigning politeness.

Ann was cautious at first. "Lauren's here. Yeah, she's fine. Did you say she was stalking you? That's what it says." Then, "How did this happen, Autumn? You need to fix this." Then "Okay. You remember the address?" And to me, "She's on her way."

When Autumn arrived with my dog and phone, Jay wouldn't talk to her. He'd taken a position by the window where he could cross his arms and let her know he was not having her shit. I tried to introduce them, but he wouldn't make eye contact, said something to my sister under his breath that no one needed to hear to understand. Some version of "This bitch."

I admired his loyalty, but I wanted them to be friends. Maybe because I'd only just found Jay again, and I was losing Autumn. She'd been apologetic at first—said she had meant to meet me at the jail, never meant any of this to happen. She explained Karen was a fundraiser for the Gay Liaison Unit. They all knew her.

That's when things started making sense—the felony charge, the made-up additional charges, the attempt to lose me in a cell for thirty days, long enough to lose my job, my dog, my mind.

Ann showed Autumn the charge sheet, where it said

I'd lifted Karen off the ground and thrown her down, like either of us was qualified to perform stunts in movies.

Autumn just said, "I know. I tried to tell them. But they're cops." Then, for no reason whatsoever, she laughed and said, "I was stoned. Sorry."

Ann and Jay shared a look like, *Are you hearing this shit?* Autumn shrugged, said she had to work in the morning. I realized then that I'd never really know how she felt about any of it. She'd probably been apologizing to Karen just as earnestly. The only thing that mattered to Autumn was that no one was mad at Autumn, which also happens to be how she'd ended up dating two people at once.

By the time my case went to court, I would've pleaded guilty to anything that kept me out of jail. But Autumn did get the stalking charge dropped. I pleaded guilty to assault and got two years' probation, and orders to stay away from Karen. I didn't think that would be a problem. My probation officer let me volunteer at a dog shelter for my community service.

At first I thought I could maintain some semblance of a social life. But D.C.'s a small town if you're gay. Seemed like anytime I went to a bar, Karen would walk in ten minutes later with a full posse and I'd have to leave. When Pride came around, I spent the day standing with a couple friends on one sidewalk of Pennsylvania Avenue. Karen set up camp on the other side of the street. I did my best version of "Having a very good time. Who? Don't even see her," like you'd do with an ex at a party when the host accidentally invited you both.

My last attempt at being gay, as I knew it, which involved being around gays on Friday and Saturday nights, was the Badlands Christmas party. My old boss always invited anyone who'd ever worked at Badlands. I was there maybe an hour before one of the bouncers came up behind me and said, "Karen's here."

I stupidly said, "She didn't even work here," like it mattered. I knew it didn't matter. I ran out the back door like I'd robbed the joint and drove home.

I stopped going out after that. Which, by default, meant I stopped socializing. Didn't actually know how else to socialize. I'd go to work, come home, hike with my dog, volunteer at the dog rescue, sign up for a couple programming classes at the community college. I was being good. I could be good. Someone fucking notice I'm good.

I was barely speaking to Autumn when she asked me to meet up for the traditional "I want my blue hoodie back, and I have some of your mail," the final dissolution of any relationship.

My probation was almost over. I was thinking of moving to New England, to be closer to my family. We ordered beers and I went outside to answer my phone. And another member of the Gay Liaison Unit gayly bent me over the hood of his cruiser and cuffed me. My friends were still inside. I managed a text message, in cuffs, "I'M ARRESTED." I also managed to swallow a gram of coke that was in my wallet.

Karen arrived while I was being read my rights. I'll never know if she was in the bar at all. I doubt it. I'm tall enough to see across a crowd. Either way, her entourage sang happy birthday to her as I was hauled off to jail again. Surprise.

Once again, Autumn had to call my supervisor to

explain why I would not be coming into work. At least this time, it was only for a night.

Karen said I'd been circling and threatening her for hours, in the bar I'd entered fifteen minutes beforehand. All I had were three witnesses and an ATM receipt from a bar blocks away from when I withdrew money and had a shot for liquid courage to prove it was impossible I'd been threatening Karen for an hour. Karen had her own personal police force.

The judge added another year to my probation, but thank fuck I didn't have to spend any more time in jail. I decided I should probably think about moving.

For a long time, I didn't tell anyone but my closest friends that I'd been to jail. When I did, the fact fazed no one in my working-class circle.

Jail, convictions, violence, drugs, police, prison, and judges are facts of a life in the margins. In the world I inhabit, a record can mean you're an asshole or you *were* an asshole or you met an asshole. In the world I inhabit, you're more than the record. But that record won't let me leave the world I inhabit. Because there's another world where the record is all that matters. It's why they made the records, to keep people out. As long as I keep to my station, they won't use it against me.

In that world, I would meet a writer with a trust fund who would say, "They don't just lock people in jail. You see a judge. You can make bail. You call a lawyer."

The problem is, people like me, white people with even a little agency, aren't usually the people who get locked in solitary for a week because they assaulted the wrong person who was friends with the wrong cop. But it does happen. In most cases, someone like me could've pleaded down to disorderly conduct. We pick up trash on the highway or work at a dog shelter, and our probation officers warn us a full month before asking us to pee in a cup so they don't have to bother with the paperwork.

When we do fall through the cracks, we're more likely to get a second chance. As damaging as it was to me, I still got another chance. I probably couldn't get a job at a day care, certainly nothing white-collar. But if I were to tell a potential boss I have an assault conviction, shrug and add, "Stupid lesbian drama," I can get a job at a bar—no problem.

There are levels of privilege. Now that I've jumped a level, from blue-collar asshole, possibly crazy veteran with a criminal record, to writer who no one would suspect has a criminal record, or if they do suspect, they don't care, I do have to talk about it. Or nothing will change. Because people still believe, despite all evidence, that cops don't lie, that the system is just, that people in jail deserve jail, and, mostly, that it won't happen to them. I can tell you solitary confinement is torture. I can quote the stats on who's in jail, how many are serving serious time who haven't been convicted of anything at all. But unless you understand it can happen to you, to someone who looks like you, that you can end up in solitary, guilty or not, and lose your goddamn mind, unless I can make you feel it, you won't fucking care.

I wonder still about the voices. I haven't heard them again. But I have a pretty good idea which voices were real. And I think about them sometimes. I wonder if the lady with the kidney stones made it home for her daughter's graduation. I hope the woman who did sex work got clean. I hope Billie Holiday sings to her boys when she puts them to bed. And every time I read the news and it says a jail's lowered its suicide rate, I'll think of the girl in the elevator blanket who sang Aaliyah.

Leaving Isn't the Hardest Thing

The first time I found others who'd been raised like me, I felt a little like Robinson Crusoe must have when he finally encountered another human. It was 2005. I was watching the news with my sister Ann and saw that the Family's heir apparent was dead.

The words took a minute to sink in. I didn't know him personally. To me, he was Davidito, the adopted son of David Berg, a hero in the comic books we read, the main character of the Family's manual on raising children, the Davidito Book. He was a celebrity, a teen idol, like Prince Will or Harry, or Jonathan Taylor Thomas. The kind you grow up with, sort of—parallel lives. And you think you know them. The girls used to brag they'd grow up and marry him.

I was twenty-seven and hadn't thought of him in ten years at least. But CNN said his name was Ricky. They said he'd tracked down one of the inner circle, murdered her, then shot himself. My first thought on the murder-suicide involving the kid who was supposed to grow up to lead us through the End Time, my very first thought, was *Hey. Holy shit. We're on CNN.* My second thought on the murder-suicide, on seeing real-life Family members on the screen, those old stock photos—the faded black-and-whites, the grainy harvest golds leaking into the lime greens and chocolate browns of my youth, hippies kneeling in prayer with the hands raised to touch God, the beards and sackcloth and middle parts and chunky glasses, the guitars and twirling skirts and the kids—my second thought was *Oh, fuck, people can see this.* Fuck. Fuck. Fuck. Fuck. Was that Dad?

Ann said she didn't think so. She said no one would recognize us. Then she said she'd met him once.

I said, "Wait. Davidito?" in the same tone you'd use if your sister told you she used to play soccer with the Obama girls.

She waited a beat and said, "Yeah. He was in the teen home for a while. We weren't supposed to know who he was. But everyone did."

"What was he like?"

"Quiet. Kind of nerdy." She was playing with her phone like she should call someone but couldn't decide who to call. Just clicking through the menu. "They were horrible to him," she added. "It was like he'd been banished to come live among the peasants."

I just stared at her. She decided to drop this now. Where I chose being affable, and lying about my past to fit in, Ann chose mystery. You'll never know a damn thing about Ann she hasn't decided to tell you. And you'll still know only the half of it. Or maybe that's who we've always been.

We watched the news, flipping channels during commercials in case another station was covering the story. We hardly spoke, our minds cycling through a blend of horror and fascination and nostalgia. Then someone she knew was on the screen. And I thought it would be cool to see an old friend. A face I actually knew. Wouldn't that be something.

I'd searched before, not for others, just the name itself—the Family, the Children of God—some proof we even registered in the social conscience. But even if social media had been as widely used back then as it is today, I didn't know my old friends' real names. I could barely remember my own Family names, much less what the other kids were called at any given time. Fun trick they played on us. Change the kids' names. Change homes, new kids, new names. Change the fucking kids too. Wake up one morning, and there's a Josh where Jen should be. Or was it Jules. Who's to say. You're not allowed to ask. So no, I wasn't searching anyone's name. For fuck's sake, I thought the founder, our prophet, was named David Brandt. That's what it said in the books. There was nothing to find except a notation in a listicle—"Top Ten Weird Cults." We always make the list. Christ, that's an odd thing to be proud of. But it was the only proof I had that any of it had happened at all.

I was fifteen years old when we left the Family for good. Escaping a cult isn't nearly as exciting as they make it sound, not the Family anyway. We walked out one night after dinner. No big deal.

All I have to mark the occasion is a single line in the diary I'd been keeping: "Mom came in to pray with me." No one reading my diary would've known what I'd meant. But I'll never forget. She asked if I'd leave with her. It was bad enough my sisters were in different homes and we'd have to leave without them. I was fifteen, old enough, she said, to decide for myself. I made the note in my diary, and I tried not to hope.

She'd been planning it for a while. We'd been living in a smaller home outside Munich, just Mom, Gabe, and Mikey. My sisters had been sent to a teen home in some other city. It's not a bad retention tactic. Harder to leave when you don't know where your kids are. With a gun to my head, I couldn't tell you what my sisters' names were then.

Of all the Family homes, that last one was my favorite. We'd rented it furnished, this chalet on a hillside overlooking a pristine alpine lake in Bavaria. My parents' bedroom was the sort of library I still fantasize about. Three walls of books and a rolling wooden ladder to reach the top shelves. It was a home where the guy in charge was more scared of my mom than he was of the Family. Where my mom let us borrow books to read. Where I could get away with things like keeping a diary. Where we could take walks into town where Mom could call our grandma and ask for help with plane tickets. Where we could just walk out one night, take the train to Munich, and fly back to Texas. I'm not even sure we told anyone when we left.

My grandmother in Amarillo took us in, as always. We'd lived with her for three years when we left the cult the first time. I was six then. This time I was a teenager and had been living in a cult for six years. After Bavaria, and Switzerland before it, lands colored in with crayons—green meadows dotted with splotchy cows, pink and purple geraniums overflowing their window boxes on brown chalets, turquoise lakes and blue skies and mountains left white at the top of the page— Amarillo looked like coffee spilled on a brown Formica table.

It's a city where the weather is matched only by the meanness. My forebears moved out there in covered wagons in search of cheap land. The land tried to do what the natives couldn't. But the Scots-Irish are a stubborn, stupid sort. They stayed despite the blizzards, tornadoes, hail, fog, freezing fog, heat, floods, and drought. They farmed dirt through the Dust Bowl and the wind that blows forty miles an hour on a calm day, coating the city in dried cow shit from the feedlots west of town. It's a town where a year after I graduated high school, a punk, a sweet oddball named Brian Deneke, was killed, run over by a rich kid in a Cadillac during a fight. (If you think that sounds like murder, you'd be mistaken. See, the rich kid was a good Christian and a football player. Brian, a punk. Amarillo sentenced his killer to probation.) It's a town where they sued Oprah. When you think about it, Amarillo's reason enough to join a cult.

I got off the plane and looked out at the endless prairie, an ocean of brown nothing, and felt like I was lost at sea. I don't know that I ever did get my bearings again.

Assimilating back into a "normal" teenage world was an adjustment. For the first few years my brother and I were homeschooled, which just meant we filled in some quizzes before our parents got home from work, after we'd watched MTV all day.

Most of the day, we tried to learn how to dress, talk,

and act like humans. We quizzed each other on the lyrics to "Baby Got Back" because everyone else knew the
words. We quizzed each other on sitcom and movie
characters. We'd steal the *People* magazines from Grandma's bathroom and memorize the important facts—ask
me anything about Julia Roberts. We called this class
"humanities," because the ancient shit in the textbook
wasn't going to help us in Amarillo. We played basketball
at a nearby Christian school. My brother was tortured
for his bikini briefs in the locker room; I was teased
for my giant red Sally Jessy Raphael glasses. We wore
clothes my aunt bought us at garage sales. While Mom
cleaned houses, Gabe blew money on pyramid schemes
and make-your-first-million seminars.

We enrolled in high school when I was a senior. My
brother was cute and funny. I was weird and invisible.
The one time anyone did pay attention to me was when
a football player who wore a belt buckle the size of my
head cheated off my algebra test and failed. I wasn't even
useful as a nerd.

I'm certain there were parties to attend on the weekends. But if I wasn't working at the fast-food restaurant
where I held a part-time job, I'd toss a couple books
and a sack of tacos in the old Pontiac my grandpa gave
me when I'd turned seventeen and I'd drive to the edge
of the canyon singing along to Toad the Wet Sprocket
and Pearl Jam songs blasting through my one working
speaker. Then I'd drive home to make sure I wasn't late
for my pointless curfew.

There's a specific time period you're supposed to learn
how to make friends, how to have a conversation, what
role you play in the social order. I didn't learn any of that

because I was in a cult. And once I was out of the cult, I couldn't explain any of that, because I'd been in a fucking cult. That I didn't fit in even in the cult wasn't much help.

The distance between me and everyone around me, the disconnect, only served to reinforce what I'd learned in the cult: I didn't belong.

It's not all that complicated. A cult needs control to function; people are easier to control when they're isolated. Remove natural allies—parents, siblings, friends. Make people distrust authority. Convince the kids if they say anything, their parents will go to jail. You speak a different language. Never mind that you're in a foreign country. Even if you speak the language, you don't. You use the cult language now.

An entire war is being waged to make you fearful and avoidant of anyone or anything that causes doubt— "Come out from among them and be ye separate." It's why evangelicals avoid secular books and movies and TV. You don't have to be in a cult. There's an entire society built to insulate those with faith—bookstores and music and movies, everything.

Even our fundraising methods served a purpose. You knock on doors or block pedestrians all day, try to sell them posters or tapes, try to save their souls, people don't always take it well. Any evangelical kid who was told to try to lead their friends to Jesus can tell you how popular that'll make you. People get annoyed because you're fucking annoying. How do you react to Jehovah's Witnesses knocking on your door, the "God Hates Fags" assholes at the Pride parade? You ever notice their kids are watching you? It's by design. Every shitty interaction with an outsider reinforces what you were taught. They, those others, those Systemites, are mean, sometimes cruel. You're different. You don't belong out there.

So I worked at trying to fit in, and failed, because the very act of trying is the definition of uncool. I read my books and lived in my head, and my past faded into something like a movie I'd seen once, of someone else's life.

In the years prior, when we were homeschooled, when my brother and I weren't "studying," Gabe would order us to go play outside. Sometimes we'd walk to the library. Or we'd walk to Albertsons and buy a Coke from the vending machine and walk back home.

We used to climb the dogwood tree in the backyard, scoot down the branch that overhung the sunroom, and drop onto the roof, where we'd read and talk.

I was picking at the splinters the cedar shingles left in my legs. We'd carried our little radio up with us and played the Top 40 station just loud enough for us to hear—quiet enough so Gabe wouldn't hear it if he stepped outside to check on us.

Mikey asked, "What do you want to be? When we're older. What do you want to be?"

I was sixteen years old and I'd never considered the question as anything more than an abstraction. One of the things that had been my saving grace during all those years in the Family was that my bed was on the top bunk, where I was usually safe from the pervy uncles. I'd hide books under my mattress, a radio for a time, and I'd tell myself stories about who I really was—a secret agent, a spy, a lunatic locked away, a normal girl. I'd escape. I'd

grow up and live the life I'd seen in movies. I'd be a cop.
I'd be a soldier. I'd have friends. I'd have a whole shelf
full of books. I'd have a dog.

But I'd never thought about what I wanted to do
with my life. We were told the world was going to end.
I hadn't known I would grow up. Far as I can tell, my
brother was the first to ask me.

"I don't know. What are you going to be?" I asked
him.

"An artist, I guess." He studied his abs. Douchebag
was a more likely career path. "I could probably be a
bartender. That looks like fun. People have to talk to the
bartender." He had a point.

"I think I want to be a writer. Maybe a reporter," I
said. Reporters got to travel wherever they wanted. And
they didn't have to work in offices. They could eat whatever they wanted. I'd seen them on CNN. "I guess a
writer." It seemed like a less competitive field.

He said, "We'll probably both be bartenders."

One morning, during senior year, Mikey got to the newspaper before me and stripped out the comics section. Left
with the rest, I flipped through the A-section and saw
David Berg's face. David Berg, Moses David, Mo, Dad,
Grandpa—the insane prophet of God. He looked like a
taxidermied opossum in one of those tourist trap junk
stores off Route 66, pointy and beady-eyed. I realized I'd
never seen his face. I'd never even met anyone who had
met him. He lived in undisclosed locations with an inner
circle. In all our books, they always covered his face by
pasting on a cartoon lion's head or a cartoon version of

him that didn't look a damn thing like him. I felt like I was underwater. I couldn't hear Mikey chewing his cereal. I couldn't hear anything.

He didn't look much like a prophet. He looked more like one of the guys who hung out at the library during the day, smelling like booze and boiled sweat. When the words stopped fluttering on the page, I read them. They said he died in his sleep.

I took the entire page, folded it, and stuffed it into my backpack. Told Mikey we'd leave in five minutes. My voice sounded weak behind the sloshing sound of my pulse. I walked to the bathroom and quietly closed the door. I read his obituary again. And again. They said he died. He was dead. They said his wife, Maria, would lead the cult. He was dead.

The only thing I remember about school that day was that David Berg's obituary was in my backpack. I couldn't stop thinking about it. And what I thought, after the initial desire to find his grave and piss on it, was that everything I remembered was real. I was real. You can forget after a while, when no one sees you. I felt like a ghost, wandering the halls, sitting in class, memorizing facts to pass tests, wishing someone would just talk to me, just for a moment. But now I had proof—a page from the *Amarillo Globe-News* that said I was real.

After the final bell, I had an hour to kill before Mikey got out of soccer practice. So I drove down to the Texaco station and bought a pack of Marlboros. My plan was to drive around the block, smoke a couple, become a Systemite. The fucking Family. The utmost Systemite thing I could do was smoke a cigarette. (I wish I was kidding. But when big shot family leaders met in a public place, they'd smoke. They claimed the cigarettes were camouflage, but maybe it was just a convenient excuse to sneak a smoke. Obviously anyone looking at a group of adults standing together could think, *You know, those people might be in a cult. Nope. Never mind. They're smoking. Couldn't possibly be a cult. Had me fooled for a second with those shitty haircuts.*) I suppose I could've just eaten a bag of white sugar with a spoon, but smoking seemed cooler.

So I lit a Marlboro. And I choked on the first inhale. I had to pull over in the Wienerschnitzel parking lot to finish. I thought I'd throw up, and I'd have to reconsider that white-sugar thing. But I fucking did it.

When I picked Mikey up from practice, I drove across the street to the bowling alley and parked (I wasn't getting expelled for smoking on school grounds), lit another cigarette, and showed him the obituary. I expected shock, the same feelings that had overwhelmed me all day. What I got was a shrug. "You didn't show that to anyone, did you?" He stripped off his socks and threw them onto the back seat.

"Who am I gonna show?"

"Are those any good?" He picked up the cigarette pack.

"The first one sucks. After that it's okay." I passed him the matches and he lit one. Choked. Threw it out the window.

"Just don't show Mom," he said. He might've meant the cigarettes, but I think he meant the obituary.

Gabe had bought into some franchise that treated restaurant and hotel floors with acid etching that was supposed to prevent slips, but all it did was stain the tile and sear your lungs. After dinner, he loaded his truck and left. Mom was watching *ER* in the living room. I took the now fuzzy page from my back pocket and handed it to her. She stared for a minute, then walked to her bedroom, the page dangling from her hand like she might drop it. Mikey was sitting on the floor, surrounded by his homework. "Don't," he said. But I've never been able to take good advice. I followed her.

She was sitting on the edge of the tub, her face in her hands. "Did anyone see that?" she asked.

"It was in the paper," I said. But I knew that wasn't what she meant. "What did you do with it?"

"I flushed it. Jesus, Lauren. How could you be so stupid?"

"Mom, I didn't show anyone but Mikey." I lifted the toilet lid. Hoped I'd see the page floating. "Did you see him?"

"I thought he looked different," she said. "Pass me the tissue."

I handed her the box and sat on the floor, said, "Maybe if he'd shown his face, people would've left earlier." Somehow I knew this would be the only time we'd talk about the Family.

"You can't ever tell anyone." She was desperate. She grabbed my hand and repeated it. "No one. Not your friends. Not your husband. They'll never understand. We'd lose everything."

I dug my toes into the pink shag carpet my grandmother would never replace. I thought that someday I'd have friends. I thought if I did have friends, they'd understand.

"But you left," I said. "You got us out."

She said it wouldn't matter. They'd never understand.

"Mom, I don't understand," I said. And I didn't. I didn't understand any of it.

"Neither do I," she said. "I know I should apologize to you and your brother. But I don't know where to begin." Her shoulders shook, and I sat beside her, put my arm around her. I told her it was okay. "Are you smoking?" she said.

My first thought, always my first thought, was to lie. "Yeah. I bought a pack today," I said.

She asked if I had any left. So we went outside and I dug the cigarettes and matches out of my glove box, lit one for both of us. We leaned against the trunk of my car, shivering in the cold, and watched the smoke curl in the frigid air. I'd always seen my mom as someone proud, my fierce protector. And she was. But underneath the calm on the surface, she was already more broken, more tortured than I'd ever be. She was fucking terrified. I agreed then to the charade we'd perform for the next twenty years. We would pretend nothing happened. We would lie until we began to believe our own lies.

For years, I kept the secret. Even if I'd wanted to tell someone, there's no handbook to announce that sort of thing. I thought sometimes, back when I thought of it at all, that I should make a poster, like the ones we used to hand out. Maybe a picture of me on the front, like a lost kid poster: *My name is Lauren. I was in the Family. It's a cult. Nope, not that one. No Kool-Aid. Just an old guy who thought he talked to God.* But what can I really tell you to explain my life? I know it's fascinating because it's so different. But it's so fucking different. And no matter what I say, it'll still be foreign to you.

I can't tell you what it feels like to live in a constant state of alert unless you've lived it. We watch horror movies because they're fun. There's tension. The dark room. The building music. The ominous threat. Then release. A cat jumps out of the cupboard. There's no one behind the shower curtain. But in a cult, just like in any abusive relationship, there's no release. It's a constant threat. That sort of prolonged terror leaves a mark. But the problem with any sort of fucked-up childhood, just like any abusive relationship: you can't talk about it because it's a secret.

All those secrets we keep and the lies we tell to keep them rot into shame. That shame isolates us. We're shaped by our experiences, but when we see those experiences through shame, all those experiences feel like failure. Cults, evangelical Christianity even, teach you that God will break you to re-create you in his image. So they break you. And all you have are the pieces. You patch yourself together. But all you see are the flaws.

The thing about being part of something like a cult is it fills something inside you. You have a reason and a certainty in that reason. You need that purpose because they take everything else, everything that defined you, down to your fucking name. Kind of hard to make friends when you don't know who the fuck you are.

I didn't even know where to start. I asked the guidance counselor for guidance. She said I should consider the meatpacking plant and junior college. Gabe told me inspiring stories of entrepreneurs who'd started from nothing, rode the bus to New York, and didn't give up. We didn't have Google to search for career options, or how to pay for college when your dad's investing in Primerica. The Air Force recruiter said I could be a translator. I figured I'd be an airman. I'd have friends, a shared purpose. That's how it worked in books.

And it sort of worked. I did have some friends in the Air Force—a roommate who hung out at the basketball courts because basketball shorts reveal the exact size and shape of a dick. She called it window shopping. Then we moved rooms, new roommates, and never spoke again. I didn't get along with my next roommate. But there were two girls from Idaho down the hall who I hung out with. I was in love with one of them because she challenged me to arm wrestle the first time we met. And she won. Then I was transferred to another training base in Mississippi, traded those friends for a few airmen in my class. We'd drive to New Orleans on weekends, share a shithole motel room where the stamps on the phones said they came from another shithole motel, where we'd lie on our sleeping bags atop the stained sheets. When I transferred to South Carolina, I made friends with the guys in the room next to mine. Then moved off base and made friends with my roommates. Moved again. New house. New friends.

My friendships, if you could call them that, were built on all the depth and intimacy of a fourth-grade relationship that starts and ends with "We sat together at lunch for a week" and lasted about as long. We never stayed up all night talking. I never knew a thing about their hometowns or families. Never told them a damn thing about myself that wasn't a lie. I couldn't.

All my life, friends came and went, or I came and went. When I was younger, there were kids I played with and talked to more than others. But I'd wake up one day and their bunk would be empty, or they'd wake up and find mine empty. We were never allowed to say if we were going and when, certainly not where. Never allowed to say goodbye. Might be why as an adult, I considered acquaintances with the same sense of object permanence as a dog whose squeaky toy is taken away. I'd wonder what happened, and then they'd simply ceased to exist in my mind.

Don't get me wrong, I desperately fucking wanted the sort of friends everyone else seemed to have. I just didn't understand how anyone formed those bonds. I wish I could say that it occurred to me maybe the problem was that I was lying to them about everything, that my entire past was fiction, that I'd pretend to know and remember things I didn't because I was so fucking concerned with fitting in. In fairness, you people do get irrationally mad when someone hasn't seen *Star Wars* or *E.T.* And it's a little fucking unnerving that a common response to someone whose childhood memories aren't an exact replica of your own is "What, did you grow up in a cult or something?"

It would've been so easy, so many times, to just say yes. But I didn't know how. I was too fucking ashamed of it.

My only permanent contemporaries were my siblings. When I was in the Air Force, any three-day weekend at Shaw Air Force Base, I'd drive the fourteen hours up to Massachusetts to see Valerie. I'd pull into her drive-way sometime around seven a.m. on a Saturday, knock on one of the kids' windows to let me in. They'd watch cartoons while I tried to sleep a couple hours. And I'd spend the weekend at the only place, around the only people, I didn't have to be anyone but me.

Still, my family rarely talked about the Family. There was one time I can remember, one summer weekend when I was twenty-three or twenty-four. I was bartend-ing at Badlands in D.C. and working on a healthy coke habit. Mikey had just moved up to Massachusetts after college and was bartending at one of those happy hour bar and grills with a random collection of vintage sport-ing goods nailed to the walls. (Turns out, he was half right about our futures. We've both spent years sling-ing drinks. But he still paints. And I never could stop writing.) Ann had long since left the Family on her own and was waiting tables to put herself through nursing school. Valerie and her husband had just bought their first house, a drafty little ranch with brown shag carpet and a park bench on the front porch.

We were down in the basement, all four of us, sit-ting on a futon couch, the floor, Valerie's husband's com-puter chair, drinking wine after the kids went to bed. Valerie brought down a photo album she'd swiped from Gabe's house after our grandma's funeral. I'd never seen it before. Mom must've forgotten it when she left. We started flipping through those old photos and kept grab-bing the album from each other. I'd find an old picture from Chile—our sun-bleached hair looking like it'd been cut with a steak knife. I forgot we were blond once.

These were the photos we mailed home to Grandma. Most are posed. Those awkward smiles that stay the same though your face ages—this is my picture smile, the smile I'll hate every time I see it. But point a camera at me and my brain no longer controls my face. "Say cheese." I remember having to brush my hair for the pictures. Mom fixing it after my failed attempts to make it look nice for the camera. "This is for Grandma. Wear those earrings she sent you for Christmas, Lauren. Stand up straight, Ann. Valerie, don't make that face. Mikey, you're perfect." The backgrounds change. Cherry blossoms in Osaka. A glacier on the Gotthard Pass. A castle in Munich.

We don't have our old art projects, those bowls you made in third grade. We don't have yearbooks or scrapbooks. We don't have a box of mixtapes and ribbons, no trophies, no spelling bee certificates. And up until that moment, I didn't know we had many photos.

We kept passing those old pictures around, checking the backs for dates, telling those half stories each one of us remembers differently, or not at all, staring at those images of us like one of those optical illusions in the mall—relax your eyes and you'll see a tiger, or figure out what the fuck happened to your family.

But we didn't talk about the pictures that weren't in the album, the pictures we'd never have sent back to Grandma—pictures from inside the homes, in our rooms with those fucking triple-decker bunk beds in the background or pictures of a prayer meeting or pictures of us on kitchen duty or selling posters. Those pictures don't exist. If they did, we probably would have burned them.

Still, if there were any time to discuss it at all, the four of us together, it was that night. But we didn't. The Family had become a secret we kept, even from one another.

When Ricky died, Ann showed me a website, a message board. I'm pretty sure social media at the time was still just classmates.com. But finally, I had a way to talk to others who'd grown up in the cult.

For weeks, I spent every spare moment on that website. Racing home after work. Still in my cable company work uniform, insulation stuck to my shirt. The ashtray by the keyboard overflowing onto my desk. Every night, I'd watch the same scene play out. One of us, a cult baby, logging in to ask the same question: "Do you remember me?" The details varied. "My parents were Happy and Mercy. I have an older brother, 5 younger sisters. I was in Osaka. I was in a home in Poland by a lake. I was in Brazil, the big home on a hill." But the question was always the same: "Do you remember me? Does anyone remember me?"

I'd asked the same question when I first logged in. I got an answer almost immediately, an older girl who remembered me from Osaka. Holy shit. I was a real girl. She pointed out others who'd been in the same school. Then a girl from Switzerland, Jen, who knew another, a whole cluster of cult babies in Berlin. Another from a different home in Japan. We shot questions back and forth faster than we could answer them all. Those first few moments of finding a witness to your life. The fucking rush of it. Questions about the homes, about siblings, about shepherds, about parents. "Wasn't there a park down the street? Yeah, with the bamboo forest. Where's your little brother now? Oh, my parents are never leaving. Your mom was nice, though. Do you remember that nasty-ass homemade yogurt? Hey, what ever happened to that asshole who they put in charge of us for like ten minutes before the Elgg home got raided?"

We had our own inside jokes. I'd tell you some, but, I mean, you're not going to get them. We wrote down lyrics of Family songs just to put the bug in someone else's ear. We complained about our jobs and debated why so many of us joined the military and shrugged at how all of us can cook and do basic carpentry. And honestly, we spent a lot of time making fun of you crybabies. How you can't even change a diaper while holding another baby. How you can't fix anything. How you could never have choked down boiled liver. How you think your mom gaslit you because she returned shoes she couldn't afford to buy you. How you suck at camping and we don't even want to go with you anymore. How you're actually proud you can't cook an egg. How the worst thing that happened to you was something you saw happen to someone else on the news.

And then the rush was gone, as soon as it came. We were real. Our lives were real. Cool. The fuck were we supposed to do with any of it. We weren't much help to each other in the how-to-function-out-here department. Might as well have asked our parents for career advice. But what I wanted—someone to remember me—wasn't what I needed. It rarely is. What I found, I didn't recognize right away. I should have, considering. But I'm a slow thinker, and a slower learner.

We were telling our stories on that board. And I

started realizing just how much the cult had shaped me—from the way the words "can I talk to you" would send ice down my spine, to the way I hate hearing music or television when I'm trying to sleep, to my obsession with socks. (We lived off donations. And no one ever donates socks.) We all had a story about sharing a contraband pink razor with twenty other girls. We compared what we'd bought with the money we pilfered from selling posters. I blew mine on candy and books that my mom let me hide in her closet. My friends who'd stayed in longer spent theirs on birth control pills and escape plans. But what I wanted to know, how to heal, how to be normal, no one could answer.

That older girl I'd known in Japan, though, Taylor Stevens, was writing a book, a thriller. And she asked me to look at it. We kept talking. And she kept telling me I should write. I kept telling her I do write. She said I should write about my life. I said she was crazy. No one knows about that.

I bought her book when it came out. And there, on the back of it, "raised in the Children of God." You'd have thought I was a closet case buying lesbian erotica the way I carried that book through the Crystal City Barnes & Noble. I had to buy three other books just so it wouldn't stand out. Someone might see it and think, *You know, I bet that there is a cult member too.* Thank god I was a smoker.

I was also a fucking closet case, just not about the lesbian thing. Like I said, you'd think I'd have known. And like any closet case, I was just swimming in the putrid shame of it. Seeing someone live openly, god, I was so fucking envious. There were plenty of others who were out, so to speak. Many never bothered with the closeted stage, didn't give a shit who knew, showed up for interviews, participated in documentaries, wrote essays and books. I admired the hell out of them. I was fucking in awe. And as sure as a closet case evangelical miserably married to a beard she fucks once a year watching the Dykes on Bikes ride by in the Pride parade, I was fucking disgusted. I mean, god. If you guys could just act normal for one goddamn minute. I'll stay in my closet, thank you very much.

I was going to be normal. I had a head start; I got out of the Family earlier than most of those weirdos. I could be a Systemite. Goddamnit.

By the time I was thirty-five, I'd scraped and saved and used my veteran's loan to buy a fixer-upper in one of the suburbs of D.C. that Realtors refer to as "up-and-coming," and my neighbors described as "might want to stay away from windows on New Year's Eve." I rescued dogs and friends who fought for space on my couch. I made friends with the first people who were nice to me. I tried like hell to care about football and video games and zombie movies. I watched football. And zombie movies. I mean I had friends who were motherfucking Republicans who prayed before meals. One of them was a goddamn cop. I held onto a job I hated. I even got promoted a couple times because that's what a good Systemite does.

Turning off my mind turned out to be a useful skill as an adult out in the world. A more useful thing would have been to live a life I didn't want to shut off. I was still struggling in that department. It was fine. I could live in my head. I could read books about the lives I wasn't living. I always had. I would be happy. I would be normal. I'd been blotting out my past, clinging to anything else to define me—jobs, hobbies, friends and relationships. It'll work all right for a while, until you lose something. I mean your identity is glued together with scraps of meaningless pop culture, and your supposed friends only like you when you're funny at parties, and you're so fucking broken inside you're a fucking Jell-O mold held together with duct tape. One leak and it's all coming out.

The leak in this case was a shitty breakup. She was hot and loved books and hated scary movies and loved Patty Griffin and wanted to buy a house with me and have a baby and make a family. And it was all a lie. It's not a great story, really. You're missing nothing here. She's the same as me. She does what she needs to survive. So she agreed with me on everything. We both disappeared. And by the time it ended six months later (lesbians do move fast), there really wasn't much left of me.

Jay showed up one day to find me sitting in the dark, gnawing on a raw zucchini from the garden I'd so carefully planted that spring, now overgrown with weeds. The only reason I was eating anything at all was some deep-seated lizard instinct to survive. The lizard was fucking exhausted.

The fundamental misunderstanding of depression is the idea that the suicidal want to die. I didn't want to die. But some misfire in my brain treats existential pain like a dog reacts to vomiting: *Fuck it. I'm gonna dig a hole to die in.* Even on a good day, my brain will point out a few easy ways out: *Take a hard left in front of that truck. It'll be over before you feel it.* But when it's dark, when I'm hopeless, I'm just white-knuckling my way through the nights for no reason but instinct.

Jay opened the curtains and started collecting the bottles and cans off the coffee table, muttering something like, "Girl. Smells like a dang Wu-Tang Clan concert in here." I might've been going a little heavy on the weed. I told my dog to bite him. My dog refused to bite his favorite uncle.

We brought my dog to the park and sat on a bench smoking while the dogs checked that every dog did indeed have a butt hole. I told Jay I wanted to die. Then I told him I didn't, not really. I wanted to live. I just couldn't find a reason.

Jay said, "Honey, you just need to get laid." (He's a lot better at making me laugh than he is at advice.) But he started telling me about a trip he and his boyfriend were taking. And I thought, *I could go back to Europe.* I must've said it out loud because Jay lit up. I tried to crush the idea with, "I can't afford it." And he said, "Put it on a credit card. So what. You're gonna die anyway, right?" He had a point.

I bought tickets to Europe as a bargain with myself: *Go back, and if you still want to die afterwards . . .* I figured I could mitigate the damage if I slept at campgrounds and hostels. Then I thought, holy shit, I actually know people in Europe.

By 2013, the message board I'd found back in 2005 had moved to a Facebook group.

Listen, there are innumerable reasons to bash social

media, to worry our brains are being rewired to crave likes and retweets like fucking junkies. And like the junkies we've become, we lack the attention span to even read the many well-deserved critiques on social media.

In any case, sure, social media's unraveling our very social fabric. But for cult babies scattered around the globe, not to mention queer kids in Amarillo, social media's allowed us to reach out beyond our little worlds, to talk to others who might understand, to hear voices besides those around us and those in our heads that fill us with shame.

I'd only intended to find a few couches to surf. But in doing so, I found people who understood where I'd been. All that time hiding my past, lying about it to nearly everyone, I'd been constructing a completely false narrative about who I was. With the cult babies, I dropped the pretense entirely. I didn't need them to think I was a good Systemite. I didn't need to pretend I caught that pop culture reference from 1989. I didn't need them to think I was happy. I didn't need them to believe anything at all about me. I could simply tell them the truth. And the truth was, I was completely fucking lost.

I was thirty-six years old and didn't have the first clue how to function as an adult. My dating history was only useful as a cautionary tale. I was stuck in a dead-end, soul- and joint-crushing job in the dying cable industry. And every night, as I sat in traffic on the Wilson Bridge, staring at the spot where she'd proposed to me, I had to fight the urge to floor it into the Potomac.

I couldn't begin to find my identity, much less heal, until it was safe to excavate it from all I'd piled on to hide it. Coming out as gay was easy once I left the military. It was the early aughts; gays were everywhere. I could and did move to a city with a massive gay population, where the shame I felt about my sexuality could be danced away in a sea of others like me.

Cult baby was a little harder. Like I said, I didn't know any. And seeing as how we tend to find any groups suspect, I don't see a cult-pride parade being organized anytime soon. I became adept at blending in, surviving in hostile territory. If someone asked about my childhood, if I couldn't change the subject, I'd claim my parents were hippies. I'd tell stories that were truth adjacent. I really was in Chile under Pinochet, but I'd say my parents were missionaries. I really was near Berlin when the Wall fell, but I'd tell you that I was at boarding school. I just couldn't bring myself to say the real reasons why I knew what I knew. It's a little difficult to connect with other people when you're hiding. But logging into the Facebook group for cult babies was like chatting on Gay .com when I was still in the military. I could be out. I could be me. But it wasn't enough. I needed to feel real offline too.

I landed in Zurich, rented a car, and drove down to Italy, along the sea to Nice. Then I flew to Berlin. Berlin was an afterthought, a cheap way to stay in Europe another week. But I wanted to find the flat where I was born, see my old friends, some new friends I'd been talking to online.

It was strange enough leaving the cult, but a lot of kids never learned their own languages, never lived in their home countries. When they got out of the Family, those who could moved to cities where they had a chance of survival. Berlin being Berlin—a city of immigrants, a haven for artists and anarchists and queers, where everyone speaks English and often three other languages, with free education and a cheap cost of living—an inordinate number of cult babies ended up there.

I'd always loved Berlin, though more in theory than anything else. We left when I was two. But "I'm from Berlin" was a load-bearing part of my story because I couldn't tell the rest. Turned out I loved that city even more in reality—the graffiti, the history, the Wall, the public drinking, the dogs in bars and restaurants and trains, the sense that no one in this city would ever belong anyplace else.

I was staying with a friend of mine I'd known in that other life, where we lived in a chalet in Switzerland and snuck down to the pantry to stick our hands in the Ovaltine jar reserved for pregnant and nursing moms. We'd lick the sticky, delicious crumbles of sugary chocolate protein powder off our hands, check each other's faces for evidence, and scramble back to hang laundry before we were caught.

When Jen picked me up from the airport, she looked the same, hair the color of orange Fanta and freckles on her nose, just a little older, maybe a few more freckles.

That afternoon, Jen's boyfriend, a German DJ named Victor, met us for beers on a footbridge in Kreuzberg. Late summer evening. Everyone in Kreuzberg was out that day, worshipping the sun, everyone carrying an ice cream cone or a beer, or both.

When Jen walked over to the kiosk for more beer, Victor asked me why Berlin. I said I was born in Berlin, and I have friends here. He asked me why I was born here. The first guess is usually military parents. Whatever someone guessed, I'd just half-heartedly nod and change the subject.

I didn't know how much he knew. Jen and I hadn't talked about it. I didn't want to out her, but I didn't feel like stretching the truth too far. So I told him, "My parents were missionaries." It's like the pronoun game, for cult babies.

"You must think of a better story," he said. "If someone has to meet more of you than one or two. They tell me the same stupid thing."

That was not a problem that'd ever occurred to me. "So you know," I said.

"It doesn't take long. She has to say something before I meet her friends? Some are not so . . . You are sometimes odd, I think." I appreciated that he was trying to tamp his German bluntness.

Jen returned with the beer. "You should say maybe the circus," Victor said. "Can you make these animals, from balloons?" (In case clowns don't already give you the creeps, sometime after I left, the Family's next big push, their new fundraising method, was "clowning.")

I told Jen I'd given him the missionary line. She laughed. "No one cares," she said. "We're not even that interesting here." As if to prove her point, an old woman shuffled over to us. In her arms, she carried a stuffed hedgehog on a leash, a hedgehog identical to the toy my dog played with at home, but she had no dog that I could see. She set the hedgehog down, picked up our empty bottles, and shuffled off, dragging the hedgehog behind her. No one seemed to notice her.

I thought, if that were true in Berlin, it could be true anywhere. That week in Berlin, not having to hide, my past just being a thing about me as interesting as, well, my being a dyke, it was like driving up to Provincetown for the weekend when you're a closet case stationed in South Carolina, holding hands with a girl in public, making out with a stranger. Makes it really goddamn hard to go back to the closet. I finally had to admit I wasn't who I'd been trying so hard to be. All that time surviving, I'd forgotten to live. I'd been pitying myself for a past I couldn't change, and I'd refused to consider that I still had a future.

I started writing the truth. Just little stories at first. I'd never show them to anyone. But I'd told myself to get my shit together. Writing was my way of taking a nightmare, studying it in the daylight, and realizing the monsters were just shadows, or, in my case, hippies at that second location you're supposed to avoid. And the thing is, I wasn't even the one who followed the hippies. The fuck was I so ashamed of. I started telling friends, "By the way, I lied to you about everything."

My technique needed finessing. But among the many problems with hiding my past, refusing to think of it, is I'd reduced my story to that entry in a listicle. "Weird Sex Cult." Everyone still wants to know about the sex. But now I know how to tell them that you can get used to anything. It's not like girls outside a cult are spared adult men groping them or boys being generally gross. Mostly it just meant I changed a lot of diapers.

All those memories that plagued me and filled me with

self-loathing and self-pity, when I wrote them down, said them out loud, tried to explain them to someone else, they were too fucking absurd to hold the power I'd given them. I mean some of it, a lot of it, is objectively fucking funny. I'd been terrified of people so paranoid they prayed against evil spirits hiding in grocery bags and burned Dolly Parton tapes to prevent feminist influence. I'd made monsters of people who believed in a fucking drunk who told them heaven was in the moon.

It turns out I have a second coming out story. Because I'm fucking proud of the kid I was. I'm proud I resisted. I'm proud I smuggled a radio into my room. I'm proud that I punched boys who got handsy. I'm proud I read hidden books in the bathroom at night. I'm proud that I was a stubborn, defiant little lesbian who made them work so hard to break me. I'm proud of every time I patched myself together and kept going when I was broken.

The last thing I expected was that once I told the truth, I'd find that others with their so-called normal childhoods could relate. I mean, the Republicans and the cop I knew don't talk to me anymore. But those are historically the kind of friends you lose when you come out.

I found there's always been a place I belonged; I just needed to expand the borders of my world from coworkers and friends I'd made for no other reason than they were nice to me. It started with finding other cult babies. But telling the truth about my past is a pretty effective asshole test. Allowing myself to be exactly who I've always been, not feigning interest in video games or zombie shows, means I end up with the sort of friends I once fantasized of having—people who read books, people who've been other places, people who tell the truth, people on the edges who've never fit in and were way ahead of me in accepting that—but I never noticed them because I was trying so desperately to be normal. I don't know what normal is anymore. I know I don't want any part of it.

Pet Snakes

The first time I tried to buy drugs in Austin, I ended up sitting on the edge of some guy's waterbed while he explained the belt drive on his record player. Or maybe his record player was better because it didn't have a belt drive. I wasn't listening because I didn't give a shit. He said the waterbed was vintage, but I think I've got it beat. When did they start adding bookshelves to the headboards, mid-'80s? It doesn't matter. The point is, I'm too fucking old to be sitting in a studio apartment, pretending to be impressed by a record collection. But this is what we do in states run by evangelical zealots who won't legalize marijuana.

I'm lucky this is my problem with buying drugs. There's little chance I'll get pulled over on the way home. If I do, it's unlikely a cop will search me. If he finds drugs, I probably won't get worse than probation. Seems a little cavalier considering I've actually been to jail. But it's been a while.

———

After jail, I was as paranoid about cops and drugs as a QAnon believer is about the deep state. I treated that paranoia the same way I dealt with my fear of snakes. I learned everything there was to know, which wasn't all that hard since I'd accidentally made friends with a cop. (I mean, he wasn't a cop when I met him.) But being friends with a cop meant hanging out with cops because cops are like the kids in high school who lived at the mall. They cannot be alone.

Cops watch *COPS* and talk about cop stuff and ogle pictures on the Internet of cop cars and trade cop patches and unironically argue donut brands. (Do not, if you ever find yourself surrounded by cops debating Krispy Kreme vs. Dunkin', ask if they hold strong opinions on bacon. It's like making a zombie-Jesus joke around Branch Davidians. Your chances of being shot for it are about the same.)

As a friend of a cop, I went on ride-alongs to watch cops be cops—mostly run the plates on any car they deemed suspect. A suspect car, according to cops, is any car that looks different, driven by anyone who looks nervous or Black. And any car with a Cowboys bumper sticker if the Redskins lost last night. (I'm not kidding. Imagine the most rabid sports fan you know. Now give him a hangover and a gun. Might be wise to remove your bumper stickers.)

This is what I learned from my research: Cops are dumb as shit. They're insular and thin-skinned and get off on making people cry. They're misogynists. They're racists. And they don't generally give a shit about pot.

But pot has a strong smell and they'll use the excuse if they need to make quota, or if they don't like you.

Mostly I learned that I cannot be friends with cops.

I can, however, drive a boring vehicle and keep it reasonably clean. I can live in cities where weed busts aren't a priority, because even in a state like Texas, a local liberal electorate has a little bit of sway over cop priorities. And I can make sure I'm never carrying enough for a felony. Felony busts are worth a lot of points on a cop's monthly quota.

What I'm saying is I live in Austin, and the only time I carry anything close to an ounce is driving directly home from a dealer's shitty studio apartment. And having driven a work van for ten years with a complaint number on the back of it, I long ago lost the inclination to speed. I fucking use a turn signal pulling into a parking space. That's not to negate the main reason I feel safe: I'm white. And I can scrape together enough for a lawyer.

That doesn't mean it's not a pain in the ass to have to sit on a waterbed in a cloud of patchouli listening to Ryan tell me I've never really heard Fleetwood Mac. I mean, really *heard* them, you know?

It's always some guy named Ryan or Greg or Brad. Waterbed guy's a Ryan. As far as Ryans go, he's not the worst. Last Ryan I had was back in Virginia, right after I'd quit my bar job to move to the suburbs. That Ryan had a pet lizard and a lot of questions about my sex life.

After pet-lizard Ryan, my next guy was a Brad who owned a pet snake. And I hadn't yet gotten over my fear of snakes. A good rule is if your new pot dealer has a pet snake, find a new pot dealer. He's going to make you watch him feed the snake. It's only a matter of time. But I had to keep going to Brad because he was my girlfriend Autumn's buddy from back in high school.

He and Autumn talked once about how he'd make a great sperm donor. But he wanted to do it naturally. Autumn never mentioned it to me. Brad made it a point to fill me in while I watched his on-screen character bum-rush another heavily armed soldier, then teabag the corpse. The shirtless guy on the couch laughed.

There's always a guy on the couch—shirt optional—smoking free pot. The couch guy rarely talks. He mostly sits there, breathing heavily, fondling the Xbox controller in his lap, trying to hide the fact he's in love with Ryan or Greg or Brad. Anytime a couch guy does talk, I immediately miss the heavy breathing.

This guy—who had opted out of the shirt—was waiting for Brad to go into the bedroom to get the pot so he could ask me the next question on his list of shit that douchebags on couches ask lesbians: "Like, if you're using a dildo, what's the difference anyway?" He'd have to wait until next time. Brad wanted me to watch a squeaking mouse drop to a certain death in a terrarium.

I managed to leave with the bag before the snake felt hungry.

I was glad I was already stoned. Pot dealers like you to smoke on arrival. It makes them feel safe. It makes me feel a little less like screaming.

I was buying pot to numb the panic attacks. I didn't know they were panic attacks at first. I knew sometimes I couldn't breathe and the world closed in around me. I knew a simple thing like a roommate playing the radio while cleaning the apartment or people talking over music at a house party could overwhelm me, cause my hands to shake and my skin to piss sweat. I knew a smell like patchouli or rotten leaves could make me hide in a bathroom to beat my fists against my legs and vomit. I knew if I smoked before I lost the ability to flick a lighter, I might be okay. I knew this all began after some drunk asshole raped me back when I was in the Air Force. I just didn't like naming the problem. Naming the problem felt like acceptance. I was fine. I smoked a little pot. Who doesn't.

Having to then hang out in some asshole's apartment—minimally furnished in early-aughts Ikea, '90s left-on-the-curb, my-mom-gave-me-that, and a bong collection—watching guys build out their *Call of Duty* load, listening to jokes over the rage-rock playlist while a usually shirtless guy asked me questions about my sex life, in order to get the drugs I needed to deal with some guy who'd copped a feel at work seemed a little fucking excessive. But there was no other fucking option. This was the Maryland suburbs, and pot wouldn't be legal in even California or Colorado for several years.

The panic attacks had been getting worse because I was working as a cable tech, walking into strangers' houses and all too often completely at the mercy of some guy. Then I went to jail, where they locked me in a cinder block cell for a week. I stopped smoking pot because I was on probation.

I stopped sleeping, staying up later and later each night to avoid falling asleep, only to wake up paralyzed, a nightmare I couldn't remember just at the edges of my mind. I'd sleepwalk through my workday, stay up until four a.m., sleepwalk through another. The way my shifts

were structured—two on, one off, two on, two off—
every other day was Friday. I slept through my days off.
The sunlight through the window told my mind I wasn't
in a cell.

That lasted a couple weeks, until it didn't. I was con-
necting a ground wire to the cinder block wall of a customer's basement, tears streaming down my face. The
tears had become a regular occurrence. I hid my eyes
behind sunglasses when I could. When I couldn't: "It's
just allergies. I need to see if I can get a shot. Honey
works? Wow. I'll try that."

Anyway, I was screwing this little ground wire into
place. The next thing I knew, I was sitting on the concrete floor of a basement with a profoundly kind woman's hand on my chest telling me I was okay. I was safe.
A broken glass of water on the floor next to her skirt.
A laundry basket she'd dropped next to the unfinished
stairs. I'd pissed myself.

She told me not to worry about it. She was pregnant.
She did it all the time.

I'm grateful it was her. My last customer had been a
gun nut who sprayed cologne on that morning like he
was trying to kill a cockroach. I don't know how comforting he'd have been during a panic attack.

My boss sent me home and told me to get a doctor's
note. I could file for temporary disability for PTSD.
The VA doctor signed the paperwork and said, "I'm just
going to write that you can't be in basements or near
men. Unless they can figure out how you can do your
job without that, you can take some time."

I figured I'd do what I'd always done, any goddamn
chance I got. I would read. Escape to another world,

another life, until I could face my own. But in an unusu-
ally dick move, even given its long history of sabotage,
my brain forgot how to recognize words. I don't mean
that I forgot the word "aphasia." I mean that I couldn't
remember the word "book." I'd have to read a page five
times for anything to make sense. And I'd forget it all
halfway through the next page. But I didn't want to
be around people on account of my eyes leaking, and I
wasn't all that big a fan of most people. I tried television. But daytime television is geared toward the unem-
ployed, and the ads for mesothelioma lawsuits, for-profit
college grifts, and disability scams made my depression
seem like a reasonable condition, considering my future.
Luckily my roommate had an Xbox.

My experience with video games was that I'd often, in
supposedly social settings, had to watch people, mostly
guys, play video games. People who play video games
universally assume this is something anyone would
find entertaining. I'd rather shove lit cigarettes into my
vagina. But my roommate wasn't home. I turned on the
machine, waited for something to load, and there it was,
Call of Duty. I had to sit through some patriotic music,
run through the tutor setting, and I was born again, a
gamer. I tried live action first, but I could hear those
other fuckers talking about me: "Look at this faggot.
The fuck is he even shooting at." I backed out and played
the campaign mode. At least the game didn't call me a
faggot.

Turns out shooting Nazis is a great way to waste a
month of your life. It requires no thought whatsoever.
You run up a hill. Shoot some Nazis. Die. Respawn and
shoot some more Nazis. Take the pie out of the oven. The

pie's not in the game. I'd started baking things because I wanted to feel like I could do anything at all. So I baked. I didn't eat any of it. I had no appetite. But my roommate was more than happy to take pies and cookies and muffins and cakes to work.

I didn't talk to anyone. I didn't leave the house except to walk my dog. I was barely alive, like my system had shut down to save the battery. And once a week, I'd shower so that they wouldn't think I was too far gone, and I'd go see my doctor at the VA.

I'd already been diagnosed with PTSD after the breakup with Autumn, before jail. The doctor who diagnosed me handed me the first of many bottles of correct, legal, get-your-shit-together drugs. Prozac didn't work, so we tried Wellbutrin. When that didn't work, we added Zoloft. Switch one out for Cymbalta. Let's add trazodone. Still crazy? Okay, up the Wellbutrin. You haven't slept in four days and you're seeing patterns in everyone's behavior and you think they're watching you? Maybe we should add Xanax. Oh, you've written a hundred-thousand-word manifesto and think bugs are crawling under your skin. I see. That's no good at all. Let's switch to clonazepam. Have we tried citalopram yet? Let's switch that to Paxil. Tell me more about losing time. Do you mean you can't remember doing things? "Other than actually fucking assaulting someone?" And when you say you're not in your body . . . Maybe we should try lithium.

Here's the thing: these drugs work miracles for most people. Maybe they did work as antidepressants. I could no longer tell if I was depressed. I had that same numb feeling I'd had before, but on the pills, I couldn't laugh, couldn't cry, couldn't fucking scream. I felt nothing except the electricity firing through my brain that had me convinced I was having a stroke. At first the zaps only happened when it was quiet, while I flipped my pillow to the cool side to try to sleep. Then they grew louder. I was shocked no one else could hear them. My brain felt like touching an old console TV. I was trapped behind the screen like a shitty horror movie, screaming at anyone and everyone to let me out. But they just went about their day because all they saw was the blank stare of the heavily medicated. I couldn't sleep. I couldn't eat. I could think about wanting to die, but if I took enough trazodone or clonazepam or whatever they'd given me that week, I could fall asleep without taking any action on the whole wanting-to-die thing except to hope maybe I wouldn't wake up. I fucking dreaded waking up each morning to another day of nothing. Most days I don't remember at all. But I kept taking the pills.

The pills had to work. I was raised by hippies who smeared my feet with chopped garlic to cure the measles and prayed to cure the flu and stuffed garlic in my cheeks to cure swimmer's ear. So I fucking believe in medicine. I believe in vaccines. (Not to mention Q-tips after swimming.) And I truly believed the doctors who told me they just needed to find the right combination.

I went back to work after a month. My eyes had stopped leaking and the panic attacks had subsided, but I was a fucking shell. There was a guy I worked with named Andre, a fat guy with a goofy smile. We were work friends because he'd been in the Navy and his dad

was gay. (Work friends don't require a long list.) He
called me to help out on a job, and afterwards, we were
smoking out by his van and he asked me what I was on.
I told him I wasn't on anything.

He cocked his head like I was full of shit. He said I
was full of shit. "Are you even awake?"

I said I couldn't tell either. I needed to adjust my meds.
I fucking hated that I talked like that now, like a crazy
person whose meds needed to be adjusted. He asked
what I was on and I started listing things. I'm pretty sure
naming more than three items on a list of "What are you
on?" is a sign your doctor might not be listening to you.

He said, "Dude. What are they, trying to make you
happy? You're not a happy person, Hough. It's okay. I
like you grouchy and funny."

I'm not advocating taking medical advice from a dude
at work. But I couldn't get it out of my head, partly on
account of racing, obsessive thoughts being a new side
effect of one or three of the pills I was taking. So I called
Amy, my old bartender friend, and asked her to meet me
for a drink.

Amy was already out for a drink with a couple bartenders I vaguely knew. I met them at Badlands because
we could get a free drink. The guys wanted to go to a different bar, they just had to make a quick stop, and that's
how I accidentally went to a meth deal.

I always did feel cool hanging out with bartenders—
the nods from bouncers, the free drinks, the occasional
wave from someone you only know as "vodka soda,
doesn't tip after the first round." I was glad there were
four of us or I'd have ended up walking a step behind,
which is decidedly uncool. We wound up at an English

basement off Logan Circle. The bartender, who we'll just refer to as Mike because he was one of the bartenders, who were mostly named Mike and if they weren't, they got used to it—anyway, Mike had called ahead but still had to beat on the door for a good five minutes before it was answered by a tweaker whose bones looked ready to break through his skin. He stared at the four of us, looked up and down the street, and said, "Did you bring the batteries?"

Batteries? I looked at Amy, who just shrugged like, *Meth dealers, am I right?*

The tweaker flung open the door, and there, all across his living room floor, were cop-style flashlights in various states of disassembly. The tweaker was rattling off his findings on lumen variations between lenses and bulbs. He was close to figuring it all out. What he was figuring out, you'd have to ask him. I walked out and waited on the steps.

When the bartenders came out and said they had to run to a store to buy batteries, I decided to wait in Logan Circle. The sex workers in the circle, who were smoking my cigarettes, thought this was the funniest, whitest thing they'd ever heard. They told me, "Crack dealers will kill you. Sure. But at least they don't send you on errands."

I tuned them out. I was trying to think and trying not to think all at once. Trying to think about anything else, but I couldn't. I'd just seen myself in the mirror. And it scared the shit out of me. I was down to about 160 pounds. I'd been picking the same scab on my arm for months, convinced it would never heal, which it wouldn't because I couldn't fucking stop picking at it.

And while I wasn't taking apart flashlights, I'd been just as manic about everything from researching cameras I'd never buy, to googling names of everyone who'd ever wronged me. I was as glassy-eyed as a meth head, but my drugs weren't even any fun.

When we were finally alone and I was driving Amy back to her apartment, I asked her if she thought I was acting strange. She'd known me about as long as anyone in D.C., and I figured she'd tell me the truth. She waited a minute and I knew the answer. But it was worse. She said, "I almost didn't answer when you called." It was all I could do to keep the car between the lines.

I flushed every pill I had.

This is not how to come off psychiatric medication. You're supposed to wean yourself with the help of your doctor. But I think we've established that I wasn't exactly thinking straight. So instead of a calm, slow return to something like my normal brain chemistry, I rode out a week of a lightning storm in my brain and mood swings that scared my dog. That poor fucking dog really didn't get the good years of my life. But he slept on my chest when I couldn't stop shaking and head-butted me awake from nightmares and made sure I went outside, whether I liked it or not.

I told myself I was going to feel something again, even if it was pain. I was going to fucking feel it. I just wanted to be me again. I missed me. After months of not even being able to cry, I broke down sobbing one day, sitting in traffic, weeping because my iPod played "Southern Cross." And I was so fucking happy to feel again, I started laughing. I felt like a fucking crazy person. But the thing is, I like being a little crazy, as long as I can feel.

When you've been depressed as long as I have, you get good at it. You develop survival skills or you don't last very long. I know to go outside. I know a sleep schedule helps. I know to make myself exercise, even a little. I know who to call when things get too dark. I know to make myself call. And I know my brain's full of shit. It's like being on psychedelics. You can talk yourself down, tell yourself you're on drugs, none of this is real, it'll pass. I don't know that when I'm on pills. It's hard to tell yourself you'll feel joy again when you don't remember what feelings are.

I was still on probation. Still had to pee in a cup every other month. Which, when I did the math, meant I could smoke pot for a month, suffer thirty days, pee in a cup, and smoke again. Fucking marijuana. It's the least goddamn harmful drug, but goddamn if it doesn't hang out in your pee the longest. I could've been clean from coke, heroin, barbiturates, meth, codeine, PCP, ecstasy, or LSD in one to three days. Smoke a little pot because it actually does fucking help with every goddamn symptom of PTSD, from the constant alertness to pissing myself in a stranger's basement, because I can control the dosage of pot, know how high I'll be and for how long, because I can still feel joy, and my urine is dirty for seven to thirty days. Violation of my probation, which had nothing to do with drugs.

I decided it was worth the risk. Which meant I had to wait in a Greg's apartment watching his avatar wander around a map, picking up random shiny objects, until Greg felt like weighing out a bag. When that Greg stopped answering text messages, because that's what pot dealers do, I got a Brad. Then a Greg, or a Ryan. Then a Brad again. Sometimes back-to-back-to-back Ryans. Maybe a Brian just to mix things up. You get the point.

I have to switch dealers a lot because I don't smoke enough to buy regularly and keep up with their lives. An ounce can last me six months. The downside is, I tend to run out at the worst goddamn times. Like, after a breakup.

I was heartbroken. I tried drinking. I gave it everything I had. But I'd just end up hungover and still heartbroken. The VA offered me pills and a therapy appointment in a few months. I texted every known pothead in my phone but couldn't find a plug.

This is how it goes as you get older. You finally have a little money, enough to blow on a bender. And you cannot fucking find drugs. Everyone's so closeted about their drug use, you don't know who to ask. You're still a little paranoid and don't want your responsible adult friends thinking you're some sort of drug user. You can't just go down to the local high school and ask the stoner crowd. You're a goddamn adult. The only drug users I knew were into coke and meth. They're great if you want someone to clean your house and occasionally scream at you about politics or cry about *Buffy the Vampire Slayer*. Not great at finding weed.

They say when you're heartbroken, it's good to distract yourself, volunteer, find something meaningful to devote yourself to. I devoted myself to finding weed. I got a little from a friend at work. But when that ran low, I tried stand-up gigs. I'm serious. I had a friend, this local comic named Lars, who thought stand-up might be good therapy for me. I actually went to open mic nights, got up on stage, and asked if anyone was holding, explained why I couldn't find drugs because I look like a cop, told them the story about walking into a bar one night and watching the obvious drug dealer with the backpack panic and run out. The crowd thought it was hilarious. But it wasn't exactly a bit. Not one person fucking offered me drugs.

I would like to add, for the record, that since I'm now open about my drug use, I'm now the person every responsible adult who'd like to use drugs—relatives, bosses, neighbors and friends—asks for drugs. Be the change.

One place I did know to find weed was a concert. And I had tickets. (The moment this occurred to me included a pathetic sob because "we were . . . supposed . . . to go . . . together.") I was a goddamn mess. No one in my condition needed to attend a Citizen Cope concert. But I had two tickets to his sold-out show at the 9:30 Club. Even in a better time, I couldn't go alone. I don't like crowds, but I'm usually all right with another person. So I put an ad on Craigslist: "Face value or whatever you have to start my bender." Within an hour my inbox was a cornucopia of drugs. Every Cope fan in D.C., and it's his hometown, was sending me pictures of fucking drugs—weed, ecstasy, coke, acid tabs—mostly weed and acid. It's a tribute to Citizen Cope's music, really.

I was proud of my ingenuity until the guy showed up. His polo shirt was tucked neatly into his Dockers and his shoes had been shined, actually hand-shined. He wore wraparound Oakleys. He looked like a cop. I told him so.

He said, "Yeah, well, so do you."

I'd tried to not look like a cop. I really did. I mean that my jeans had holes in them and I'd tousled my hair.

What else can you do. My roommate and I had smoked some of the little we had in the living room just before the guy's arrival. But it didn't help. And he wasn't wrong. I do look like that dyke cop who mocked you for crying about the speeding ticket. It's the haircut, mostly.

Anyway, we were at an impasse. I couldn't smoke in front of him to assuage his fears. He sure as fuck wasn't going to smoke in front of someone who was definitely a cop. We probably stood there in my living room for a solid ten minutes trying to solve the problem when my sketchy roommate with the cock-ring gauges in her ears came up from the basement to ask me for a lighter. She saw the obvious cop in my living room and startled, dropped the bowl, and dropped to her knees, picking at the carpet, saying, "My drugs. Oh no. Not my drugs."

Someday I'll move somewhere where weed is legal, or they'll legalize it everywhere. Someday. Until then, at least the current guy doesn't have a snake.

After Ryan with the waterbed, I got a job bouncing at a gay bar. Part of my job was telling people to please not smoke pot on the patio. Are you serious? Go around the corner so you're not on our property. I simply waited until a regular lit up on the patio, and I asked him for his plug, and to please go around the corner to smoke. I finally have a pot dealer who doesn't own a reptile or a record collection or a waterbed. And the guy on his couch is a drag queen, who has a lot of scissoring jokes.

While I can feel relatively safe buying drugs from a dealer, and while you can walk into a store in LA or Portland or Denver, show your ID, and pick out a designer brand of weed, some gummies, and a new vape pen, there are people sitting in cells for years, for fucking decades, because a cop didn't like them, because of the color of their skin, because he saw the bumper sticker of a team he hated on their car and ran their plates and found a dead inspection. And when he searched their car, because of the color of their skin, because they hurt his delicate ego by not calling him "sir," the cop found a long-forgotten roach under their seat.

If I lived in nearly any state but Texas, I could get a medical license for PTSD and depression—not at the VA, though. While my current VA doctor knows how I treat my symptoms and would gladly prescribe marijuana based on countless studies proving its efficacy, she's barred by federal law from prescribing it. They can prescribe me anything but the one thing I know helps. And every time I drive home from a dealer's house, I risk going to jail, not to mention a small fortune in lawyer's fees, because the pills didn't work.

Cable Guy

I can't tell you about a specific day as a cable tech. I can't tell you my first customer was a cat hoarder. I can tell you the details, sure. That I smeared Vicks on my lip to try to cover the stench of rugs and walls and upholstery soaked in cat piss. That I wore booties, not to protect the carpets from the mud on my boots but to keep the cat piss off my soles. I can tell you the problem with her cable service was that her cats chewed through the wiring. That I had to move a mummified cat behind the television to replace the jumper. That ammonia seeped into the polyester fibers of my itchy blue uniform, clung to the sweat in my hair. That the smell stuck to me through the next job.

But what was the next job? This is the shit I can't remember—how a particular day unfolded. Maybe the next job was the Great Falls, Virginia, housewife who answered the door in some black skimpy thing I never really saw because I work very hard at eye contact when faced with out-of-context nudity. She was expecting a man. I'm a six-foot lesbian. If I showed up at your door in a uniform with my hair cut in what's known to barbers as the International Lesbian Option No. 2, you might mistake me for a man. Everyone does. She was rare in that she realized I'm a woman. We laughed about it. She found a robe while I replaced her cable box. She asked if I needed to use a bathroom, and I loved her.

For ten years, I worked as a cable tech in the Virginia suburbs of Washington, D.C. Those ten years, the apartments, the McMansions, the customers, the bugs and snakes, the telephone poles, the traffic, the cold and heat and rain, have blurred together in my mind. Even then, I wouldn't remember a job from the day before unless there was something remarkable about it. Remarkable is subjective and changes with every day spent witnessing what people who work in offices will never see—their coworkers at home during the weekday, the American id in its underpants, wondering if it remembered to delete the browsing history.

Mostly all I remember is needing to pee.

And I remember those little glimpses of the grotesque. The one that comes to mind now is the anti-gay lobbyist whose office was lined with framed appreciation from Focus on the Family, and pictures with Pat Buchanan and Jerry Falwell, but whose son's room was painted pink and littered with Barbies. The hypocrite's son said he was still a boy. He just thought his sundress was really cute. I agreed, told him I love daisies, and he beamed. His father thanked me, and I wanted to tell him to go fuck himself. How the fuck do you actively work to ensure the world's a more dangerous place for your beautiful little kid? But I didn't ask him that. I just stood and glared at him until he looked away. I needed the job. I assumed his kid would grow up to hate him.

Maybe the next job that day was the guy whose work order said "irate." It's not something you want to see on a work order. Not when you're running late and you still have to pee because "irate" meant that the next job wasn't going to be a woman in lingerie; it was going to be a guy who pulled out his penis while I fixed the settings on his television.

I know after that one, I pulled off the side of the road when I saw a horse. Only upside of Great Falls: Not too long ago, Great Falls was mostly small farms and large estates. The McMansions outnumber the farms now, but there are still a few holdouts. I was sent to the area often enough that I'd started carrying carrots or apples in my lunchbox. Doesn't take a horse long to recognize a work van. I called the horse over to the fence, and he nuzzled my hair. I fed him my apple. Talking to a horse helps when you can't remember how to breathe.

Maybe that "irate" was an "irate fn ch72 out." Fox News. Those we dreaded. It was worse when the comment was followed by "repeat call." "Repeat" meant someone had been there before. If it was someone I could call and ask, he'd tell me: "Be careful. Asshole kept calling me 'boy.' Rather he just up and call me a [that word]. Yeah, of course I told them. Forwarding you the emails right now. Hang on, I have to merge. Anyway, it's his TV. Dumbass put a plasma above his fireplace. Charge the piece of shit 'cause I warned him. Have fun."

I'd walk in prepared for anything. There was sobbing, man or woman, didn't matter. There were the verbal assaults. There were physical threats. To say they were just threats undermines what it feels like to be in someone else's home, not knowing the territory, where that hallway leads, what's behind that door, if they have a gun, if they'll back you into a wall and scream at you. If they'll stop there. If they'll call in a complaint no matter what you do. Sure, we were allowed to leave if we felt threatened. We just weren't always sure we could. In any case, even if we canceled, someone else would always be sent to the same house later. "Irate. Repeat call." And we'd lose the points we needed to make our numbers.

The points: Every job's assigned a number of points—10 points for a "my cable's out" call, 4 points to disconnect a line, 12 to install Internet. We needed about 120 points a day to make our monthly quota.

A cut cable line was worth 10 points, whether we tried to fix it or not. We could try to splice it if we found the cut. Or we could maybe run a temp line. But you can't run one across a neighbor's lawn or across a sidewalk or street. That's what happened with the guy who was adding a swimming pool. The diggers had cut his line. I knew before I walked in. But he still wanted me to come stare at the blank cable box while we talked. I did because the Fox News cult loves to call in complaints about their rude techs.

The tap, where the cable line connects, was in a neighboring yard. There was a dog door on the back patio of that yard. I like dogs, but I'm not an idiot. I told him it would be a week, seven to ten days to get a new line. He said through his teeth he needed an exact day. I gave him my supervisor's number. This whole time, his wife was in the kitchen wiping a clean counter.

I was filling out the work orders and emailing my supervisor to give him a heads-up on a possible call from a member of every cable tech's favorite rage cult when his wife knocked on my van window. She stepped back and called me "ma'am." Which was nice. Her husband with the tucked-in polo shirt had asked my name and I told him Lauren. He heard Lawrence because it fit what he saw and asked if he could call me Larry. Guys like that use your name as a weapon. "Larry, explain to me why I had to sit around here from one to three waiting on you and you show up at 3:17. Does that seem like good customer service to you, Larry? And now you're telling me seven to ten days? Larry, I'm getting really tired of hearing this shit." Guys like that, it was safer to just let them think I was a man.

She said she was sorry about him. I said, "It's fine." I said there really wasn't anything I could do. She blinked back the flood of tears she'd been holding since god knows when. She said, "It's just, when he has Fox, he has Obama to hate. If he doesn't have that . . ." She kept looking over her shoulder. She was terrified of him. "I'm sorry," she said. "I just need him to have Fox." I got out of my van.

The neighbor with the possible attack dogs wasn't home. The next-door neighbor wasn't either. But I looked up his account. I got lucky. He didn't have TV service.

I pulled up his modem on my laptop, perfect signal. There was an attenuator where the cable connected to his house wiring to tamp down the signal—too much is also a problem. I got enough running a line from the neighbor's house to theirs so the asshole would be able to get his rage fix from Hannity. I remember leaving a note on the neighbor's door, some ambiguous lie about their Internet service being urgent. I figured the neighbor might be more understanding about Internet service than Fox. I sure as fuck was.

Maybe the next job was unremarkable in every way. I liked those jobs. Nothing to remember but maybe a cute dog. Maybe a few spiders. But I'd gotten used to spiders. I don't feel mosquito bites anymore either. If the customer worked any sort of manual job, they'd offer me water. I wouldn't usually accept. But it was a nice gesture.

Blue-collar customers were always my favorite. They don't treat you like a servant. They don't tell you, "We like the help to use the side door." They don't assume you're an idiot just because you wear a name tag to work and your hands are calloused. The books on their shelves aren't bound in leather. But the spines are cracked. Most of them, when you turn on the TV, it's not set to Fox. They're the only customers who tip, and the only customers who won't fuck you for accepting one.

We weren't allowed to take tips. But every so often, a favor like setting up surround sound or an especially hard job like wrapping a house in cable line to get to a back bedroom or extra time in an attic could pay off. Not always. Take a tip from the wrong asshole and they'll mention it when they call in a complaint because they forgot which input their cable's connected to, and, well, that's why you're not allowed to take tips.

Maybe the next job I had to climb into an attic. Maybe it was above 90 outside and 160 up there. I'd sweat out half my body weight, and my skin would itch like hives from the insulation the rest of the day. At some point, I'd blow something black out of my nose. You have to work fast in an attic. You don't come down, not all of these customers would even bother to see if you're at medium rare yet. If the customer had a shred of humanity, you could ask to reschedule for the morning.

Humanity is rarer than I imagined when I first took the job. One woman wanted me to shimmy down into a crawl space that held three feet of water and about a foot to spare under her floorboards. A snake swam past the opening. She said it wasn't a copperhead. Like I fucking cared.

We had a blizzard one year—a few, really. Snowmageddon and Snowverkill and Snowmygod, I think WTOP named them. We had to work. I went to one call where the problem was dead batteries on a remote. They didn't think batteries were their responsibility. The next, they wanted me to replace a downed line. Yes, that's the power line in the tree too. Well, sure the telephone pole's lying in the street, but we figured you could do something. I didn't explain why I didn't get out of my van. I took a picture and sent it to my supervisor with "Bullshit."

Most of the streets were blocked. Thirty-five inches is a lot of snow. A state trooper told me to get the fuck off the road. My supervisor said, "We can't. We do phone, so we're considered emergency service." I didn't have any phone jobs. No one else I talked to did either.

The supervisors made a good show of pretending to care that we made it to jobs. The dispatchers canceled everything they could. The techs, we didn't talk much. Every so often someone would mic their Nextel to scream: "This is bullshit! They're going to get us fucking killed!" And someone else would say, "They don't care, man. They won't have to pay anyway. They'll piss-test your corpse and say you were high. Motherfuckers."

"They'll fucking care when I plow my van through the front of their building."

"Dude, I'm gonna ram the next little Ford Ranger I see." Supervisors drove Rangers.

"Fuck that. I'm ramming a cop."

"Bitch, how you gonna know what you're ramming? Can't fucking see the snowplow in front of me."

I couldn't respond. My voice would stand out. We had to hope for the humanity of others, the customers, because corporate didn't care. They didn't have to drive through a blizzard. The blizzards, I remember.

The other days, they all blended together. Let's go back to imaginary day. Maybe next I had the woman with the bullmastiff named Otto. I don't remember much about her because I like bullmastiffs with their giant stupid heads. I told her I needed to get to her basement. She said, "Do you really? It's just it's a mess." (That's never why.) I explained the signal behind her television was crap. The signal outside her house was great. With only one line going through the cinder block wall, there was probably a splitter. She was taller than I am. That's something I

remember because, like I said, I'm tall. Height was probably a useful trait for her considering what I found next.
I told her what I told everyone who balked about their
privacy being invaded: "Unless you have a kid in a cage, I
don't fucking care." Kids in cages were an unimaginable
horror then. A good place to draw a line.

This is a good time to say, if you're planning on growing massive quantities of marijuana, look, I respect it.
But don't use a three-dollar splitter from CVS when you
run your own cable line. Sooner or later, you'll have a
cable tech in your basement. And you'll feel the need to
give them a freezer bag full of pot to relieve your paranoia. Which is appreciated, don't get me wrong. Ston-
ers, I adore you. I mean it. You never yell. I can ask to
use your bathroom because you're stoned. You never call
in complaints. But maybe behind the television isn't the
most effective place to hide your bong when the cable
guy's coming over.

Anyway, Otto's mom laughed and said, "Not a kid." It
took me a second. She went down to get his permission.
And I was allowed down into a dungeon where she had
a man in a cage. I don't remember if she had a bad splitter. So that was probably early on. After a few years, not
even a dungeon was interesting. Sex workers tip, though.
Not that it's always obvious.

Some houses, I could tell you from the kitchen with
absolute certainty there was a sex swing in the basement,
piled with laundry next to that elliptical machine they
bought with similar intentions, also now used exclu-
sively to hang laundry. I could tell before I knocked on a

door whether or not anyone was home. I could tell you, just standing in their living room, if they had a swastika hanging in the basement. The Nazis weren't always that subtle, even back then. The preppers, Nazis or otherwise, rarely surprised me—their tactical boots and tactical belts tend to give them away—but I never stayed longer than I had to.

At one such house, I found a mini-cult of preppers. I knew there were too many people living in one house by the shoes piled next to the door. A teenage boy with a tragic case of acne had been assigned to escort me through the house. The living room had been retrofitted as a classroom, complete with a blackboard, times table charts, a Christian flag for morning allegiance, and a row of computers along the back wall.

Five kids, all about eight or nine, were sitting on the carpet, debating the finer plot points of one of those rapture novels. My jaw tightened just hearing them. I wondered if we were that obvious when we were kids. Probably.

The computers were useless because they'd tried to run their own cable with shitty RadioShack wiring that had basically become an antenna, feeding every radio and television signal into their modem. No modem in the living room. I trailed the body odor of my teenage escort as he led me down the hall, past rooms full of bunk beds and a room that held more than one crying baby being calmed by a teenage girl. I wanted to run before we got to the basement stairs. Maybe if I started shouting "God is dead," they'd throw me out, and it would sound just crazy enough as an accusation that my boss wouldn't believe them.

The basement was a prepper's wet dream—rows upon rows of metal shelves stocked with everything from tubs of lard to sacks of whole wheat, boxes upon boxes of batteries, and an entire shelving unit of gauze and bandages. And there, above the flashing modem on the back wall, a fucking armory.

My only strong opinion on guns is most people who want them shouldn't own any. I spent many an Air Force Saturday night shooting bottles lined up on cinder blocks out in the country. It's fun. We told ourselves we were responsible because we yelled "clear" and "firing" a lot. My dad and my uncles and cousins and friends hunt. I have friends who collect guns, fewer these days. More than a few got rid of them after Sandy Hook. But I've read enough and seen enough to know the "good guy with a gun" is a masturbatory fantasy right alongside "we're just preparing in case we have to defend ourselves from a tyrannical government." And I know a goddamn cult when I see one.

I told the kid I could charge him something outrageous for the work, or he could rip out all those wires they'd added, connect our line to the modem, and he'd be a hero. He chose the correct option. I got the fuck out of there without asking if he wanted to subscribe to HBO.

I wouldn't have tried anyway. I hated selling. I thought knocking on doors would be my problem. I'd lasted about four hours knocking on doors for the Sierra Club, never went back after lunch. And I never quite got used to it. I'd have to pause every time before I knocked, shift my tools to my left hand, back to the right, breathe, count to three . . . knock. Like jumping from the high board. But it was the selling—my hard limit. I just couldn't do it.

Maybe it was all those days selling posters and tapes as a kid, preying on people kind or annoyed enough to buy something they didn't want or need. But I cannot sell. I couldn't tell someone whose Internet hadn't been working right for months that if they just upgraded to the faster tier, the problem would be solved. I couldn't tell someone who couldn't afford a bed frame that the sports package was what they needed to sleep at night. And I sure as fuck couldn't lie and tell them I'd hook them up with free premium channels for their troubles, and not mention if they didn't call to cancel in a month, their next bill would knock the air out of them. That's how I was told to sell. Every guy who thought he'd give me a little advice because my sales were down and somehow the techs meant to fix your cable are also required to sell you more cable: "Just tell them you're hooking them up. They can get it taken off if they call. Who gives a shit." I did. Selling something to someone, asking someone to buy something they didn't want and I didn't believe in, it tasted like after you've gone too far in an argument, said that one thing you know landed and hurt them and you can't take it back. It tasted like shit. So I didn't sell. I'd make my sales numbers by fixing the ridiculous packages our sales reps shoved into new orders. *Do you, gaming nerd, and your Korean grandma actually watch a lot of football? If I take that off, you can get the Korean channel for two dollars less a month. Did you request the news package, frazzled single mom who doesn't have time to do her roots? There's a kid's package you might get more use out of, same price.* Maybe the next house was a finance guy who didn't need movie channels but didn't know he could get even more news.

Maybe my next job was a short little fucker who walked like a little teapot and beat his kids. Sometimes you can tell. Some of us recognize the look in their eyes, the bite of fear in the air. He followed me into the office. And he rubbed himself against my ass when I leaned over to unplug the modem. I let it happen that time. Sometimes you know which guys you can't fight back against.

There were a lot of those. Those I never forgot. They seep into your skin like cat piss. But you can't shower them off. It's part of why I didn't mind most people assuming I was a man. Each time I had to calculate the odds of something worse against the odds of getting back to my van.

Once it was an El Salvadoran guy in a tiny two-bedroom apartment full of El Salvadoran guys. Those apartments were common. Day laborers crowded into apartments to save money to send back home or pay off coyotes. Their pallets folded against the walls. Cheap Walmart steel-toes piled by the door. The kind of boots that break down within a month. A saint and prayer candles above the television. The apartment smelled like sweat and tortillas. I liked those apartments. The buildings were roach-infested shitholes. But the day laborer bunk rooms, they usually helped tack down the lines I had to run from the single living room outlet to the bedrooms.

That time, the guys heard me yelling and barged

in. Their roommate had copped a feel, ran his hand between my legs while I was bent over the television. I had him pinned against the wall. One of them, the English speaker, took charge. He said they'd take care of it. A couple guys dragged him to the back room. The foreman said, "Please, no police. We will make him stop this, yes?" I liked the look in his eye. I needed the points for the job anyway.

They helped finish the install. The foreman offered me a beer. I turned him down. He helped me carry my tools and step ladder back to my van. He said he was saving money for his wife and his daughter to come. They were safe. But only for so long. He showed me a picture of his daughter. I knew he was showing me why I shouldn't call the police. If I had, it would've been the first time. No one deserves what our government will do to them—the guys who helped me, who were just trying to survive, who no one minds hiring for jobs we wouldn't lower ourselves to do, who our leaders happily vilify so you don't notice they're fucking you too. But I worry even telling this story, if you're an asshole, you think they're all the same.

The foreman promised me again he'd take care of it. I believed him. We shook on it.

One of those creeps, his suit cost more than my car. I can't fathom what his smile cost. He had an elevator in his three-story McMansion. Maybe he thought he owned me too. I broke his nose with my linesman's pliers. Nice heft to those linesman's pliers. He'd called me a dyke. I hope I ruined his suit. I lost the points.

I made it back to my van. My van became my home,

my office, my dining room. I was safe in my van. In my van, I could pull off near a park for a few minutes, smoke a cigarette, read the news, check Facebook, breathe until I stopped shaking, until I stopped crying. That's only if there was someplace to pull over, preferably in the shade. We were monitored by GPS. But if I stayed close enough to the route, I could always claim traffic. This was Northern Virginia. There was always traffic.

Maybe that's why I was running late to the next job, and my dispatcher, my supervisor, another dispatcher, and the dispatch supervisor called to ask my ETA. No, that job canceled.

"Irate" doesn't always mean irate. Sometimes it just means he's had three techs out to fix his Internet and not one has listened to him. They said it was fixed. He was bidding last night on a train. It was a special piece. He'd seen only one on eBay in five years. One. He showed me his collection. His garage was the size of my high school gym. But his sensible Toyota commuter box was parked out front. His garage was for the trains. He had the Old West to the west. And Switzerland to the east. But the train he wanted went to someone in Ohio because his Internet went out again and he lost the auction. He wasn't irate. He was heartbroken, and no one would listen.

I remember he started clicking a dog-training clicker when I said the signal was good behind the modem. He said he was sorry. The clicker helped when he was feeling overwhelmed. I said I should probably try it. My dentist didn't like the way I clenched my teeth. He said, "They all come here and say it's okay, but it goes out again."

This was probably around the time my supervisor realized I was pretty good at fixing the jobs the guys couldn't, or wouldn't. And really good with the customers who'd had enough. The guys looked at cable as a science. Name a channel, they'd tell you the frequency. They could tell you the attenuation per hundred feet of any brand of cable. The customers were just idiots who didn't know bitrate errors from packet loss. I looked at cable like plumbing, or something like that. I like fixing things. Some customers were idiots. Most just wanted things to work the way they were promised. This guy's plumbing had a leak. I didn't pay attention in class when they explained why interference could be worse at night, or I forgot it soon after the test. I knew it was, though. So when he said the problem only happened at night, I started looking for a leak. One bad fitting outside. Three guys missed it because they didn't want to listen to him. Because he was different. Because he was a customer. And customers are all idiots.

I remember training a guy around the time I was six years in. He'd been hired at five dollars more an hour than I was making, 31 percent more. I asked around. We weren't allowed to discuss pay. But we weren't allowed to smoke pot and most of us did. We weren't allowed to work on opiates either. We were all working hurt. I can't handle opiates. But if I'd wanted them, there were plenty of guys stealing them from customers' bathrooms. I could've bought what I needed after any team meeting.

That's the thing they don't tell you about opiate addiction. People are in pain because unless you went to college, the only way you'll earn a decent living is by breaking your body or risking your life—plumbers, electricians, steamfitters, welders, mechanics, cable guys, linemen, fishermen, garbagemen, the options are endless.

They're all considered jobs for men because they require a certain amount of strength. The bigger the risk, the bigger the paycheck. But you don't get to take it easy when your back hurts from carrying a ninety-pound ladder that becomes a sail in the wind. You don't get to sit at a desk when your knees or ankles start to give out after crawling through attics, under desks, through crawl spaces. When your elbow still hurts from the time you disconnected a cable line and your body became the neutral line on the electrical feeder and 220 volts ran through your body to the ground. When your hands become useless claws thirty feet in the air on a telephone pole and you leave your skin frozen to the metal tap. So you take a couple pills to get through the day, the week, the year. If painkillers show up on your drug test, you have that prescription from the last time you fell off a roof. Because that's the other thing about these jobs: they all require drug tests when you get hurt. Smoke pot one night, whether for fun or because you hurt too much to sleep, the company doesn't have to pay for your injury when your van slides down an icy off-ramp three weeks later. I chose pot to numb my head and body every night. But it was the bigger risk.

I probably should've stolen pills. It would have made up for the fact I was making less than every tech I asked. They don't like you talking about your pay for a reason. Some had been there longer. Most hadn't. I was the only female tech because really, why the fuck was I even doing that job? Because I didn't go to college. I joined the

Air Force. They kicked me out for being gay. I'd since worked at a gay bar, Home Depot, Starbucks, Lowe's, 7-Eleven, a livery service, construction, a dog groomer, and probably ten more shitty jobs along the way. Until I was offered a few dollars more, just enough to pay rent, as a cable guy.

My supervisor hadn't known, said he didn't know our pay. But he said he'd take care of it, and he did. He said the problem was my numbers were always lower than most of the guys. All those points I mentioned. So my raises over the years had always been lower. The math didn't quite work, but it was mostly true. My numbers were always lower. Numbers were based mostly on how many jobs we completed a day. On paper, the way we were rated, I was a terrible employee. That I was a damn good tech didn't matter. The points were what mattered. The points, I'm realizing now, were why I spent the better part of ten years thinking about bathrooms.

The guys could piss in apartment taprooms, any slightly wooded area, against a wall with their van doors open for cover, in Gatorade bottles they collected in their vans. I didn't have those options. And most customers, I wouldn't ask. If I had to pee, I had to drive to a 7-Eleven or McDonald's or grocery store, not all of which have public bathrooms. I knew every clean bathroom in the county. I knew the bathrooms with a single stall because the way I look, public bathrooms aren't always safe for me either. But they don't plant a 7-Eleven between the McMansions of Great Falls. One bathroom break and I was already behind.

The guys could call for help on a job. No problem. If

I called, some of them wouldn't answer. Some I'd asked before and taken shit for not being able to do something they couldn't have done either. One of them told me my pussy smelled amazing while he held a ladder for me. One never stopped asking if I'd ever tried dick. Said I needed his. And for the most part, I liked to tell myself I could handle their taunts and harassment. But I wasn't calling them for help. Sometimes I'd have to reschedule the job because there was no one around I could ask for help. Rescheduling meant I'd lose even more points that day.

So my numbers were lower than the men's. I never had a shot at being a good employee really, not by their measure. Well, there was one way.

I worked with an older guy, a veteran like me. I usually got along with the veterans. He was no exception. Once, after I explained why I called him for help, he told me that he understood. He said he found vets were less likely to treat him like shit for being Black. Higher odds they'd worked with a Black guy before. That made sense. But when I asked him how he kept his points up, seeing as how he worked slower than the other guys, he said he clocked out at seven every day. Worked the last job for free. It brought up his average. I wasn't willing to work for free.

One year, though, the company tried a little experiment: choose a couple of people from each team, let them take the problem calls, those jobs a couple of techs had failed to fix, and give them the time to actually fix the problem.

Time was the important thing. Time is why I can't tell

you what day or week or year a thing happened. Because for the ten years I was a cable tech, there was no time. I rushed from one job to the next, sometimes typing on the laptop, usually on the phone with a dispatcher, supervisor, customer, or another tech. Have to pee, run behind, try to rush the next so the customer doesn't call and complain you're late, dispatch gives the call to another tech, lose the points. The first few years, I was reading a map book to find the house. Then crawling down the street, counting up from 70012 because I needed house number 70028 but no one else on the street thought it important to put numbers on their house. They'd tell me I needed to pick up my numbers. One more bad month and I was out of a job. Maybe you can understand why I avoided canceling anything but the most dangerous jobs.

After a few years, I spent most of my days off recovering. I'd get home and couldn't read a page in a book and remember what I'd read. I was depressed. But I didn't know it. I was too tired to consider why I couldn't sleep, why I'd stopped eating, why I was so ashamed of what my life had become.

Sometimes at night, when I couldn't sleep, I'd think of the next ten years doing the same fucking thing every day until my knees or ankles no longer worked or my back gave out. I thought maybe the best thing that could happen was that if I got injured seriously enough, but not so seriously I'd forget the synthetic urine I kept in my lunch cooler, I could maybe try to survive on workers' comp. Most mornings, I woke and it took a minute to decide: Do I want to die today? I guess I can take one more day. If I can just make it to my day off. I tried to go to school for a while, but I was too tired to learn coding. And anyway, I missed most of the classes because I'd have to work late.

That one year, though, being a cable tech wasn't all that bad. I'd start in the morning with a couple of jobs. And the rest of the day they'd throw me one problem job at a time. And I had all the time in the world to fix them. It's how I became the Cheneys' tech.

My supervisor called and said, "Look at the work order I just dropped you. You're gonna thank me." I recognized the name: Mary Cheney, the former vice president's daughter. I didn't know why he thought I'd thank him. I called him back. "What the fuck are you doing to me here?"

"I thought you'd be happy. They're lesbians."

"Dude. They're married." He didn't say anything. I said, "Google her and tell me you still think you're doing me a favor."

He said I was just pissed because they were Republicans. I said I was pissed because Dick was a fucking war criminal. He called me a communist. Said a couple of guys had been out. Internet problem. Read the notes. I didn't really have a choice. But with the pressure off to complete twelve jobs a day, I found I could have fun at work, joke with my boss about whether or not the Cheneys constituted a favor just because, hey, we're all lesbians.

Mary Cheney wasn't home. Which was good. The further I was from Dick, the more likely I was to keep my mouth shut. Her wife was friendly and talkative in the way old people are friendly and talkative because they haven't had a visitor since Christmas. The house had a few problems. I'd fix one. She'd call my supervisor and I'd have to go back to fix another. But I finally got it fixed.

A few months later, my boss called and started with, "Don't kill me." He was sending me to Dick Cheney's. Dick was home.

He had an assistant or secretary or maybe security who followed me around while I checked connections and signal levels. I'd already found a system problem outside. I just wanted to make sure I never had to fucking set foot in that house again. Dick walked into the office while I was working. He was reading from a stack of papers and ignored me. I told the assistant it would probably be a week or so. I'd put the orders in. He had my supervisor's number.

He said something to the effect of, "You do understand this is the former vice president."

Cheney looked up.

I panicked and said the first thing that came to mind: "Yeah, well, waterboard me if it makes him feel better. It'll still take a week." And I walked out.

It was my last call that day. I drove the entire way home thinking of a hundred better things I could've said. Finally, I called my supervisor and told him I might've accidentally mentioned waterboarding. He laughed and said I'd won. He'd stop sending me to the Cheneys'. I don't actually know if they ever complained. If they did, he never mentioned it.

That was the year I met a Russian mobster whose name was actually Ivan, a fact that on its own made me laugh. There were rumors of mob houses. The guys said they'd been to others. My original trainer pointed one out in Fairfax and said, "If you have to go in there, just don't try to see shit you don't want to." I pressed him for details. But he wouldn't tell me. I thought he was full of shit.

The Russian mob house was off Waples Mill Road. It was a massive McMansion, looked like a swollen Olive Garden. I parked behind a row of Hummers.

Ivan was a big kid with cauliflower ears. He met me at the door. Told me, "Please follow." I followed him to an office. Same collection of leather-bound books on the shelf in most McMansions. I think they come with the place. The modem was in the little network closet. The signal looked like they had a bad splitter somewhere. (Remember what I said about cheap splitters?) I told Ivan I thought there was a bad splitter somewhere. I needed to check the basement. He said, "Is not possible."

I said, "I can't fix it then." He didn't say anything, and I wasn't clear on where we were with the language barrier. So I added, "No basement, no Internet."

He seemed worried. Kept looking at the door. Looking at me. Like a puppy trying to figure out where to pee, a large, heavily tattooed puppy. I said, "Look, unless you've got a kid in a cage, I don't fucking care."

He nodded and said, "You stay. I ask for you." I told him I'd stay. I heard him down the hall. Heard Russian, garbled words. A couple of doors opened and closed.

Ivan came back and opened his paw to show me a gram

bag of coke. He'd helpfully brought a caviar spoon. He said, "You must taste." I actually laughed. He seemed sad that I was laughing. I told him: "Look, I can't. I'm at work. I'll take it home, though, for tonight." This was one of my first jobs that day. I did not want to find out what climbing a telephone pole felt like on cocaine.

He said, "No. You must taste." This time he emphasized the word "must." I told him I get sinus infections. (This is true and extremely annoying.) He didn't understand. I pantomimed and explained a sinus infection in words like "nose, coke, bad, no breathing." This made him happy. It was a problem he could fix. "Stay." I was the puppy now.

He came back with a little round mirror and a little pile of coke. He said, "This is better. No cuts." I was just standing there. I really couldn't figure out what to do. I hoped this was some weird mob thing like when every Russian I'd ever met forces you to do vodka shots and then you're friends. But I'm not great with vodka. And I'm really not great with coke. Drugs affect me.

He stepped closer and he looked older and very sad. He said, "I am trying to say, is safe for you if you taste. You do not taste, is maybe not safe for you now." I figured it was probably his job to kill me and he honestly felt awful about it. I took a bump.

He was visibly relieved. He smiled all goofy and lopsided and said, "Okay. Yes. This is smart decision you make." And he took me to the basement.

I think my heart attack started on the stairs. It was good, though. Best heart attack I'd ever had. I could hear it. I didn't know my eyes could open that wide. Which didn't help me see.

They had a bunch of sweet gaming computers lined up on a table. But with no Internet, all the guys were hanging out on a couple of sofas watching soccer. The World Cup was on. One of the guys pointed at me and asked Ivan something. Ivan said, "Yes, of course." I understood that much Russian. And the guy gave me a thumbs-up, said, "Good shit, yes?" I agreed that it was good shit. And I changed their splitter and got the fuck out of there. I don't know what they were up to that they didn't want me to see on those computers. (If you're reading this, Ivan, I do not know what y'all were up to. I didn't see shit.)

We got a new regional manager after that. He called me "young lady." I told him not to. My old vet buddy said he'd called me an entitled dyke after I left the room. The company was bleeding money with the whole no-one-fucking-needs-cable-anymore thing. And I was back to chasing points. Eventually, my ankle went out.

I remember my last day. There was a big meeting. I hated these. The only potential good part was that they'd play happy messages from happy customers about their cable tech. If you got one, you got a twenty-dollar gift card to Best Buy. I got lots of calls, mostly because little old ladies liked me. I programmed their remotes. They never played mine in the meetings because no one ever figured out what to do about customers thinking I was a "nice young man." That last meeting, they gave a guy an award. For ten years, he'd never taken a sick day, never taken a vacation day. He had four kids. I thought maybe they'd have enjoyed a vacation. But that mentality is why I was never getting promoted in that company.

I couldn't go back after surgery. My ankle never

healed right. I needed a letter from HR to continue my disability. Just a phone call. But they moved their HR team somewhere else. They never answered my emails. So I work at a gay bar. The pay is shit. But I like going to work. I don't spend my nights worrying about where I'll pee. And no one has called me Larry in years.

Everything That's Beautiful Breaks My Heart

It's helpful, in the midst of an existential crisis, to find yourself driving a bread-box Winnebago down a two-lane road winding through Texas farmland. Not a car to be seen for miles. No cell service for hours. The only colors, the wildflowers gathered around fence posts and the impossibly blue sky. The only sounds, the wind, a rattle in the back you can't identify, and an old iPod full of LimeWire downloads circa 2007. It was like skipping through a time capsule of bad relationships—a lot of Korn, Daughtry, and Papa Roach and a surprisingly thorough collection of John Denver. But it was that or the old-time Gospel hour or the cattle auction on AM radio. And I fuckin' love John Denver.

It was September 2016. A few days before this, I'd gotten a call from a friend, another cult baby (don't throw that term around), who asked if I could go to Dallas to pick up a box of Family literature someone had found. I said yes because I had nothing better to do. And I was curious.

So I drove up to Dallas. I texted something friendly like, "Hey, it's Lauren. Sara's friend. Prob 20 mins away? Where do you want to meet?"—like I was buying a coffee table off Craigslist and didn't want to sound like a possible serial killer. The replies came in a string, without any attempt at friendliness.

Turn down the alley.

Flash your lights.

Once. Don't honk.

Leave it running.

Don't get out until I'm back inside.

Meth dealers aren't this paranoid.

The handoff looked like something out of a bad spy movie, like they ran out of money and didn't bother scouting for a cool location, just filmed the pivotal scene in their mom's suburban cul-de-sac, dogs barking in the background.

I don't know how the fuck a box of Family literature ended up in a suburban garage in Texas, not exactly. Most of it should've been burned long ago.

When I was maybe fourteen, in Switzerland, other homes in Europe kept getting raided, the children carted off to foster care. If any authorities got their hands on those books, they would be evidence, pretty damning evidence—*Heaven's Girl* (a sort of YA novel about a teen girl who fights the Antichrist and enjoys being gang-raped by soldiers—how else would you tell them about Jesus); Mo Letters, the meaty stuff; the how-to manuals on Flirty Fishing, sex, and training teens; and *The Last State* (how to tie a kid to a bed and beat her with sticks until the demon comes out).

We had always been on edge about Romans, the police. But with news of the raids, we knew the Romans were finally coming. Just a matter of time. So every night, for months, we would burn books.

I didn't care. I was hoping for the police, for any authority, to save me. I knew my grandma's number by heart.

Either way, burning books was a cake assignment—outdoors, no one listening to you talk, keep the fire low so the neighbors don't see and you don't burn down a fucking chalet, tell a joke and toss another section of *Heaven's Girl* on the fire.

Clearly we missed a few copies. Some members hated that we were destroying them and held on to their libraries. My guess—based on familiarity with paranoid older cult members—is one of those people who kept their books eventually stashed them in their daughter's garage during a move or a divorce. All I know is the daughter wanted them out of her house before her kids or, god forbid, her husband found them. She called a friend, who called a friend, who called me.

We have our own reasons for preserving the books that have nothing to do with their holiness and a lot to do with custody cases should someone need to get their kids from a parent who won't leave the Family. Strange as it may seem, these books are our history. It's proof of the stories we tell and the stories we can't explain to our therapists and the stories we don't tell the people who love us, because we love them and don't want to hurt them. But I like to think that someday, people will gently fold their MAGA hats and All Lives Matter T-shirts, stuff them into a box, and shove them in the back of the closet next to the box that holds Grandpa's white hood we don't talk about anymore. I want to believe that eventually, finding someone who supported Trump will be as difficult as finding someone who supported the war in Iraq, or a prominent member of a doomsday cult, QAnon, if you will. You can't change everyone's mind. Sometimes it's enough to know they feel shame.

I suppose it helps to explain what the hell I was doing in a Winnebago in Texas. I was having the sort of midlife crisis that causes people to quit their jobs, sell their houses, move into RVs, and drive across the country. Normal shit. You've seen movies. All of this had been an urge for a while. All it took was Springsteen on the radio during my nightly hour-long commute and I'd think, *Fuck it. Just keep going. You can be in California by Tuesday.* Some nights the only reason I didn't keep driving was they'd put transponders in our work vans.

I had been doing what was expected of me, the job, the house, the modest forty-two-inch flat screen, the gym membership, the sensible Ikea sofa, lawn tickets to concerts twice a year, the two-week vacation somewhere cheap but nice.

For a moment, I had it all, the American dream.

My house, perpetually in some stage of renovation, as is the rule of fixer-uppers, was finally almost presentable.

I'd patched and painted the once Pepto-pink walls in slate blues and grays, hung curtains, replaced the grout in the bathroom; both toilets flushed, the patched and sealed chimney had stopped leaking into the fireplace, most of the closets had doors, the porch railings were scraped and painted, I'd coaxed grass to grow between the weeds and planted a garden, you could even turn on a few lights without shorting out another light.

So I did what you're supposed to do, as a fine upstanding American homeowner in the Maryland suburbs: I invited everyone over for a crab boil. I was stuck outside in 100-degree heat steaming crabs. But I'd look in every so often and watch my friends standing around the living room, drinks in hand, making small talk. A few boyfriends and husbands were missing, and I assumed they were in the spare bedroom, watching football with my girlfriend.

I kept looking in because I was waiting for this guy to show up. I'd known him when we were kids in Switzerland. Now that I think about it, we'd burned books together a few times. It doesn't matter. His name was Tom. And I used to know him. He was always a nice kid, always in trouble. (If you want to ponder the nature vs. nurture of it all, it's kids like him I get along with now. The tattletales and rule followers and spiritual kids grew up to be assholes.) Tom said he was in town and I'd invited him, but hadn't heard back. Then he walked in, and he looked like an overgrown version of the thirteen-year-old boy I used to know. His hair still sticking up around the same cowlick. Same half-dimple in his chin. Someone pointed to the back door and I waved.

What happened next was the saddest goddamn game

of Show Me Your Life I've ever played. He showed me pictures of his kids. I introduced him to my dogs. He scrolled through pictures of his house, stairs he'd refinished, the deck he'd just built. I gestured around with the crab tongs—walls. He showed pictures of his vacation to Europe where he'd found these old ruins where we used to play Antichrist vs. Heaven's Girl. I opened his beer with a bottle opener someone gave me when they got back from Croatia. He told me about his construction company. I might've told him something about work. Probably not. He'd already seen my work van out front.

We weren't competing. And I'm not just saying that because if we had been, I'd only have won the first round. But it wasn't a competition. He was genuinely happy for me. I was thrilled for him. He gave me some tips on refinishing the floors. I gave him the names of some bands he'd like. Then he admitted he'd only worn a Black Keys T-shirt because he thought I'd think it was cool. I assured him it was very cool. I didn't need to impress him. He's a cult baby. It's a little like knowing someone from AA or group therapy or basic training. You've seen each other cry.

That we'd seen each other break was why we were trying so earnestly to assure each other we were okay. They didn't win. We'd done all right. We'd survived, thrived even. We'd made it. We were happy. They were wrong. We were okay. And happy.

I don't know if he was happy, or if he is happy. We're friends because we share a common past. The extent of our relationship is that we hit like on each other's pictures. He was probably happy. I was fucking miserable.

I had done what I was supposed to do, most of it anyway. He may have been ahead, but he's a straight white German male who lives in Canada. He got free university. I was still proud I hadn't been to jail in a couple years. But like I said, we weren't competing. And we grade each other on a curve. He was, however, extremely impressed with jail stories. Guys always love the D.C. lockup advice—"If you have to shit, take one leg out of your pants so you can still fight if you need to." Still, I'd done it. Here's my house, that's my job, there are the people and animals who love me. I got my shit together. I'm someone people can love.

In the weeks after he left, I couldn't sleep. I let things go long enough, haircuts and personal grooming and laundry, that friends started asking if I was depressed, and I probably was. But sometimes what looks like depression is your brain slowing down enough to think, like a freezing body draws oxygen away from your limbs. I wanted so bad for someone to just tell me what to do. But I was thirty-five. I was already quickly realizing that no one has the first fucking clue, that all those people you thought had their shit together were simply hoping they hadn't just made that one choice that ruins everything. Fingers crossed.

When it comes down to it, everyone—your parents, your friends, that clickbait article, the self-help books, your therapist, Beverly Cleary, and Dan Savage—has the same advice anyway. Doesn't matter the question, they tell you to listen to your inner voice, trust your instincts. Everyone likes to give advice, but no one wants to be responsible for the outcome. It's an easy way to sound wise, and drop a chit for a future "told you so," while keeping clear of blame when everything goes to shit. Truth is, no one fucking knows what else to say.

Was it a midlife crisis I experienced that put me in that Winnebago, or is that what we call it when most of us hit the wall and realize we'll never get ahead, even if we manage to catch up? Did I just see it a little early? Like everyone else, I'd been working forty to eighty hours a week most of my adult life. And not once was I more than one missed paycheck, one vet bill, one bad trans-mission, one natural disaster, one injury or illness away from losing it all.

Maybe "midlife crisis" is what we call it because that's about the time we realize working hard and staying out of trouble doesn't change the fact we'll be working until we're eighty—unless we get sick first, or shot. (You really do have to account for that possibility in this country.) And we're already fucking exhausted.

We're all so busy struggling to survive that we don't have time to live. The only joy we experience is by pur-chasing objects meant to make our lives easier. Buy a house. Homeownership, that's the ticket. Quit throw-ing your money away on rent. In reality, you might own one room after ten years of payments. Not the kitchen. Maybe the smaller bedroom. Make your payments on time for twenty years of a thirty-year mortgage, get laid off, miss a few payments, and you'll find out exactly what you own.

But sure, let's play along. Now you have a house. You're almost there. But you have to fill the house. Only a psychopath leaves their walls unadorned. You need things to sit on and things to sleep on and things to put things in. You need things that'll make your life easier. The robot vacuum that'll do the work for you so you have time to pay your taxes. The tax product that'll do your taxes for you so you have time to make dinner. The dinner ingredients shipped in a box and all you have to do is prepare them. The app that allows you to order dinner so you have time to relax. Never mind the commercials you can now skip with the premium cable package, the television show you're watching on your sixty-inch LCD screen that was supposed to make you happy is just an ad for something else you *need*. Buy it. It will make you happy.

But only a for a moment. So you post a picture of it on Facebook. That little bell lights red and you got a notification. Someone liked your picture. A sweet, sweet hit of dopamine hits your brain because we're all fucking lab rats. Another notification. Someone commented, "I'm so jel." Because we no longer have time to write full words. Who cares. It's another hit either way. You give back to the community. Scroll through and like someone's vacation photos they're posting every 2.3 hours because actual experiences are no match for the hit we fucking need and can only feel when someone likes the pictures of our experiences.

It's no wonder we're all depressed. Our culture doesn't value experiences or living. We value work so you can buy things. We don't even value our mental health and inner lives enough to not call buying things "retail therapy."

The last company meeting I attended, they gave a guy

an award for never missing a day of work in ten years—not a single sick day, not a snow day, no vacation. And he has kids. I thought he should be publicly shamed, and long ago. Maybe the first year he hadn't used any vacation. Sure, you can sell some of it back. But not all of it; they're not a charity. But ten fucking years? In a sane society, he would be a cautionary tale. In our society, he got a plaque and a fifty-dollar gift card to Best Buy.

It's no longer enough to show up every day, do your job, and go home. It's like every company bought the same self-help book on how to save money by skipping raises and get the same loyalty by turning your company into a cult. But it wasn't loyalty that kept me there. I simply didn't see another choice. This was what I was supposed to do.

Until that visit from Tom, the mirror of having to explain my life to someone else. I couldn't ignore it anymore, could no longer shut my mind off and watch TV. The problem was, it wasn't me that was failing. Like I said, I was doing what I was supposed to be doing. Living the fucking dream. The problem was, I didn't want any goddamn part of it.

Once I saw it, it's like a stain on the ceiling. It's all you can see anymore. You start noticing all the other stains. That line where the drywall's about to come loose and it's going to cave in. You just don't know when. The narrative we're sold works for a while, until you see the holes. We work. We consume. We get sick. We die.

I couldn't sit through another meeting praising company values, company culture—don't just show up to work every day, tell your friends and neighbors about us, and let's bring out the one guy who started as a tech but made it to management so he can tell you all how he bleeds blue, the company colors, and let's hold a moment of silence for Ronnie, who worked in the warehouse for thirty years and every morning he'd tell you how many days until retirement. He was going to move to North Carolina, be close to his people. Do some fishing. He was supposed to retire four years, three months, and seven days ago. But the company got bought out, the new company didn't count his time. Still, he fucking made it. Finally. He retired, and he dropped dead a month later.

I felt like I did back when I was a kid, surrounded by true believers, and for so long I'd thought I was trapped. But I was only trapped by my own fear of losing it all. And when I added it up, "all" was just stuff I didn't need anyway.

So I trusted my instincts because the one thing my instincts know is a cult. I decided that day was as good a time as any to schedule a long-overdue ankle surgery. I listened to my inner voice when it told me to use the time off to hop around on crutches, hanging crown molding and scheduling the flooring crew. I sold the Ikea sofa and the TV and dresser. I gave away what I couldn't sell. Then I sold the house.

I figured I could live off the savings a little while. (I maybe had been *going through some shit*, but I'm not stupid.) I never actually quit my job. I didn't go back either. I was in California by the time the disability ran out. Maybe my inner voice is just the remnant of that wild kid who grew up all over the world, leading me on a fun but ultimately lonely path to destruction. But that kid didn't want *things*.

I wanted to fucking live. I wanted to be a writer.

That's how, at thirty-seven years old, I ended up driving around the country in a Winnebago, with a worn-out banana box of cult literature that somebody had failed to burn, stashed back in the shower that didn't work. That's why when my inner voice had an even crazier idea, like *I bet I can find the ranch*, I pulled over into a strip mall, parked next to a Panera to borrow their Internet, pulled up Google on my laptop, and typed in "Texas Soul Clinic."

The Soul Clinic if you're cool, the TSC if you're a cult baby—the ranch was where my parents joined the Family. Some people visit Civil War battlefields. My dad stops and reads historical markers on the highway. Apparently I try to find old communes.

You won't find Thurber, Texas, on a map. It's a ghost town with a diner and a brick museum, made of Thurber bricks, where, if you're interested in bricks, I'm sure you can learn about Thurber bricks. (I spent a lot of time on Google that day.) My Winnebago, propelled by a four-cylinder Toyota pickup with a house crammed on top, topped out at about fifty miles per hour, downhill. So I took the back roads until I got near the old town.

I pulled over at the diner called Restaurant, ordered a tea and a salad, thankful for some healthier options than Subways in gas stations. A few old timers were slow-sipping coffee at the next table. I thought to ask them.

I was sure they'd remember. Thurber isn't the type of place people move to. But I chickened out. I didn't belong—that much was obvious—and I didn't know how to explain what I was looking for or why. I knew the looks I'd get.

I felt a little better asking at the brick museum, so I drove over and parked in a nearly empty lot. No one was studying the history of Thurber bricks that day. The docent's face looked like it hadn't seen water since the Dust Bowl. She asked if I was looking for the RV park. "No, just passing through, ma'am. I was wondering, back in the '60s, early '70s, there was a cult out here."

I was speaking softly because I was in a museum, not because I was asking about a cult. But I was worried she'd assume the latter or not hear me at all. So I was relieved when she didn't whisper when she answered, "The Children of God." Then she stared at me for a moment like she was trying to figure out if I was a lunatic or a cult member, or someone chasing a dose of trauma porn, just stopping by on the way to Waco.

"Not the first, huh?"

She smiled. "First Texan, though. Every couple years. Always 'bout your age."

I was absurdly happy to be called a Texan. I could still speak the language. This is what I did miss about Texans. My grandma used to say, "Words cost." Which is a perfectly Texan way of saying, *We expect you to pick up the rest in context. If you can't, well, that's on you.* It had been a problem on the East Coast, where I am expected to not only fill in a full sentence but also add a smiley face to any jokes to avoid confusion.

The docent's directions made perfect sense in that

they made no fucking sense at all. "Two dirt roads, but don't count the first, or the gravel. Might be gravel now. Go down that. Close up to the ridge. Nothing's there anymore. You were brought up in that mess, honey?" And there it was, the look I was afraid of: pity.

I counted the miles on the odometer. But when I saw the ridge, I knew I was in the right place. It felt like I'd been there before.

There was no historical marker. But something happened here. We all have those places where something happened to make us, or change us. I'm here because of this place, and all the places that came after. But this place was the beginning of me. I swear even now that I could feel it, as real as the mesquite-dotted ridge ahead. Something happened here. My parents were here.

I'd seen so many pictures of the place in black and white and sometimes color, old newsreels and stuttering '70s home videos. Hippies in shacks and bunkhouses. A few wild-haired toddlers running around in overalls. Lanky men in flared jeans. Women in long dresses. Long hair. Long necklaces with yoke pendants hung next to toothbrushes. Baby-faced and bright-eyed. Smiling from ear to ear. They were doing something, brother. They'd dropped out. Given up their worldly possessions. They were going to change the world. It's a revolution for Jesus, man. Then they started preparing for the end of the world.

I kept heading toward the ridge, but something was off. It wasn't that I was expecting hippies. They were long gone. If anything remained of the old buildings, I couldn't tell from the fence line. But I thought I'd find a real ranch, maybe an oil field. This was Texas. There wasn't a long list of options. But as I neared the ridge, I slowed to a crawl.

The fence was all wrong. Ranch fences are barbed wire strung between posts. A farm might not have a fence at all. But this fence was black steel and eight feet tall. I was busy staring at it when a family of ibexes with their twisted antlers bolted out of a mesquite clutch. That's not a sentence found in nature. Then I looked up. Towering above us all stood a single fucking giraffe, probably wondering why the trees wouldn't grow tall enough to chew. I rolled to a stop and stared at the poor animal, awkward, lonely, and completely fucking lost. You're not supposed to identify with a fenced-in giraffe that doesn't belong in Texas.

My parents had come to this place because they'd been seeking something more meaningful, a way to do good, to help. My dad didn't want to kill Vietnamese farmers on the other side of the world to save nothing. By the time they tried to send him, the war was already over. We just hadn't admitted it yet. My mom was tired of seeing her friends' names on the lists of the dead. They'd been raised during the most prosperous decades in our history. They came of age when it seemed ready to unravel. All they saw was the misery wrought by greed—the poverty and war, the loneliness and the fucking cruelty of it all. So they joined a commune, a community where people shared what little they had, where people spoke of love and peace, a world without money, a cause. A family. Picked the wrong goddamn commune. But who didn't.

Texas may have more than its share of cults—Branch Davidians, Church of Wells, Yearning for Zion, and Rajneeshpuram are just a few. For a while in the '70s, joining a cult was as common as signing up for Cross-Fit a couple years ago. Cults, new religious movements, whatever you call them, they're not a new phenomenon. Most fizzle out. Some last. Some grow enough to be called religions. People join because they're longing for a sense of community and a higher purpose. They stay because they usually find that sense of community, with all the ties that bind it, and a higher purpose, unless and until they see through it.

One of the most effective cult strategies is to keep everyone too busy to notice what is happening to them. There's always a big change, a new crisis, a new mission, a new Gospel. A community has needs—food and housing and, in the Family's case, hungry kids and babies whose diapers needed to be changed. We struggled constantly just to make rent and pay our tithe to keep the home in good standing with Family leadership. You don't want to leave. Never mind figuring out what you'll do on the outside, you don't want to abandon your community. That trick doesn't only work in cults.

"Cult" is one of those words thrown around a lot these days—all over Twitter and Facebook. It started some-

time around the summer of the 2016 Republican convention and has continued right up through 2020, and I
doubt this year will be the end of it. I don't know who
said it first. But goddamn if you didn't catch on quick.
It's like a cult, you said. You posted a photo of rabid
white boys in red hats. "This is a cult." Took a screen-
shot of the local news comment feed. "They're a death
cult." You watched an emaciated blonde lie through her
veneers and said, "It's like arguing with cult members."
You watched him ranting, bragging about his intellect,
his crowd size, his deals. You said, "He's going to bring
about the Apocalypse." It reminded me of watching my
stepdad in a turf war with a Hare Krishna. That was
our corner, right in front of the zoo. Gabe told the Hare
Krishna his crew needed to move on. "You look like a
cult, guys. I mean, come on. You're a cult. The cops are
going to make all of us leave." The Hare Krishna lost his
shit, threw one of his books at us, screaming about how
we were a cult. It's always someone else, never you.

Then I watched the members of that shitweeble's cab-
inet, each in turn, each trying to outdo the last, lavish
praise on the . . . Messiah? And I thought, *Well, fuck.*

After I left the ranch, I mailed the books to my friend
who runs the Safe Passage Foundation, a group that
helps people who grew up in cults. But I didn't mail
them all. Maybe I'm not the most trustworthy person,
but in my defense, I only kept a book if there was more
than one copy. As such, I ended up with a bunch of the
comic books we used to read. And because the Children

of God was a doomsday cult, many of them were about the End Time, the End of Days, the Apocalypse.

These are the stories I return to time and again. I don't know why. I'm not looking for answers. They're not interesting. They're not particularly funny even to my warped sense of humor. Maybe I just need to remind myself the Family was wrong.

The problem is, I'm not entirely sure they were wrong about everything.

I've never been much of a fan of apocalyptic fiction. The only Family comics I used to enjoy weren't about the Apocalypse itself. They were the survival manuals. How to build a Dakota fire so your enemies won't see the glow. How to build a shelter. How to make water with a plastic bag and a tree branch. How to build snares with wire and sticks and rocks. Did you know you can eat bees? Just pull off the stinger. Absent in those comics was the voice of our leader casually throwing in a little side note of his greatness, "I scored a 179 on the Army IQ test. Highest score they'd ever seen."

The lack of David Berg's usual insanity might've been why I liked those books. Or maybe I liked them for the same reason people fantasize about a zombie apocalypse or fighting for the resistance in a dystopian fascist dictatorship—that is, my real life was fucking miserable, and I was surrounded by people who were mean to me. Most of the people around me were supposed to die? Good riddance.

It wasn't that I necessarily believed the prophecies. But I didn't *not* believe them. I don't know anyone my age who didn't spend most of the '80s convinced early death was all but a given. If it wasn't Chernobyl, it would be the next meltdown, if the hole in the ozone layer didn't fry us first, or the Russians launched and then the Americans would have to launch, or a computer exercise could go wrong and make NORAD think the Russians were launching and Ferris Bueller couldn't stop it. Those were just the big ones. Our world was a death trap of razors in candy, men in vans, swimming within thirty minutes of eating, talking on phones during thunderstorms, AIDS needles in bus seats, crack pipes in playgrounds, quicksand, leaving the curtains open for serial killers, swallowing too much gum, bathing during thunderstorms (I wouldn't even pee during a thunderstorm, just to be safe), spontaneous combustion, rusty nails, hiding in a fridge, the Bermuda Triangle, Colombian drug lords. I really did watch too much *Miami Vice*. So when the Family said the world was going to end, I thought, *Tell me about it.*

The strangest goddamn thing when I got out of the Family was finding out evangelicals believe a lot of the same crazy shit we were taught, actually believe that if the temple is rebuilt on its eponymous mount in Jerusalem, Jesus will come back; believe that if the earth is no longer able to support human life, they'll be raptured; believe in an Antichrist and a Mark of the Beast.

I'd dropped the belief in the Antichrist, along with most Family doctrine, by the time we landed back in Amarillo. It wasn't really a conscious decision. I stopped hearing about it, so I stopped thinking about it. I didn't notice I'd stopped believing until we went to church one Sunday. My parents had decided we probably should believe in something. So they brought us to a mega-

church with a live band. The intensely shiny pastor
started talking about the End of Days, and I froze, like,
Oh. Hey. Uh. We don't talk about that weird stuff out here.
We never went back.

I suppose the Family version of the story had to come
from somewhere, and I appreciate that I don't have to
give David Berg points for creativity. He was raised a
Pentecostal. All he did was add a couple notes to the
already weird interpretation of Revelation.

Since the world began, people have been predicting
its end—the Mayans and Mesopotamians and, of course,
the Christian Bible. Somewhere, deep down, we've
always known that it's not just us but our entire society
that balances one misstep away from unraveling. It's why
prophecies of the Apocalypse work so well on Americans, why postapocalyptic fiction has never seemed
entirely fictional.

The end of civilization has been a constant in our col-
lective conscious, not to mention our entertainment.
Through stock market crashes and housing crises, and
the accelerated warming of our planet, we've treated
ourselves to the comfort of watching our world end on
our screens, over and over again—*The Road, Children of
Men, The Day After Tomorrow, Zombieland, Armageddon,
Extinction, Deep Impact, Independence Day, I Am Legend,
The Walking Dead* and all its spinoffs. Maybe it's just
catastrophe porn. Maybe we've been trying to numb ourselves for what we've always known is inevitable. After
all, we grew up mourning the future we'd never see.

The Apocalypse has always been a fantasy to some.
Those who believe Jesus will ride down from the clouds
on a white horse never cared as much about joining him

in paradise as they did daydream of the perverts and sinners suffering in lakes of fire. To the equally cruel and no less delusional, the marauding hordes of brainless zombies weren't a nightmare but masturbatory fuel that one day they'd finally get to fuckin' shoot someone. Men would be men again. Women would be forced back into their godly role, serving the needs of manly men who protect them. And that bitch, Kevin in HR, won't survive the first round. Fuck that guy. To the rest of us, the end of the world sometimes felt like relief. Maybe we could outrun and outsmart the violent gangs roaming our blackened cities. Maybe not. Who gives a shit. At least we'd never have to pay off the student loans and credit cards. At least we could skip the second shift. At least we'd see it coming.

It's not that we didn't hope for a better outcome. We watched a Black man win an election promising change, and we hoped. We actually believed. We really fucking did. But this country wasn't built for change. This country was built, from its very founding, to maintain the status quo, to protect the rich, to protect the powerful, the white men and their money.

And this is where the Family was fucking right. God damn them. In one of those books, there's a comic called "The American Dream Is a Nightmare." Like a lot of the early comics, it looks like a Chick tract. And they probably did hand it out on the street back in the day. And skipping the doctrinal part, it's fucking true. There is no getting ahead in this country unless you're extremely talented, connected, and lucky.

We work. We consume. We get sick. We die.

Instead of freedom, instead of a chance, instead of peace, we're sold lies. They teach you hard work and patriotism and greed are virtues. They keep us so busy struggling every goddamn day just to stay alive that we don't have the time or energy to fight back. They tell us we have all the power, all we have to do is vote. Then they close polling locations and require ID, and only one machine works, and they won't even give us the day off. And when we do put them in power, they're really sorry about that vote, they're sorry we couldn't outbid the white men with money. They needed the money to win the next election. They'll remember us then.

This is the greatest country on earth. Pledge your allegiance to the flag. Just don't ask any questions. Keep your head down. Work hard. You see that guy over there? He's worth a billion dollars. He started from nothing. You could make it too if you tried a little harder. You could make it if it weren't for that other guy, that immigrant, those poor white trash, those welfare queens holding you down. Keep working hard. You owe it to your country, your community.

Cults fucking wish they could pull it off.

They've had help recently, the guys who pull the strings. Sometime back in 2007, you took a quiz to find out which *Brady Bunch* character you really were. And you've been fed a version of reality ever since. Which reality? The one the algorithm knew would keep you online longer. The news that confirmed your beliefs. You were right all along. Everyone you see on your feed agrees with you. You don't even need to look outside. It's all right there on your screen telling you the truth as you see it. Every time you clicked, the algorithm learned a little more about what that was. You think it's like arguing with cult members? Fucking tell me about it.

All these things you take for granted—access to books, music, the simple ability to find an answer to a question, that what you were taught is true, that your heroes and idols weren't predators, that the institutions you trusted wouldn't fail you. I long ago had to question everything I'd learned, everything I thought I believed, to deconstruct an entirely false narrative of history and the world, of my country, of my life and who I thought I was. It's fucking infuriating now to see you believe a meme or clickbait when a world of information is right there in your hand. It's fucking surreal to watch the same confirmation bias, the same belief persistence, the same goddamn cognitive dissonance that stole my childhood turn an entire nation into blank-faced true believers. But then, if you don't leave a cult, you'll never know you're in one. America is the greatest country on earth.

What does it say about us then if the only change, the only escape, the only end we can envision, is violence and annihilation? Let the motherfucker burn. They'll kill a million of us and stack our bodies in the streets to protect the status quo. They enslaved and jailed and slaughtered entire peoples to build this nation. What's a few million more? As long as they keep us busy, as long as it's the other guy, as long as Facebook tells us a nice story about ourselves, we've been happy to go along. Until something happens, one crisis too many, a pandemic maybe, and all those systems were exposed at once—our healthcare system that never was, our economy that only works so long as we consume, our police

who'll only protect us so long as we allow them to murder with impunity, our service industry that requires the
blood sacrifice of its lowest-paid workers to thrive, our
food chain that's always been a row of bleeding dominoes
ready to tumble, and our governing bodies that cannot
handle even the smallest crisis without sacrificing the
poor and the vulnerable. Once more, on our screens, we
watched it unravel. Then we took to the streets to let
them know we finally were seeing it laid bare.

Apocalypse never meant the end. It's called Revelation
for a reason—the unveiling of the truth. When we finally
realize the systems and institutions we've been told exist
to protect us are designed to control us. When those systems fail, and the truth is unmasked, they have no real
power, and we outnumber them. We always have.

That home in Switzerland where I burned books with
Tom did get raided. We were long gone, all the kids
packed into vans in the dead of night, driven around for
twelve hours, making nonsensical turns to shake anyone
tailing us. We ended up in an old hostel in the mountains. The drivers dropped us and our go-bags, and left
to pick up another load, maybe the younger kids. I don't
remember. I remember there were about thirty of us
JETTS, the Junior End Time Teens, and two adults.
When we woke up the next morning, the pasture and
trees behind the hostel were covered in a foot of snow
like a fairy tale. I don't think anyone said a word. We all
just filed down the stairs, pulled our jackets and boots
on, single file out the door, through the cow gate, and
we held a massive, loud, boisterous snowball fight in the
pasture. One of the adults came outside to collect us and
we just kept playing. Fuck him.

Sounds like a small thing. But for Family kids, who never walk past a street-facing window during the day, never raise their voices if they're allowed to speak at all, never play at violence, and never, ever disobey an authority, it was a fucking prison riot.

We realized, if only that one morning, they had no power. The same holds true now. They only have power because we believe, because they've taught us to need them.

Those are the moments I'm proud of. The times I saw through them. The times I made them work to break me, even though I knew they would. The times I questioned the lies being fed to me, though everyone around me believed. I learned early that if everyone around you has their head bowed, their eyes shut tight—keep your eyes open and look around.

I'm reflexively suspicious of anyone who stands on a soapbox. Tell me you have the answers and I'll know you're trying to sell me something. I'm as wary of certainty as I am of good vibes and positive thinking. They're delusions that allow you to ignore reality and lay the blame at the feet of those suffering. *They just didn't follow the rules, or think positively enough. They brought it on themselves.*

I don't have the answers. Maybe depression's the natural reaction to a world full of cruelty and pain. But the thing I know about depression is if you want to survive it, you have to train yourself to hold on; when you can see no reason to keep going, you cannot imagine a future worth seeing, you keep moving anyway. That's not delusion. That's hope. It's a muscle you exercise so it's strong when you need it. You feed it with books and art and dogs who rest their head on your leg, and human connection with people who are genuinely interested and excited; you feed it with growing a tomato and baking sourdough and making a baby laugh and standing at the edge of oceans and feeling a horse's whiskers on your palm and bear hugs and late-night talks over whiskey and a warm happy sigh on your neck and the unexpected perfect song on the radio, and mushroom trips with a friend who giggles at the way the trees aren't acting right, and jumping in creeks, and lying in the grass under the stars, and driving with the windows down on a swirly two-lane road. You stock up like a fucking prepper buying tubs of chipped beef and powdered milk and ammo. You stock up so some part of you knows and remembers, even in the dark, all that's worth saving in this world.

It's comforting to know what happens next. But if there's one thing I know, it's that no one fucking knows. And it's terrifying.

I don't dream of a home and a family, a career and financial stability. I dream of living. And my inner voice, defective though it may be, still tells me happiness and peace, belonging and love, all lie just around the next corner, the next city, the next country. Just keep moving and hope the next place will be better. It has to be. Just around the next bend, everything is beautiful. And it breaks my heart.

Acknowledgments

Thank you to my absolute force of an agent Jamie Chambliss, who found me when I was flailing, who believes in me when I lose faith, who always finds a story in my rambling words, who makes me believe I can write—for your incisive editing, for your infuriating queries, for your friendship, I am forever in your debt. To my agent Steve Troha for telling me to make it funnier, for always answering my panicked texts, for fighting my battles, and for only laughing a little bit when I fell on my ass and broke my phone, thank you. Thank you to the team at Folio.

Tim O'Connell, my editor at Vintage, who took a chance on me and convinced me to write in essays. Thank you for your faith in me, for your patience and keen edits, for insisting I mention the fucking giraffe. It's been an honor, truly. To Anna Kaufman and Rob Shapiro, thank you for your notes, for keeping me on something of a schedule, for answering my endless questions. Reagan Arthur, thank you for believing in me and for pretending you don't see half my tweets. A huge thank-you to the entire team who worked to make this book happen: my publicist, Julie Ertl; Dan Novack; Mark Abrams—thank you for my amazing cover design; Nick Alguire; Edward Allen; Beth Lamb; Suzanne Herz; LuAnn Walther; Antoinette Marotta; Melissa Yoon; Barbara Richard; and Jessica Deitcher.

I am grateful for Sandra Newman, who took me seriously long before I considered myself a real writer. For your encouragement, for always being willing to read another draft, for your notes, for talking me off more than a few ledges, thank you. I am honored by your friendship. Howard Mittelmark, who can somehow edit me without breaking me, who always makes me sound and sometimes even makes me feel a little smarter, thank you. Elizabeth McCracken, I will never comprehend your kindness. For guiding me and mentoring me and believing in me, for your constant encouragement, I cannot possibly express my gratitude except to say thank you. I would consider myself forever indebted, if it weren't for Pandemic Cat.

Leta Seletzky and Andrea Avery, thank you for reading these half-baked words and finding something to praise. It's an honor to be in the trenches with you. Squaw Valley group ten, I could not have imagined a better workshop. Jennifer Graham, thank you for getting my ass to the coffee shop, for the tacos, the beer, and your friendship. Thank you to Moira Donegan, for your friendship, for helping an old dyke with her homework. Heather Havrilesky, for reading this crap, for volunteering as my personal advice dispenser, for the constant support. To Roxane Gay, thank you for being my champion and friend. Thank you to Andria Williams for reading early versions, for publishing my story in *The Wrath-Bearing Tree*, for your friendship.

Thank you to the many writers, artists, and freaks who've supported me, read essays, blurbed me, lent advice, listened to my whining, shit-talked my nemeses, and made this possible: Megan Stack, Julie Powell, Janet Fitch, Tanya Tarr, Michael Schaub, Andrea Pitzer, Alexander Chee, Charlotte Clymer, Lucas Schaefer, Vincent Scarpa, Thomas Pluck, Benjamin Dreyer, Duchess Goldblatt, Alice Anderson, Tammy Ingram, Jennifer Bendery, Ashley Ford, Leah Hampton, Adam Savage, Nicole Cliffe, Whitney Brown, Julia Park Tracey, Erin Khar, William Fatzinger, Lyz Lenz, Cari Luna, Nick Arvin, Mary Childs, Amy Bloom, Jason Roberts, Kate Mannion, and Seamus Bellamy, sup.

A special thank-you to my friend Taylor Stevens, who all but forced me to keep writing, who encouraged me to write the truth, and who never let me give up. I owe you a debt I can never repay. Thank you to my fellow cult babies, especially Whisper, Sara, Jennifer, Janet, Kylie, Juliana, and Dia. Thank you to Gretchen Ramke, for your friendship, and the acid, but not the horror movies. Thank you, Ty Brewster. Thank you, Cate Blanchett. Thank you, Lars Loving. Anita Sterrett, Jay Johns, Archer Hellick, and Joey Oldaker, thank you.

Thank you, Karl Poss IV, my web designer and photographer, who managed to feed me enough tequila that I smiled in a picture.

Thank you to the entire staff and a few of the patrons at the Iron Bear. I could not have asked for better bosses than Jason Grodzinsky and Ben Besh, who paid me to sit at the front door and read and write, and occasionally check an ID, and who somehow didn't shitcan me that month I showed up an hour late for every goddamn shift.

To my parents, siblings, niece and nephew, my aunts, and Carly, thank you for supporting me. Though I know you probably wish I'd been a painter, plumber, anything but a writer. Thank you for the dog-sitting, reading, and conversations that weren't about this book.

These essays were written mostly at Once Over Coffee and Radio Coffee & Beer in Austin. I hope I get to sit on your patios again one day. Thank you to the cast and crew of *Schitt's Creek* for the therapy; Jason Isbell, John Prine, Emmylou Harris, and Patty Griffin for the music; Sour Patch Kids for the sugar rush; my Patreon subscribers for the vet bills; and you know who you are for the weed.

To the love of my life, Teddy, thank you. If it weren't for you, I might've finished this six months earlier. But it would've been boring as shit. You're the best dog.